First World War
and Army of Occupation
War Diary
France, Belgium and Germany

36 DIVISION
Headquarters, Branches and Services
Commander Royal Engineers
6 October 1915 - 14 February 1919

WO95/2495/1

The Naval & Military Press Ltd
www.nmarchive.com
Published in association with The National Archives

Published by

The Naval & Military Press Ltd

Unit 10 Ridgewood Industrial Park,

Uckfield, East Sussex,

TN22 5QE England

Tel: +44 (0) 1825 749494

www.naval-military-press.com

www.nmarchive.com

This diary has been reprinted in facsimile from the original. Any imperfections are inevitably reproduced and the quality may fall short of modern type and cartographic standards.

© Crown Copyright
Images reproduced by permission of The National Archives, London, England, 2015.

Contents

Document type	Place/Title	Date From	Date To
Heading	WO95/2495/1		
Heading	36th Division C.R.E. Oct 1915-Feb 1919		
Heading	36th Division H.Q. 36th Div: C.R.E. Vol I Oct 16		
Heading	War Diary of Hd Qrs R.E. 36th Divn From 6th October 1915 To 31st October 1915 (Volume 1.)		
War Diary	Longueau	06/10/1915	06/10/1915
War Diary	Flesselles	06/10/1915	12/11/1915
War Diary	Arqueves	12/11/1915	16/11/1915
War Diary	Arqueves	17/10/1915	31/10/1915
Miscellaneous	Move of 16th R.I.R (P) & 121 122 & 150 Field Companies.	11/10/1915	11/10/1915
Miscellaneous	C Form (Original). Messages And Signals.		
Heading	H.Q. 36th Div: C.R.E. Vol 2 Nov 15		
Heading	War Diary Of H.Q. R.E. 36th Division From 1.11.15 To 30-11-15 (Volume 2)		
War Diary	Arqueves	01/11/1915	26/11/1915
War Diary	Changing Area	27/11/1915	28/11/1915
War Diary	Pontremy	29/11/1915	30/11/1915
Miscellaneous	C.R.E. 36th. Division.	21/11/1915	21/11/1915
Heading	C.R.E. 36th Div: Vol: 3 Dec 15		
Heading	War Diary December 1915 Headquarters 36th Divisional R.E.		
War Diary	Pontremy	01/12/1915	31/12/1915
Miscellaneous	A Form Messages And Signals.		
Miscellaneous	C.R.E. 36th Divn H.Q 144. Q	18/12/1915	18/12/1915
Heading	War Diary Of C.R.E. 36th (Ulster) Division Month Of January 1916		
War Diary	Pont-Remy	01/01/1916	03/01/1916
War Diary	Domart	03/01/1916	18/01/1916
War Diary	Bernaville	18/01/1916	31/01/1916
Heading	CRE 36th Div: Vols. 4/5		
Heading	War Diary Of C.R.E. 36th (Ulster) Division For Month Of February. 1916		
War Diary	Bernaville	01/02/1916	01/02/1916
War Diary	Acheux	02/02/1916	29/02/1916
Heading	War Diary Of CRE 36th (Ulster) Division For Month Of March 1916 Vol 6		
War Diary	Acheux	01/03/1916	31/03/1916
Heading	War Diary Of C.R.E. 36th (Ulster) Division For Month Of April 1916		
War Diary	Acheux	01/04/1916	03/04/1916
War Diary	Harponville	04/04/1916	20/04/1916
War Diary	Hedauville	21/04/1916	30/04/1916
Heading	War Diary Of CRE 36th (Ulster) Division For Month Of May 1916		
War Diary	Hedauville	01/05/1916	31/05/1916
Heading	36th Divisional Engineers. C.R.E. 36th Division June 1916		
War Diary	Hedauville	01/06/1916	30/06/1916

Type	Description	Date From	Date To
Miscellaneous	This account has been sent in by-Colonel P.T. Denis de Vitre DSO. (late C.R.E. 36th Division)	21/05/1930	21/05/1930
Miscellaneous	Statement Of Work Carried Out By The Royal Engineers Under Divisional Arrangements During The Months Of April, May, and June 1916		
Miscellaneous	H.Q 36th Division "Q"	19/07/1916	19/07/1916
Miscellaneous	A.D.M.S. No. 663. d/19.7.16 (36th Division)	19/07/1916	19/07/1916
Heading	36th Divisional Engineers C.R.E. 36th Division July 1916 Engineer arrangements for the offensive.		
War Diary	Divisional Report Centre at Q.31.B 10.9	01/07/1916	01/07/1916
War Diary	Div. Report Centre	02/07/1916	02/07/1916
War Diary	Hedauville.	03/07/1916	05/07/1916
War Diary	On March	06/07/1916	06/07/1916
War Diary	Rubempre	07/07/1916	09/07/1916
War Diary	Bernaville	10/07/1916	12/07/1916
War Diary	Serques	13/07/1916	21/07/1916
War Diary	Esquelbecq	22/07/1916	23/07/1916
War Diary	Montnoir	24/07/1916	31/07/1916
Operation(al) Order(s)	C.R.E's Order No. 2	20/06/1916	20/06/1916
Map			
Miscellaneous	Movement Order by Lt. Col. P.T. Denis de Vitre. C.R.E. 36th Division.	15/06/1916	15/06/1916
Operation(al) Order(s)	Operation Order By C.R.E. No. 3	28/06/1916	28/06/1916
Miscellaneous	108th Infantry Brigade Operation Order No 1	23/06/1916	23/06/1916
Miscellaneous	Appendix "A". Signal Communications.		
Miscellaneous	Appendix "B". Prisoners Of War.		
Miscellaneous	Ammunition Supply And Accounting For Ammunition. Appendix 'C'		
Miscellaneous	108th Infantry Brigade: Dumps And Stragglers Posts Will Be Found By Battalions As Follows:- Appendix "D"		
Miscellaneous	108th Infantry Brigade. Appendix "E"		
Miscellaneous	Appendix "F"		
Miscellaneous	Carriage Of Tools And R.E. Stores. Appendix "G"		
Miscellaneous	3" Stokes Trench Mortars. Appendix "H"		
Operation(al) Order(s)	108th Infantry Brigade Operation Order No. 1	23/06/1916	23/06/1916
Operation(al) Order(s)	107th Infantry Brigade Operation Order No. 1	21/06/1916	21/06/1916
Operation(al) Order(s)	Instructions Issued With Operation Order, No. 1. dated 21st June, 1916	21/06/1916	21/06/1916
Miscellaneous	Extracts from Signalling Instructions And Divisional Artillery Orders for Attack.	18/06/1916	18/06/1916
Operation(al) Order(s)	36th Division Order No. 39	29/06/1916	29/06/1916
Heading	Appendices:- G.H.I.K.L.M.N. O.P.R.S.T.U. & Tracing.		
Miscellaneous	A Form Messages And Signals.		
Miscellaneous	C Form (Duplicate). Messages And Signals.		
Miscellaneous	A Form. Messages And Signals.		
Miscellaneous	C Form (Duplicate). Messages And Signals.		
Miscellaneous	C Form (Original). Messages And Signals.		
Miscellaneous	A Form Messages And Signals.		
Miscellaneous	C Form (Original). Messages And Signals.		
Miscellaneous	A Form. Messages And Signals.		
Miscellaneous	Signals.		
Miscellaneous	A Form Messages And Signals.		
Miscellaneous	C Form (Original). Messages And Signals.		
Miscellaneous	And Signals.		
Miscellaneous	Messages And Signals.		

Miscellaneous	Form Messages And Signals.		
Miscellaneous	A Form Messages And Signals.		
Miscellaneous	C Form (Original). Messages And Signals.		
Miscellaneous	A Form Messages And Signals.		
Miscellaneous	C Form (Duplicate). Messages And Signals.		
Miscellaneous	C Form (Original). Messages And Signals.		
Miscellaneous	A Form Messages And Signals.		
Miscellaneous	C Form (Duplicate). Messages And Signals.		
Miscellaneous	A Form Messages And Signals.		
Miscellaneous	C Form (Duplicate). Messages And Signals.		
Miscellaneous	C Form (Original). Messages And Signals.		
Miscellaneous	A Form Messages And Signals.		
Miscellaneous	C Form (Original). Messages And Signals.		
Miscellaneous	C Form (Duplicate) Messages And Signals.		
Miscellaneous	C Form (Original). Messages And Signals.		
Miscellaneous	A Form Messages And Signals.		
Miscellaneous	C Form (Original). Messages And Signals.		
Miscellaneous	A Form. Messages And Signals.		
Miscellaneous	C Form (Duplicate). Messages And Signals.		
Miscellaneous	C Form (Original). Messages And Signals.		
Miscellaneous	A Form Messages And Signals.		
Miscellaneous	C Form (Original). Messages And Signals.		
Miscellaneous	A Form Messages And Signals.		
Miscellaneous	C Form (Original). Messages And Signals.		
Miscellaneous	C Form (Duplicate). Messages And Signals.		
Miscellaneous	A Form Messages And Signals.		
Miscellaneous	C Form (Original). Messages And Signals.		
Miscellaneous	A Form Messages And Signals.		
Miscellaneous	C Form (Duplicate). Messages And Signals.		
Diagram etc			
Miscellaneous	C.E., Fourth Army. E. 619 C.E., Xth Corps. H/264	29/06/1916	29/06/1916
Miscellaneous	CRE 36th Divn	04/07/1916	04/07/1916
Miscellaneous	O.C. 16 RIR (P)	04/07/1916	04/07/1916
Operation(al) Order(s)	36th Division Order No. 43	05/07/1916	05/07/1916
Miscellaneous	Administrative Orders by Lt. Col. P.T. Denis de Vitre, C.R.E. 36th Division.	05/07/1916	05/07/1916
Miscellaneous	Communications.	22/06/1916	22/06/1916
Miscellaneous	O.C. 121.122.155 Field Coy, R.E. Extract From Administrative Instructions No. C/15/188	23/06/1916	23/06/1916
Miscellaneous	O.C., 17th N.F. (Pioneers). General Staff.	24/06/1916	24/06/1916
Miscellaneous	H.Q. 36th Division. "G".	28/06/1916	28/06/1916
Operation(al) Order(s)	36th Division Order No. 40	29/06/1916	29/06/1916
Miscellaneous	Operation Order By C.R.E. 36th Division.	30/06/1916	30/06/1916
Heading	War Diary of C.R.E. 36th (Ulster) Division For Month Of August 1916 Vol 11		
War Diary	Montnoir	01/08/1916	31/08/1916
Heading	War Diary of C.R.E. 36th (Ulster) Division For Month Of September 1916 Vol 12		
War Diary	St Jans Cappel	01/09/1916	30/09/1916
Heading	War Diary of C.R.E. 36th (Ulster) Division For Month Of October 1916 Vol 13		
War Diary	St Jans Cappel	01/10/1916	31/10/1916
Heading	War Diary of C.R.E. 36th (Ulster) Division For Month Of November 1916 Vol 14		
War Diary	St Jans Cappel	01/11/1916	30/11/1916

Heading	War Diary of C.R.E. 36th Division December 1916 Vol 15		
War Diary	St Jans Capel	01/12/1916	31/12/1916
Heading	War Diary of C.R.E. 36th Division From 1/1/17 to 31/1/17 Vol 16		
War Diary	St Jans Capel	01/01/1917	31/01/1917
Heading	War Diary of C.R.E. 36th Division February 1917 Vol 17		
War Diary	St Jans Cappel	01/02/1917	28/02/1917
Heading	War Diary of C.R.E. 36th Division for month of March 1917 Vol 18		
War Diary	St Jans Capel	01/03/1917	31/03/1917
Heading	War Diary of C.R.E. 36th Division 1st April 1917 to 30th April 1917 Vol 19		
War Diary	St Jans Cappel	01/04/1917	30/04/1917
Heading	War Diary of C.R.E. 36th Division for month of May 1917 Vol 20		
War Diary	St Jans Cappel	01/05/1917	15/05/1917
War Diary	Dranoutre Ulster Camp	16/05/1917	31/05/1917
Heading	War Diary of C.R.E. 36th Division June 1917. Vol 21		
War Diary		01/06/1917	08/06/1917
War Diary	Kemmel Hill	09/06/1917	09/06/1917
War Diary	St Jans Cappel	10/06/1917	19/06/1917
War Diary	Ulster Camp	20/06/1917	29/06/1917
War Diary	Watou	30/06/1917	30/06/1917
Operation(al) Order(s)	C.R.E. 36th Division Operation Order No. 21	28/06/1917	28/06/1917
Miscellaneous	March Table. To accompany C.R.E. 36th Division Operation Order No 21		
Heading	War Diary of C.R.E. 36th Division for month of July 1917 Vol 22		
War Diary	Watou	01/07/1917	26/07/1917
War Diary	Winnezeele	27/07/1917	30/07/1917
War Diary	Poperinghe	31/07/1917	31/07/1917
Heading	War Diary of C.R.E. 36th Division for month of August 1917 Vol 23		
War Diary	Poperinghe	01/08/1917	03/08/1917
War Diary	Mersey Camp	04/08/1917	17/08/1917
War Diary	Winnezeele	18/08/1917	22/08/1917
War Diary	Barastre	23/08/1917	30/08/1917
War Diary	Ytres	31/08/1917	31/08/1917
Operation(al) Order(s)	C.R.E. 36th Division Operation Order No. 24	02/08/1917	02/08/1917
Miscellaneous	March Table To Accompany O.O. No 24		
Operation(al) Order(s)	C.R.E. 36th Division Operation Order No 25	16/08/1917	16/08/1917
Operation(al) Order(s)	C.R.E. 36th Division Operation Order No 26	17/08/1917	17/08/1917
Miscellaneous	For 18th August 1917 March Table to Accompany C.R.E's Order No 26	18/08/1917	18/08/1917
Operation(al) Order(s)	C.R.E. 36th Division Operation Order No. 27	22/08/1917	22/08/1917
Operation(al) Order(s)	C.R.E. 36th Division Operation Order No. 29	26/08/1917	26/08/1917
Miscellaneous	Instructions For The Offensive. Employment of Pack Transport on "Z" and Subsequent Days	14/08/1917	14/08/1917
Heading	War Diary of C.R.E. 36th Division for month of September 1917 Vol 24		
War Diary	Ytres	01/09/1917	30/09/1917
Heading	War Diary of C.R.E. 36th Division for month of October 1917 Vol 25		
War Diary	Ytres	01/10/1917	31/10/1917

Heading	War Diary of C.R.E. 36th Division for month of November 1917 Vol 26		
War Diary	Ytres.	01/11/1917	30/11/1917
Operation(al) Order(s)	Amendment To C.R.E. 36th Division Operation Order No 30	17/11/1917	17/11/1917
Operation(al) Order(s)	C.R.E. 36th Division Operation Order No 30	17/11/1917	17/11/1917
Operation(al) Order(s)	C.R.E. 36th Division Operation Order No 31	18/11/1917	18/11/1917
Operation(al) Order(s)	C.R.E. 36th Division Operation Order No 32	28/11/1917	28/11/1917
Heading	War Diary of C.R.E. 36th Division for month of December 1917		
War Diary	Ytres.	01/12/1917	03/12/1917
War Diary	Sorel Le Grand	04/12/1917	13/12/1917
War Diary	Sorel	14/12/1917	18/12/1917
War Diary	Lucheux	19/12/1917	26/12/1917
War Diary	Corbie	27/12/1917	31/12/1917
Heading	War Diary of C.R.E. 36th Division for month of January 1918 Vol 28		
War Diary		01/01/1918	31/01/1918
Heading	War Diary of C.R.E. 36th Division for month of February 1918 Vol 29		
War Diary	Ollezy	01/02/1918	28/02/1918
Heading	36th Divisional Engineers C.R.E. 36th Division March 1918 Narrative of Operations attached.		
Heading	War Diary of C.R.E. 36th Division for month of March 1918		
War Diary	Ollezy	04/03/1918	21/03/1918
War Diary	Estouilly	22/03/1918	22/03/1918
War Diary	Freniches	23/03/1918	23/03/1918
War Diary	Beaulieu	24/03/1918	25/03/1918
War Diary	Roye	25/03/1918	25/03/1918
War Diary	Avricourt Guerbuigny	26/03/1918	26/03/1918
War Diary	Grivesnes	27/03/1918	27/03/1918
War Diary	Sourdon	28/03/1918	28/03/1918
War Diary	Essertaut	29/03/1918	29/03/1918
War Diary	Wailly.	30/03/1918	30/03/1918
War Diary	Allery	31/03/1918	31/03/1918
Miscellaneous	36th Division "G"	29/04/1918	29/04/1918
Miscellaneous	Narrative Of Operations Between 21st and 28th March, 1918	21/03/1918	21/03/1918
Miscellaneous	Report On The Demolition Of Bridges During Operations From 21st to 28th March, 1918	21/03/1918	21/03/1918
Miscellaneous	Amendment To "Instructions To R.E. And Pioneers In Case Of Enemy Attack"-28/2/18	28/02/1918	28/02/1918
Miscellaneous	Amendment To "Instructions To R.E. And Pioneers In Case Of Enemy Attack"-E/14/69, dated 28/2/18	28/02/1918	28/02/1918
Miscellaneous	Amendment To "Instructions To R.E. And Pioneers In Case Of Enemy Attack" No. E/14/69, dated 28/2/18	28/02/1918	28/02/1918
Miscellaneous	Instructions For R.E. And Pioneers in Case of Enemy Attack.	28/02/1918	28/02/1918
Heading	36th Divisional Engineers C.R.E. 36th Division. April 1918		
Heading	War Diary of C.R.E. 36th Division for month of April 1918 Vol 31		
War Diary	Gamaches	01/04/1918	30/04/1918
Operation(al) Order(s)	C.R.E. 36th Division Order No 2	28/04/1918	28/04/1918

Heading	War Diary of C.R.E. 36th Division for month of May 1918 Vol 32		
War Diary		01/05/1918	30/05/1918
Operation(al) Order(s)	C.R.E. 36th Division Operation Order No. 3	27/05/1918	27/05/1918
Heading	War Diary of C.R.E. 36th Division for month of June 1918 Vol 33		
War Diary		01/06/1918	30/06/1918
Operation(al) Order(s)	C.R.E. 36th Division Operation Order No 8	28/08/1918	28/08/1918
Miscellaneous	O.C. 121st Field Company, R.E.	30/08/1918	30/08/1918
Heading	War Diary of C.R.E. 36th Division for month of July 1918. Vol 34		
War Diary		01/07/1918	31/07/1918
Operation(al) Order(s)	C.R.E. 36th Division Operation Order No. 6	21/07/1918	21/07/1918
Heading	War Diary of C.R.E. 36th Division for month of August 1918 Vol 35		
War Diary		01/08/1918	31/08/1918
Operation(al) Order(s)	C.R.E. 36th Division Operation Order No. 7	04/08/1918	04/08/1918
Heading	War Diary of C.R.E. 36th Divn September 1918 Vol 36		
War Diary		01/09/1918	30/09/1918
Heading	War Diary of C.R.E. 36th Division for month of October 1918 Vol 37		
War Diary	Ypres	01/10/1918	01/10/1918
War Diary	Junction Camp	02/10/1918	20/10/1918
War Diary	Lendelede	21/10/1918	31/10/1918
Miscellaneous	C.R.E., 36th Division. Appendix A	18/10/1918	18/10/1918
Miscellaneous	Narrative of Operations on 19th and 20th Oct., 1918. Appendix 'B'	22/10/1918	22/10/1918
Miscellaneous	Narrative of Operations by 150th Field Coy., R.E., 13th Oct.-21st Oct. 1918 Appendix 'C'	13/10/1918	13/10/1918
Miscellaneous	Appendix 'D'	22/10/1918	22/10/1918
Heading	War Diary of C.R.E. 36th Division for the month of November 1918. Vol 38		
War Diary		11/11/1918	29/11/1918
Miscellaneous	G.H.Q.	07/11/1918	07/11/1918
Miscellaneous	C.R.E., 36th Division.	02/11/1918	02/11/1918
Miscellaneous	Short Description of Medium Bridge built across the River Lys at S/29.O.19.b.2.2. on the 23rd Octr., 1918, by the 121st Field Coy., R.F.	03/11/1918	03/11/1918
Heading	War Diary of C.R.E. 36th Division for month of December 1918 Vol 39		
War Diary		01/12/1918	18/12/1918
Heading	War Diary of C.R.E. 36th Division for month of January 1919 Vol 40		
War Diary		01/01/1919	31/01/1919
Heading	War Diary of C.R.E. 36th Division for month of February 1919 Vol 41		
War Diary		01/02/1919	14/02/1919
Heading	D.A.D.O.S. 36th Div Vol 4		

W051 245 1506 51

36TH DIVISION

C. R. E.
OCT 1915-FEB 1919

36th Division

H.Q. 36th Div: C.R.E.
Vol I
Oct 16

D/
7432

CONFIDENTIAL.

WAR DIARY
of
HdQrs R.E. 36th Divn.

From 6th October 1915 To 31st October 1915

(Volume I.)

Army Form C. 2118.

Confidential
WAR DIARY
or
INTELLIGENCE SUMMARY.

of C.R.E.s (Engineers regarding Royal Engineers 3rd & 5th)

From 6 October 1915

Summary of Events and Information

Instructions regarding War Diaries and Intelligence Summaries are contained in F. S. Regs., Part II. and the Staff Manual respectively. Title pages will be prepared in manuscript.

Place	Date	Hour	Summary of Events and Information	Remarks and references to Appendices
LONGUEAU	6/10/15	12.30 p.m.	Finished detraining and marched to FLESSELLES.	
FLESSELLES	6/10/15	5 am	Troops completed billetting.	
FLESSELLES	7/10/15		Nothing of interest to record	
FLESSELLES	8/10/15		The C.R.E. visited the 7th Corps and obtained instruction as to routine working of R.E. Park. He also inspected the R.E. Park and consulted Field Cashier regarding starting imprest account. The Field Companies have now carried work on in Coy. billets 132½ as follows: 12½th P.Coy at AILLY SUR SOMME, M.S.H. 12.H in MIRABAUK, 150½ in BERTANGLE (attached to the 36th Signal Coy temporarily) The XX Cable Section is at H.Q.	Dy 6 10 15 A. M. 7/10/15 Dy 8 10 15
FLESSELLES	9/10/15		Preliminary arrangements were made for starting the C.R.E.'s Park. Bought 2 hundred & pr coils for telephone lines	
FLESSELLES	10/10/15		Visited 12 & 1st P.Coy at Billets. Nothing of importance to record.	Order marked "A"
FLESSELLES	11/10/15		Marched off — during R.S.M. H/c C.R.E. Divisional Staff	
ARQUEVES	12/10/15	9.30 am	3.0 fus arrived at ARQUEVES.	
ARQUEVES	13/10/15	3.0 pm	C.E. 3rd Army arrived at 9.30 am, followed arrival in of Defence — OR CRE & OC K Balloon 9 Field Coy carried out work & defended trenches & dispose 1 M.Z & OS f TOUTENCOURT to ARQUEVES.	
		2.0 pm	2.0 pm Detailed 12th Coy to the first & 150 N/g. 6th General excavation from life south of ARQUEVES and 122°. to defences of TOUTENCOURT. Coys handed out fire trenches.	13/10/15

Army Form C. 2118.

WAR DIARY
or
INTELLIGENCE SUMMARY.
(Erase heading not required.)

Instructions regarding War Diaries and Intelligence Summaries are contained in F.S. Regs., Part II. and the Staff Manual respectively. Title pages will be prepared in manuscript.

Place	Date	Hour	Summary of Events and Information	Remarks and references to Appendices
ARQUEVES	14/9/15	8.0 a.m.	All three Coys at work on Field Defences. C.R.E. held meeting for their "abilis" with Or 16. R.I.R.P. who started work on these.	
— do —	15/9/15	8.15 a.m.	Went over "sites" of the Field Coy. R.E.	
— do —	16/9/15	6.0 a.m.	— ditto — & the work of the 16. R.I.R.P. &c &c.	
		3.30 p.m.	Rode over to see C.E. 3rd Army on Cavalry question.	
— " —	17.10.15	11.0 a.m.	Went over sites for rear defence works with C.E. 3rd Army.	
		3.0 p.m.	Inspection of Field Coy Camps & billets.	
— " —	18/10/15	8.30 a.m.	Sited three defence works for 150th Field Coy. R.E.	
		2.0 p.m.	Sited one defence work for 122nd Field Coy. R.E. & walked over some of the works in course of construction with C.E. 3rd Army.	
— " —	19.10.15	8.30 a.m. to 4.0 p.m.	Sited three defence works for 124th Field Coy. R.E. and decided on three General Sites of defence of village of VAUCHELLES	
— " —	20.10.15	9.0 a.m.	Arranged with French Army Engineers to join our line of defences S.E. of TOUTENCOURT with the AMIENS — DOULLENS line of defences. Sited more defences for 16. R.I.R. P.9	

WAR DIARY
or
INTELLIGENCE SUMMARY
(Erase heading not required.)

Army Form C. 2118.

Instructions regarding War Diaries and Intelligence Summaries are contained in F.S. Regs., Part II. and the Staff Manual respectively. Title pages will be prepared in manuscript.

Place	Date	Hour	Summary of Events and Information	Remarks and references to Appendices
ARQUEVES	21.10.15	9.30 a.m.	decided on defences of Village of TOUTENCOURT with O.C. 122nd Field Cy R.E. The three R.E. Field Cys are now employed on defence works from AUTHIE (exclusive) to TOUTENCOURT (inclusive) & the 16. R.I.R.P. from TOUTENCOURT (inclusive) to connection with the French AMIENS – DOULLENS line. Walked from bet--...	
	22.10.15	a.m.	Proceeded with C.E. 3rd Army to FORET DE VIGNACOURT, & arranged about cutting timber & hurdlework for Army Line defences and for transport of same.	
		p.m.	Office & visited defence works.	
	23.10.15		Inspected 30 huts in BOIS CREPTAL & purchased the whole of the small wood close North of BOIS CREPTAL. Received orders to employ 10th Labour Battalion on the defences Vide B.P.	
— do —	24.10.15	p.m.	Holiday of different kinds.	
— do —	25.10.15		Rode out with officers and visited works/defences in progress at BERTRANCOURT. – Recced	
	26.10.15	a.m.	Employed 8.50 men of 10th Labour Battalion on the defences – Recced & also continued & visited on further defences of villages of TOUTENCOURT. Practised Officers N.C.Os of 150 Cy in laying trenches Rode recced works/defences No 9 ARQUEVES. Five.	
		p.m.	Visited works/defences S of ARQUEVES with C.E. & Army. The small amount of rain of previous days had ceased & fairly severe frost of the day resulted, which kept up all night. Practised 150 Cy in reinstating trees for digging by night.	

Army Form C. 2118.

WAR DIARY

INTELLIGENCE SUMMARY.

H⁰. Qu. R.E. 36. Div.

Place	Date	Hour	Summary of Events and Information	Remarks and references to Appendices
ARQUEVES	27/10/15	a.m. / p.m. / night	Visited defence works. Weather fine. Eastern Battalion men reported as digging well. Enfilade Wire and N.O.P. 1/21st Field Coy is taking out trenches.	
ARQUEVES	28.10.15	a.m.	Boys' Company numbers up to 150 less out. MARIEUX. – Provided with Motorcycle car for future use, invoiced to Division H.Q. but Vehicle is clutch'd the short spare strip. Received all day. OFFICERS SERVANTS. Three men who only knew how qualifications as "valets" are not fully employed. All Private Servants – all qualify as cooks, & there are othermen	
—do—	29.10.15	night	few draw'd by & Capt. Wilkin. Reached 124th Coy is completing wiring parties along trenches. Coys on Army Line defences. N.O.P. C.R.E. 4th Div is training 1 Field Coy one at a time under fire – also re Machine Gun Emplacements.	
—do—	30/10/15	night a.m. night	Reached 122 Field Coy Officers. 122 is making trenches by night. Mustered officers with C.E. 3rd Army. Finished 122 + 124 is disabling railway tracks by night.	
—do—	31/10/15	a.m.	Tried to purchase writs & knobwork. Prices asked were absurd. Some rain. Report that I cannot keep my work up to date or how track – asked for a Motor; as I never foresees the ARMY LINE DEFENCE works. (15 works) on are 8 mile front – also the FORÊT HQ AU also some 20 miles away. Some 20 miles away by road. The C.R.E.'s Divisional that or Bri kindred or Ambulances Divisional Brigade arises taking arrangements. Purchase of	

Army Form C. 2118

WAR DIARY
or
INTELLIGENCE SUMMARY
(Erase heading not required)

Instructions regarding War Diaries and Intelligence Summaries are contained in F. S. Regs., Part II. and the Staff Manual respectively. Title pages will be prepared in manuscript.

Place	Date	Hour	Summary of Events and Information	Remarks and references to Appendices
ARQUEVES	31/10/15	—	Also supply one Pioneer Battalion. Sent Lorries Battalion. The C.O. of the letter is provided with a 2 seated Motor Car.	

J.V. Deeves white
Lt Colonel C.M.E 36. Div.
31/10/15

Headquarters,
36th Division.
11-10-15.

Move of 16th R.I.R. (P) &121 122 &150 Field Companies.
----

1. The Hdq and 3 Field Companies R.E. will march to-morrow 12th Oct. to Arqueves for duty under the orders of the C.E. 3rd Army.

2. The Coys. will be accommodated as follows:- two in tents and one in billets. the tents will meet you on arrival and are being sent by the 48th Division.

3. Advance parties to report to the O.C. Field Ambulances at Arqueves.

4. Rations for to-morrow 12th inst. will be carried with you. Rations for the 13th will follow in supply waggons from refilling point. Refilling on the 13th inst, will be at Lealvilleis.

5. Coys will march out independently.

ACKNOWLEDGE

Despatched by despatch riders at 11.50.p.m..

No.1.Copy to C.R.E.
Nn.2.Copy to O.C.121 Co.
No.3.Copy to O.C. 122 Co.
No.@4.Copy to O.C. 150.Co.
No.5.Copy to Office.

Lt.Col.
A.A.&.Q.M.G.

"C" Form (Original).
MESSAGES AND SIGNALS.

Army Form C. 2123.

Prefix	Code	Words	Received	Sent, or sent due	Office Stamp.
		£ s. d.	From	At	
Charges to collect			By		
Service Instructions.				To	
				By	

Handed in at .... Office 2.23 p.m. Received 3.57 p.m.

TO — O.C. 36 Div ARQEVES

*Sender's Number	Day of Month	In reply to Number	
B10	22/10		AAA

10th Labour Bttn moves to HERRISART tomorrow & will be available for work on Army lines & check on Monday the 23rd and ... Please see officer commanding on 24 Army to down hold of work & allot the battalion to works.

T Army

FROM
PLACE & TIME — R.E. 3 Army

* This line should be erased if not required.

AD. 36 E Div.
CRE.
Vol 2

12/
7634

Nov 15

CONFIDENTIAL.

WAR DIARY.

OF

H.Q. R.E. 36th Division

From 1.11.15 To 30-11-15

(Volume 2)

Army Form C. 2118

WAR DIARY
INTELLIGENCE SUMMARY. H.Qrs. R.E. 36th Division.

Place	Date	Hour	Summary of Events and Information	Remarks and references to Appendices
ARQUEVES	1/11/15	a.m.	Rode over to C.R.E. 4th Div'n. & went round some of his trenches & saw 3 types of machine gun emplacements. Raised most of the day.	D
"	2/11/15	all day	Proceeded to H.Q. 36 Div — thence to FOREST DE VIGNACOURT. — thence to MONTONVILLERS — thence to AMIENS & returned to ARQUEVES at 5.30 p.m. It is proposed to a C.R.E. there some means of getting about on duty other than on horseback. Total mileage 60 miles. 121' laid by starters to 4 Div for training is useful. Rained hard all day.	D
"	3/11/15		Fine. G.O.C. 36th Division inspected its defence works under construction.	D
"	4/11/15	10.0 am	Reconnoitred - Commanding French R.E. & decided on communications between defences of the village) TOUTENCOURT and the French line of defence behind it. Decided on sites for machine gun emplacement - on the defences from TOUTENCOURT inclusive to the S.E. exit.	D
		10.30 am to 5.30 p.m.	In TOUTENCOURT WOOD have unearthed an old building said to belong to the early Saxon. And old well has also been found. Weather fine.	
"	5/11/15	9.30 am	Proceeded to FOREST DE VIGNACOURT. Finally decided on Lorry Time Table. Reported to C.E. 3rd Army.	D

Army Form C. 2118

WAR DIARY
INTELLIGENCE SUMMARY.
(Erase heading not required.)

H.Q. R.E. 36th Divn

Place	Date	Hour	Summary of Events and Information	Remarks and references to Appendices
ARQUEVES	6/11/15	a.m.	Bright — sure more mushroom.	
"	7/11/15	a.m.	Visited Experiment with lack Bessy hurdle at TERRAMESNIL & reported thereon H.Q. on 36 Div. Fine — but cold.	D
"	8/11/15	a.m.	Divine service. Fine. No. 121 Field Coy relieved from training in the trenches.	D
"			Had 9 lorries of No. 3 Construction party. L. Telegraph Cy of 1st (early) mushroom. Bought more mushroom.	D
"			Weather fine. 122 Field Cy attached to 4th Division for training in the trenches & billets H.Q. & 2 sections at MAILLY-MAILLET + 2 sections at ENGLEBELMER.	D
"	9/11/15	"	Instructed by G.O.C. 36 Div to instruct a practical & portable means of throwing a 2lb bomb 50 — also a light & efficient shield & protection from to ward off bombs & hurl them back to hot trap per vehicles the trench. Rain in evening. Tried 5 coming 8 lorries are being kept for the saw mill at CANDAS — labourer demanded must at rate of 9.315 & afternoon. R.E. to supply all labour; free forage.	D
"	10/11/15		Received Hard. Men took off work to noon.	D
"	11/11/15		Received Hardie's evening myth. All day electric machine gun lab with Macauthrie's staff. Interviewed French Division re supply of engineers for saw mill.	D
"			One section of 121 Field Cy Re moved to CANDAS for use with 3rd Division.	D
"	12/11/15		Received heart - took out defensive work. Tried flying billet for 1st Cy at VAUCHELLES — decided to repair 3 ruined buildings. The billeting arrangements seem the "suggine" — each unit billets itself amongst those already there. Instead of the Village being rid of out-building areas etc.	D

Army Form C. 21

WAR DIARY
or
INTELLIGENCE SUMMARY.   HQ R.E. 36th Divn
(Erase heading not required.)

Instructions regarding War Diaries and Intelligence Summaries are contained in F. S. Regs., Part II. and the Staff Manual respectively. Title pages will be prepared in manuscript.

Place	Date	Hour	Summary of Events and Information	Remarks and references to Appendices
ARQUEVES	13/11/15	a.m.	Went to CHANDAS and arranged new site for C.R.E. Divisional Offices. Have m.g. AMIENS and arranged for making a list. Went out to PROUTH. Bought 12- Towels 22&Sheets last - Boy leaving me of all finis, a dealer afterwards asked 14 frams each. Bought Rugby Motor in AMIENS. Started at 10.20 am & got back at 5.30 p.m. Heavy thunderstorm, J.B. Wilson? at a C.R.E.'s Divisn. Slept - raw & mild.	D
"	14/11/15	a.m.	Attended a C.R.E.III Corps & Received his instrs as to Works - Hostility reference for 36th Division. Heavy but cold.	D
"	15/11/15	"	Much difficulty keeping horse fit - all round however toned to look. Legs regaining working - the stable is nearly vertical. Hard frost in a.m.	D
"	16/11/15	"	3 inches of snow at night.	D
"	17/11/15	"	Frost - sleet & hailstorm. The unevenness of the road of Soissons. Ordered for Mattress - Poulet - with stuffed mattresses. Frosty at night?	D
"	18/11/15	"	Discussion re details needed in Erecting 1 Cyclist & 4 Coys R.A.M.C. Thawing.	D
"	19/11/15	"	Rides for use of Orderlies arranged - but too heavy snowstorms bring up in more sheesteel.	D
"	20/11/15	"	Rode to AMIENS - Div.14 P.Wire- & Motor to papers - traveled 80 hails in 14 hrs, ordered 10 dist. Ammy to come out to Reliefs of me of the last 20 of this displaying me at my 11h tun. Trie-cold.	D
"	21/11/15	"	121st Field Co. R.E. (less 3 Sections) marched mobilized - at DOMART. C.R.E. motored to PONT REMY & here our mail - arrange for haltroom in new Divr H.Q. - & Workshops at AILLY. Trive- very cold & shower. Frost till midnight.	D

2353   Wt. W2544/4454 700,000 5/15 D. D. & L.   A.D.S.S./Forms/C. 2118.

Army Form C. 2118

WAR DIARY
or
INTELLIGENCE SUMMARY.
(Erase heading not required.)

H.Q. R.E. 36th Dn.

Instructions regarding War Diaries and Intelligence Summaries are contained in F. S. Regs., Part II. and the Staff Manual respectively. Title pages will be prepared in manuscript.

Place	Date	Hour	Summary of Events and Information	Remarks and references to Appendices
ARQUEVES	22/10/15	a.m. p.m.	Office and visited works of 1/B.R.1.R.P. Bad weather has brought in halt of the trenches. To lecture on recent work of C.E. 2. 34 Army & reported to C.E. XIII Corps at DOULENS. very foggy - took us 8.0 hrs. to arrive. Car commander, keen on pushing on more trainings. Office work till 11.0 p.m.	2
" "	23/10/15		All day at Office. C.S.M. Ja Turle Cy stayed with "Reconnaissance on a trade". Embankment case. Office till 11.0 p.m.	2
" "	24/10/15	a.m p.m.	Visited works of 2 Section 9/124. 7th Cy R.E. McPherson J.N.C.O. apparently established sound - more supervision. Office work. Mild.	2
" "	25/10/15	a.m.	Visited works of C.E. 3 w Army. Res. Reserved of trenchwork purchased. Mild. Recent orders arrive on 27 w. E. BERNAVILLE. met 124 & 150 T of R.E. The 122 T of R.E. removed at POR TONCOURT with C.E. 3 w Army. 1 Section 9/121 T G.B.F. from DOMBART & PONT REMY.	2
" "	26/10/15	a.m.	Some snow. Railway & aeroplane to N.E.	
CHANGING AREA	27/10/15	a.m.	8.0 am. H.Q. R.E. + 153 T.P. R.E. bench from ARQUEVES & 2 Sections 9/124 T. 22 of R.E. from VAUCHELLES & H.Q. 121" from DOMPART & 1 Section 121 Pg from CANDAS to BERNAVILLE.	2
	28/10/15		HERE to PONT REMY. 121 16 by R.E. assembled at MOUFLIERS. 150 T. by G ONQUEUSE.	
PONT REMY	29/10/15		Rain. Great G bricks erected 27 house for 1000 for respired hides. & 45 haver infact.	
" "	30/10/15		Fine. C.F. 34 Army came over. Motored to look for Sand hills & Brickfields. Bricks are being issued over 105 G above Regional prices.	2

F Garrard Lt Col CRE 36th Dn
2/11/15

2353 Wt. W2344/1454 700,000 5/15 D.D.&L. A.D.S.S./Forms/C. 2118.

695 Q.

C. R. E. 36th. Division.
~~36th. Divisional Train.~~
~~Camp Commandant.~~
~~General Staff.~~

Headquarters and 1 Section of 121st. Company R. E., strength about 3 Officers, 90 Other Ranks, and 65 horses, move from ARQUEVES on 21st. November and billet at DOMART-EN-PONTHIEU on the night 21st./22nd. and proceed to PONT-REMY on 22nd. inst., where they will remain pending the arrival of 36th. Division in that area.

Cancelled by wire

Billeting party should report to Camp Commandant 36th. Division on the morning of 21st. inst. and to A. A. & Q. M. G., 32nd. Division (AILLY) en route to PONT-REMY on the morning of 22nd. inst.

O. C. 36th. Divisional Train has been instructed verbally on telephone to arrange to ration this party at PONT-REMY.

Headquarters 36th. Division,
November 20th. 1915.

Lieut.-Colonel.
A. A. & Q. M. G.

CRE. 36th Str.
Vol. 3

121/7809

Keck 15

War Diary

December 1915

Headquarters 36th Divisional R.E.

Army Form C. 2118.

WAR DIARY
INTELLIGENCE SUMMARY.
(Erase heading not required.)

Instructions regarding War Diaries and Intelligence Summaries are contained in F. S. Regs., Part II. and the Staff Manual respectively. Title pages will be prepared in manuscript.

Place	Date	Hour	Summary of Events and Information	Remarks and references to Appendices
PONTREMY	1/12/15	a.m.	Tried to purchase wood from Count ..... owner of FRANCIÈRES. Refused sale. Said would allow us another ride in Sunday next.	
"	"	p.m.	Bought 6 trucknant wood @ 2 francs — about 67,000 feet. — Made preliminary arrangements for burying same.	Q
"	"	2/12/15	Raining. Bought 12 planks at EPÉCOURT. 12 k.by (feeling) hedaing at R.DAMME.	Q
"	"	3/12/15 a.m. p.m.	Conference with GOC. RA. at base Headquarters. — Other + bought for wood at base.	Q
"	"	4/12/15 a.m.	Returned our day, pay ny hills. Bought wood — 2 graves at .. laughed to have planking.	Q
"	"	5/12/15	Relating + purchasing timber. Bought that order of sawmill expires letter.	Q
"	"	6/12/15	Ebbey (?) precipitous timber. Saw field not yet returned.	Q
"	"	7/12/15	Hired new saw mill at FONTAINE. Owner Freeherno + bought superintendent — RE running (returning?) + formerly (?) Circular saw mill — present rates.5 124 7 ee.	Q
"	"	8/12/15	Bought planks at EPÉCOURT fr. 18 francs per cubic metre.	Q
"	"	9/12/15	Felling + purchasing timber.	Q
"	"	10/12/15		
"	"	11/12/15	Out all day in Motor. — arranging for funds.	Q
"	"	12/12/15	— dates arranged burial fr. Montreuil Provences. — repaired plates. Issued timber ale CRG/ADSS.	Q

Army Form C. 2118.

WAR DIARY
INTELLIGENCE SUMMARY.
(Erase heading not required.)

Instructions regarding War Diaries and Intelligence Summaries are contained in F. S. Regs., Part II. and the Staff Manual respectively. Title pages will be prepared in manuscript.

Place	Date	Hour	Summary of Events and Information	Remarks and references to Appendices
PONT REMY	15.12.17		Office work.	
" "	16.12.17		do.	
" "			A.A. & Q.M.G. XIII Corps came over & accompanied him to G. OFFICERS. D mouchat.	
" "	17.12.17		Portion of last 2 weeks by (71 & 72) on Artillery Training, including Gunnery. D	
" "	18.12.17		Training as above. D	
" "	19.12.17		Training as above. D	
" "	20.12.17		Friday afternoon helmets they decide — + see to 2 technical Cases — relieved 11.30 P.M. D	
" "	21.12.17		Training as above. D	
" "	22.12.17		— rain. Visited Liercourt, at Abbeville & went to find billets for 1/R. ENGINEERS D	
" "		22.12.17	2 lectures 1/122 F.A. LF. moved with PONT-REMY — rain D	A.
" "	23.12.17		No lectures cold — evacuation — Stopped ABBEVILLE — only a few billets available D	
" "	24.12.17		Tree they tells — no arrival — spent most week — + someone there must be cancelled — heavy rain D	
" "	25.12.17		Christmas Day. D	
" "	26.12.17		Office work D Sunday. 2 Septs 1/122 LFF PONT REMY for BETHUNE.	
" "	27.12.17		Office work & moved round remaining Units of Brigade. — Holiday for Xmas. D	
" "	28.12.17		Visited 1st G. Railway W. Arm. D 130 by marched to OEUFS.	

2353 Wt. W2541/1454 700,000 5/15 D, D. & L. A.D.S.S./Forms/C. 2118.

Army Form C. 2118.

WAR DIARY
or
INTELLIGENCE SUMMARY.
(Erase heading not required.)

Instructions regarding War Diaries and Intelligence Summaries are contained in F. S. Regs., Part II. and the Staff Manual respectively. Title pages will be prepared in manuscript.

Place	Date	Hour	Summary of Events and Information	Remarks and references to Appendices
PONT-REMY	29/12/15	—	Making of importance to report.	
"	30/12/15	—	— ditto —	
"	31/12/15	—	Visited the new CANADAS area in company with Field Engineer of that area	

F. Louis de V?
Lieut Col ? ONE 36 Div
31.12.15

"A" Form. Army Form C. 2121

MESSAGES AND SIGNALS.

Prefix	Code	m.	Words	Charge	This message is on a/c of:	Recd. at	m.
Office of Origin and Service Instructions						Date	
Confidential			Sent At m.		Service.	From	
			To				
			By		(Signature of "Franking Officer.")	By	

TO CRE. 36th Division

| Sender's Number | Day of Month | In reply to Number | |
| M.257 | 28/11/15 | | A A A |

Your 3 Field Coy RE which were attached to 4th Division did good work and were very keen. The 150th Co was particularly good — Officers picked up the work quickly — I consider a week is too short a time for the attachment of a Field Co but I hope that your officers considered it of value to them.

HB Jones Col RE
CRE 4th Div.

C.R.E. 36th Divn

[Stamp: COMMANDING ROYAL ENGINEER E/1058 DEC 1915 ULSTER DIVISION]

HQ
144..Q
A

Herewith copy of wire addressed
122 Fd Coy R.E, repeated 48th Division
7th Corps & 13th Corps – Wire begins –
Under instructions from 3rd Army
the 122nd Coy R.E. will leave TOUTEN
COURT for PONT REMY, 36th Division
Area on the 21st inst AAA.
They will billet en route at CAN-
APLES on the night of the 21st - 22nd
AAA.
Arrangements have been made
with D.A.Q.M.G 48th Division that
this unit be provided before leaving
TOUTENCOURT with rations for
consumption up to the night of
the 23rd AAA. message ends –

Hd Qtrs 36th Divn   (Sgd) R.F. Mayne
  18-12-15   Capt R.E
  14-35 hours   D.A.Q.M.G.

                    2
H.Q 36th,
              Noted, returned & copies kept
     CWE   (Sgd) C.H. Egerton Capt R.E
  18/11/15   for Lieut. Colonel, R.E.
                        C.R.E. 36th (Ulster) Division

CONFIDENTIAL

WAR DIARY
of
C.R.E. 36th (ULSTER) DIVISION
MONTH OF
JANUARY 1916.

"CONFIDENTIAL"

Army Form C. 2118.

WAR DIARY
or
INTELLIGENCE SUMMARY.
(Erase heading not required.)

C.R.E.
36th (ULSTER) DIVISION.

Place	Date	Hour	Summary of Events and Information	Remarks and references to Appendices
PONT-REMY	1.1.16	—	Starting [diary?] over work in new area.	
"	2.1.16	—	Enquiry into RE.	
PONT-REMY	3.1.16	a.m	Moved from PONT-REMY	
DOMART	3.1.16	p.m	to DOMART.	
"	4.1.16		Rode to CANDAS in car [with] hill — and looked over area the Mine at HALLOY-LES-PERNOIS. N	
"	5.1.16		C.E XIV Corps came over —: attended lecture at VIGNACOURT. N	
"	6.1.16		Entered into contract to supply Timber at CANDAS — Anyplr/1090th trenches at BERNAVILLE. N	
"	7.1.16		Office work till 11 o'clock. Party — a small work. Capt BOWEN R.E. joined as 14th Coy Engineer.	
"	8.1.16		Rode across to RIDEAUCOURT [?] Trenches — LONGVILLERS trees used. Proceeded [?] mills. Saw a work near DONEMONT — C.E XIV Corps called [?].	
"	9.1.16		Conference with R.E + Works Offices re hutting scheme.	
"	10.1.16	a.m	To ABBEVILLE - will etc.	
"	"	p.m	To DOULLENS to Conspect re requisitioning & work.	
"	11.1.16	a.m	Bright — lunch at FIENVILLERS —	
		p.m	Generally looked round for "horses". "Euclus" "trees" "[?]"	
	12.1.16		Ordinary routine to Army Circulars. N	
	13.1.16		Wire [?] N	
	14.1.16		[?] at BERNAVILLE, Anypt - [?]	

Army Form C. 2118.

WAR DIARY
or
INTELLIGENCE SUMMARY.
(Erase heading not required.)

Instructions regarding War Diaries and Intelligence Summaries are contained in F. S. Regs., Part II and the Staff Manual respectively. Title pages will be prepared in manuscript.

Place	Date	Hour	Summary of Events and Information	Remarks and references to Appendices
DOMART	15.1.16	—	Patrol to OUTREBOIS & other villages. D	
"	16.1.16	—	Sunday	
"	17.1.16	—	Visited the SOUTH LANCS works area. D	
DOMART BERNAVILLE	18.1.16	a.m.	Moved to BERNAVILLE	
BERNAVILLE	"	p.m.	Billeted in BERNAVILLE N	
"	19.1.16		Were out. N	
"	20.1.16	a.m.	Patrol round with S.O. 9 CE XIV Corps. N	
"	21.1.16		Office work. N	
"	22.1.16		Office work. N	
"	23.1.16		Sunday. N	
"	24.1.16		Buying horses & afternoon 230 ↑ AT by. We arrived at BERTEVICOURT & visited Hallencourt village N	
"	25.1.16		Visited 67 & 230 AE D	
"	26.1.16		Patrol round Hayaye hill D	
"	27.1.16		Office in am - Riding round village till 7.30pm. on Hutley scheme N	
"	28.1.16		Rode round villages on Hutley scheme + to look for billets. N	
"	29.1.16		Rode to look at billets - CE NW 4p with m - Gave a lecture in the evening N	
DOMART	30.1.16		Sunday Office work N	
BYHL?	31.1.16		Instead of Church, to preliminary Recut over new CRE 4thD D	

Herewith Lieut. Colonel, R. E.
C.R.E. 36th (Ulster) Division

CRE. 36th Div:
Vols: 4, 5

CONFIDENTIAL

WAR DIARY
OF
C.R.E. 36th (ULSTER) DIVISION
FOR MONTH OF
FEBRUARY. 1916.

CONFIDENTIAL

Army Form C. 2118

WAR DIARY
or
INTELLIGENCE SUMMARY

(Erase heading not required.)

C.R.E.
36th (ULSTER) DIVISION

Instructions regarding War Diaries and Intelligence Summaries are contained in F.S. Regs., Part II. and the Staff Manual respectively. Title Pages will be prepared in manuscript.

Place	Date	Hour	Summary of Events and Information	Remarks and references to Appendices
BERNAVILLE	1.2.16	—	Handing over to Scots Regiment of 114 Bde.	N
ACHEUX	2.2.16	"	Proceeded on bus with 1 officer & 4 men from East of 122 Fld. to take over new area of defences.	N
ACHEUX	3.2.16	—	Taking over from C.R.E. 4th Div.	N
"	4.2.16	—	122 do do — 150 by road moved with MAILLY-MAILLET 7. and 122 by rail - ENGLEBELMER	N
"	5.2.16	"	do do	N
"	6.2.16	"	do do	N
"	7.2.16	9.0 am	do do	N
"	"	12 noon	Took over new area.	N
"	8.2.16	—	Office. 1 section of 121 Fd. Coy. marched from CANDAS into FORCEVILLE	N
"	9.2.16	(am 5.0 pm)	Office — 121 Fd. Coy. (less 1 sect) marched into FORCEVILLE. Walked over Divisional line defences. Inspected night-working parties till 9.10 pm and office till 12 midnight.	N
"	10.2.16	"	Office till 12 midnight.	N
"	11.2.16	"	Office till 1.0 am	N
"	12.2.16	"	Office till 1.0 am	N
"	13.2.16	"	Went round infantry front line trenches with G. 17 Corps. Office till 1.0 am.	N
"	14.2.16	"	Office.	N
"	15.2.16	"	Round N. Half Div. Lines. — D	
"	16.2.16	"	Agreement for mill (saw) at LONGUEVILLERS to cut up timber for French trenches.	N

Army Form C. 2118

WAR DIARY
or
INTELLIGENCE SUMMARY
(Erase heading not required.)

Instructions regarding War Diaries and Intelligence Summaries are contained in F. S. Regs., Part II. and the Staff Manual respectively. Title Pages will be prepared in manuscript.

Place	Date	Hour	Summary of Events and Information	Remarks and references to Appendices
ACHEUX	17.2.16		Investigated supply of stores generally. Office work. N	
" "	18.2.16		ENGLEBELMER & MAILLY inspecting stores. Office work. N	
" "	19.2.16		Worked out details & wires for supply of stores - Office work. N	
" "	20		Inspected ACQUEVES MILL with view to buying as scrap materials - found meeting - no deal. N	
" "	21		Went to ORVILLE to see about a sand Quarry worked by A.L. DIVN. N	
" "	22		Agreed to buy brushwood & small trees in W.d Wds of HENBUX - Office work. N	
" "	23		Inspected Huetla & brick making at VAUCHELLES, office wk. N	
" "	24		Agreed to buy a hundred Plantation at MARIEUX.	
" "	25		Arrived - Moved office to MARIEACHEUX - Sand party which to go to ORVILLE may to opr. N	
" "	26		Demand - Motor lorries not allowed on Roads - arranged to draw stones from No3 Park by waggon. N	
" "	27		tent - visited word at point P.8. a.b. where cutting brushwood in progress.	
" "	28		slight thaw	
" "	29		visited wood N.1326. & 1722. ½6, W.8 N	

F. Beeverette
Lieut. Colonel, R.E.
C.R.E. 36th (Ulster) Division

1875 Wt. W 593/826 1,000,000 4/15 J.B.C. & A. A.D.S.S./Forms/C. 2118.

CONFIDENTIAL

CRE 36 4th Div
Vol 6

WAR DIARY
OF
CRE 36th (ULSTER) DIVISION
FOR MONTH OF
MARCH 1916

CONFIDENTIAL   CRE   Army Form C. 2118

WAR DIARY or INTELLIGENCE SUMMARY — 36th (ULSTER) DIVISION

(Erase heading not required.)

Instructions regarding War Diaries and Intelligence Summaries are contained in F.S. Regs., Part II. and the Staff Manual respectively. Title Pages will be prepared in manuscript.

Place	Date	Hour	Summary of Events and Information	Remarks and references to Appendices
ACHEUX	1.3.16	—	Pair wh. D	
"	2.3.16	—	Rode over to CRE by Bm HQters new front. D	
"	3.3.16	—	— ditto — — Acheux sector N	
"	4.3.16	—	Snow — Went round unit at AUCHONVILLERS & left sector. N	
"	5.3.16	—	Went round trenches 9 left sector. 9 108 Brigade. 121. 2nd RE troop 1 sector. Proceeded into MARTINSART. N	
"	6.3.16	—	Visited new area. D.	
"	7.3.16	—	On Leaches 9 121. 2nd RE Sector & Trenches. MESNIL N.	
			and on sector 9/22 9th RE to MARTINSART	
"	8.3.16	—	To MARTINSART to see G.O.C. 109 Bgy re work to organized stores. N	
"	9.3.16	—	To MARTINSART to inspect Adm. Area & R.E. workin front-trench system & sit. f new heavy hows. N	
"	10.3.16	—	B/y 3" trench mort. Pioneers marched to MARTINSART for work in trench trainway. 10 wagon 74 R.P. allotted to them.	
"	11.3.16	—	1 offecr — 56 O.R. 5 to beefactory from 172 to MARTINSART. Lectured C.E. 4th Army. D	
			1 offecr — 56 O.R. 5 to beefactory Pontoon to MARTINSART. front on road. 65 wag. 74 R.P. + 4 9/cs Bogad.	
			all ULSTER Divisn. & all 121 & G.R.E. allotted & wik on front trench system. D	
"	12.3.16	—	Capt Fyster. Eng. Galloway & all bries. D	
"	13.3.16	—	Round roads at MARTINSART & new communication trench. N	
"	14.3.16		Reconnoitering f crossings over R. ANCRE and adjoining trenches. Officer prisoner on deserters N	
"	15.3.16		All out.	

WAR DIARY
or
INTELLIGENCE SUMMARY

(Erase heading not required.)

Instructions regarding War Diaries and Intelligence Summaries are contained in F. S. Regs., Part II. and the Staff Manual respectively. Title Pages will be prepared in manuscript.

Place	Date	Hour	Summary of Events and Information	Remarks and references to Appendices
ACHEUX	16.3.16	—	Motored Adjt round Companies. Chose site for O.P. trench. N of MESNIL at night.	
ACHEUX	17.3.16	—	Selected site for Dro. Report Ceulté. N	
"	18.3.16	—	1 Section of 150 q. RE from M. MALLET + 1 from ACHEUX moved to MARTINSART	
"	19.3.16	—	Sunday. Office & round wood cutting parties as usual.	
"	20.3.16	—	Inspected site for trench from FORT JACKSON to CONSTITUTION HILL. N	
"	21.3.16	—	Finally settled CAUSEWAYS across R. ANCRE. N	
"	22.3.16	—	To ARSIONS to buy billing. - C.E. & Taps. N	
	23.3.16		Visiting work & office.	
	24.3.16		Going round trenches to discuss certain defensive measures	
	25.3.16		Conference with Field Coy Commander to discuss Schemes for work.	
	26.3.16		Sunday.	
	27.3.16		Report to Coy OC giving Estimate of time & men required for numerous defence works	
	28.3.16		132 2nd Coy RE moves from ENGLEBELMER to FORCEVILLE	
	29.3.16		Walked round all the front trenches of HAMEL SECTION - inspected Roadways leading from our front. Selected site for ADVANCED BOMB STORE.	
	30.3.16		Round the works east of office. N	
	31.3.16		Went round site of trench mortar battery with Col. ... + OC Field Coy RE who has to make it. N Hutts sent without parts.	

[signature] .... nel, R.E.
C.R.E. 36th (........ .....)

CRE
36 Div
Vol 7

CONFIDENTIAL

WAR DIARY
OF
C.R.E. 36ᵗʰ (ULSTER) DIVISION
FOR MONTH OF
APRIL 1916.

CONFIDENTIAL

Army Form C. 2118

WAR DIARY or INTELLIGENCE SUMMARY

CRE 36th (ULSTER) DIVISION

(Erase heading not required.)

Instructions regarding War Diaries and Intelligence Summaries are contained in F.S. Regs., Part II. and the Staff Manual respectively. Title Pages will be prepared in manuscript.

Place	Date	Hour	Summary of Events and Information	Remarks and references to Appendices
ALBERT	1.6.16	—	Round had at MARTINSART	
HENCOURT	2.6.16	—	Round trenches at THIEPVAL	
BEHENCOURT	3.6.16	—	1st & 2nd RE moved to HARPONVILLE	
MARTINSART	4.6.16		Visited 172 Co RE moved to MOTAILE CHATEAU arrived in HEILLY for R H	
"	5.6.16		Previous N	
"	6.6.16		Interviewed with French Commanding Officer at	
"	7.6.16		After working party N	
"	8.6.16		After " siting tents N	
"	9.6.16		After " visiting tents N	
"	10.6.16		Visited tents with G.S.O. N	
"	11.6.16		Office as usual. In Hosp. have trouble elephant huts – Interviews – letters letter to Br Genl R	
"	12.6.16		Visited HAMEL, walk Lt. Col. Hoy Bry to LUCK Hill – for Bry. H.Q. R	
"	13.6.16		Inspected kindred at MARTINSART in open view	
"	Sunday		Run N	
"	15.6.16		Office routine – Ave to office + fun at THIEPVAL. N	
"	16.6.16		Office N	
"	17.6.16		Office N	
"	18.6.16		7 Miners F. by machine field & dugout	
"	19.6.16		Visited trenches THIEPVAL	
"	20.6.16		party moved into billets, with infantry itself.	
HEDAUVILLE	21.6.16		H.Q. moved to HEDAUVILLE.	

WAR DIARY
or
INTELLIGENCE SUMMARY

(Erase heading not required.)

Army Form C. 2118

Instructions regarding War Diaries and Intelligence Summaries are contained in F. S. Regs., Part II. and the Staff Manual respectively. Title Pages will be prepared in manuscript.

Place	Date	Hour	Summary of Events and Information	Remarks and references to Appendices
Hedauville	22/4/16		Received Report re Trenches	
"	23/4/16		Sunday. On Report landed & New Huts supply. N	
"	24/4/16		To Toutencourt W.O. & Div. communication trenches & enemy trench. M	
"	25/4/16	a.m.	Martinsart & Aveluy trench. N	
	p.m.	Testing lights f. R.A. M	
	26/4/16		Resent enemy trench. N	
	27/4/16		11/6 & 108 Bty. re entrenching tools M	
	28/4/16		To hear talk f. inventor of gaseous recorder. N	
	29/4/16		Adm. C.R.E. Papers re enemy trench & C.H.Q. abbey - K.C.E. & R.E. French Army M	
	30/4/16		Office all am. - Issue of tools, ammo. N	

[Signature]
Lieut. Colonel, R. E.
C.R.E. 36th (Ulster) Division

ORIGINAL

CRE 36
D 3
Vol 8

CONFIDENTIAL

WAR DIARY

OF

CRE 36th (ULSTER) DIVISION

FOR MONTH OF

MAY 1916

CONFIDENTIAL

Army Form C. 2118

C.R.E.
36th (ULSTER) DIVISION

WAR DIARY
or
INTELLIGENCE SUMMARY
(Erase heading not required.)

Instructions regarding War Diaries and Intelligence Summaries are contained in F.S. Regs., Part II. and the Staff Manual respectively. Title Pages will be prepared in manuscript.

Place	Date	Hour	Summary of Events and Information	Remarks and references to Appendices
HÉDAUVILLE	1.5.16		Visited C.E. Corps D'Amel - 6th Recent army - 9pr pieces for trench mortars.	Q
"	2.5.16	"	Reclustment. N	
"	3.5.16		Ambulance tank. N	
"	4.5.16		To Amiens. Reng stores, Equipment. N	
"	5.5.16		Office work - Reception line. N	
"	6.5.16		C.E. Corps D'Amel. (Fourth Army visited units in hand + head of Bangalore torps.) N	
"	7.5.16		Visit - to - MARTINSART to see recharge in constructn of bridges. N	
"	8.5.16		Spree - HAMEL in June. N	
"	9.5.16		Office visit from units to arrange damaged trench at THIEPVAL. N	
"	10.5.16		Visited units. 9 Mess work. N	
"	11.5.16		— ditto — N	
"	12.5.16		Took officers of 18 R.I.R.(P) round to "Saps" + front line trenches to show assembly trenches.	
"	13.5.16		Office work - Arr allott relieves. Q	
"	14.5.16		Units + office W.	
"	15.5.16		Office work. N	
"	16.5.16		Visit - C.E. Colonel Armytage - France. N	
"	17.5.16		Visited 12 + by fed. Visits.	

Army Form C. 2118

WAR DIARY
or
INTELLIGENCE SUMMARY
(Erase heading not required.)

Instructions regarding War Diaries and Intelligence Summaries are contained in F.S. Regs., Part II. and the Staff Manual respectively. Title Pages will be prepared in manuscript.

Place	Date	Hour	Summary of Events and Information	Remarks and references to Appendices
18/5/16 HEDAUVILLE	18/5/16		Hedauville ⓓ	
	19/5/16		Round jobs with O.C. Pioneers ⓓ	
	20/5/16		Round jobs with GSO2 & R. Tunnelling Co. 179. RE. N	
	21/5/16		Acré – Liveday. N	
	22/5/16		Bugney Horton Answers N	
	23/5/16		Office work + tour visit. ⓓ	
	24/5/16		Office work. N	
	25/5/16		Visited Decks in Acopen ⓓ	
	26/5/16		Proceeded to AMIENS (Hoystel). ⓓ gidoes – Cantas ⓓ	
	27/5/16		Stony to charge Brigadier – a Reserve toured in from another division – arrangement	
	28/5/16		for General Tonnellion's leave. Much time spent in letting whereabouts wanted to various arms	
	29/5/16		A/J/C representation also later moved with the relies records. ⓓ	
	30/5/16		150 by RE'S obtained out of Invaluate work by 172 Co, RE. ⓓ	
	31/5/16			J Leominster Major 3? Div

36th Divisional Engineers.

C. R. E.

36th DIVISION

JUNE 1916

CONFIDENTIAL

CRE 36th
(ULSTER DIVISION)

Army Form C. 2118

WAR DIARY
or
INTELLIGENCE SUMMARY

(Erase heading not required.)

Instructions regarding War Diaries and Intelligence Summaries are contained in F.S. Regs., Part II. and the Staff Manual respectively. Title Pages will be prepared in manuscript.

Place	Date	Hour	Summary of Events and Information	Remarks and references to Appendices
HEDAUVILLE	1.6.16			
	2.6.16		2 Coy. 16 R.I.R. Pioneers arrived working party from Bath area	
			Hostile aero on ground to prevent digging of new communication trenches	
			Completion of boat and mitten stores at	
	3.6.16		Organised extra parties under infantry Brigade to deal with outbreak of fires & bouquets	
	4.6.16		Usual work with Pioneer Advanced	
	5.6.16		Lt. Faussett & 2 NCO snipers. Raid on enemies filly. Lieut. MAYNE KILLED. Three of our NCO successfully with Patrols & others in 300. Release of Lieuts. & dugouts – Lieutenant W.L. Gammon in a staff practice & loopholing transfer of 11 casualty – Lieutie found arrived.	
	6.6.16			
	7.6.16		White work	
	8.6.16		Proceeds the works in progress. N. Govt. officer reported at 10 o'clock, wishing to read the dam.	
	9.6.16		Lt. Faussett & 2 NCO snipers. Released & dugouts – How lights work completed in trenches & loopholing of deep dugouts N. officer went & discussing with Field by Lieut.	
	10.6.16		Office work & planning Defence of Brace Villiers to Redan Commandos. Lt Smith in front trenches at William Redan laying (shots) fascines. Offr ret. wounded on Causeways N	
	11.6.16		Gas Main – ordered for 2 dug outs. 6' + 6'	
	12/6/16		Received more cement – Laid afresh cement advice as a dug out at OBBLEY. N.	
	13/6/16		C. O'Conference – Field works/Contenta trenches. &	
	14/6/16		10. R.I.M.F.Pno arrived in AVELUY WOOD to dig Assembly trenches – Reto pioneer arr b 2 Coldstream. N	
	15/6/16		2.0 km. 4 W.R Regt. gave ready W. Works. 2 Toldar 11.30pm. 107 W. R.I.P. had come up. & were to work in assembly trenches next morning

1875 Wt. W593/826 1,000,000 4/15 J.B.C. & A. A.D.S.S./Forms/C.2118.

WAR DIARY
or
INTELLIGENCE SUMMARY

Army Form C. 2118

(Erase heading not required.)

Place	Date	Hour	Summary of Events and Information	Remarks and references to Appendices
HEDAUVILLE	16/6/16	a.m.	Moved H.Q.R.E. where billets ararely therein D. Told of 80 three that 2 mule carts will be later carry fans	
	17/6/16		carts. Reinforcements ordered to be	
	18/6/16		Issued to various N.Czechoslovak.	
	19/6/16		300 more men added to working parties of 6 O.I.R. 200 & 10 R.I.R. 300.	
			Tunnellers special conductors & others arrangements of battle hulks hullaies N	
	21/6/16		Res. 9 mess of 122 Res moved out of bivouacks in HENRY WOOD to make room for material requires 2.	
	22/6/16		— N	
	23/6/16		Changes in existing parties due to movements of bates N Parties v. must wanted.	
			Commander's rank of 122 & 130. Moved into MONDKEEP & THIEPVAL WOOD nockerdingly & hurnsber	
			to Divisional Bivouac area. Transport of 121 moved into Divisional Bivouac area. N	
	24/6/16		Tunnellers not being continued. N 12 midnight to midnight to ALBERT tunnel at 179 Tan by H.C.M.	
	25/6/16		parties aides.	
	26/6/16		Orders made covering in his of GOC 28th NEW ENGLAND HER - parties to parties to	
			by them. N.	
			Nine cuts N.	
	27/6/16		Handed over Cinemap & works over R.N.C.R.F. HQ.A.T.G. 10th Inn. & C. R.E. or 28/6/16. 2.	
	28/6/16		2 days holiday for 48 hours. General made a tour of O.P. in arallen line at	
	29/6/16		ENGLAND MEN - also acted day out of CRE & Stuff in Div. H.D. Rehabilitation.	
			ULSTER AVENUE further. But high earthen courses. New curbs, bridges maker weights N.	
	30/6/16		repairing mated held here. Friedberg of Div Rebel Cards & Greensher Paradis.	

This account has been sent in by -
Colonel P.T.Denis de Vitré DSO.
(late C.R.E. 36th Division)

(Typed 21st May 1930)

STATEMENT OF WORK CARRIED OUT BY THE

ROYAL ENGINEERS

UNDER DIVISIONAL ARRANGEMENTS DURING THE MONTHS OF

APRIL, MAY, and JUNE 1916.

CAUSEWAYS. Two causeways were constructed across the River Ancre. The southern one was metalled and suitable for Field Artillery; the northern one was not metalled and was suitable for infantry in fours, and handcarts, and for empty wagons returning.

The causeways were made by first building battered sandbag walls filled with chalk, resting where the ground was soft on hurdles or fascines, and by filling in the centre with chalk. Trench tramway was used for removing the chalk from other works in course of construction to make the causeways.

Culverts were made across the dykes in the marsh, and at other suitable places. Bridges were made over the River Ancre with sufficient head-room above water level to allow of pontoons passing under them. Bridges were also made on the eastern stream.

Although the ramps up to River Ancre necessitated the use of many sandbags this method was preferred instead of a timber ramp, because of the facility of repairing it in case of damage by shells, and because of distance timber would have to be brought, it not being desirable to cut down the trees in the marsh. The road bearers of the bridges and culverts were steel rails. Two service trestles and super-structure were left near Southern causeway bridge over the R.Ancre, in case of the bridge being damaged by shell fire.

RAISING AND REPAIR OF EXISTING BRIDGES. The existing bridge at Magenta Crossing, over the R.Ancre was removed to enable a leak in the river bank under it to be stopped; it was rebuilt, half with a 4'.6" roadway (half the original width) a little to south of old site, and with sufficient headroom for a pontoon to pass under it. The existing bridge over the R.Ancre at Novo Caestor Post was repaired and raised to allow of pontoons passing under it.

The half of the existing bridge over R.Ancre north of Authuille Mill bridge was raised to allow pontoons to pass under it.

FOOT TRACKS AND WADING PLACES. Eight were made and marked out by wire on posts, suitable for infantry in single file. Each of these involved one bridge over R.Ancre, with sufficient headroom to allow pontoons to pass under, and one bridge over the eastern stream. The road bearers of the bridges were steel rails.

TRACK AND QUAY. A track suitable for handcarts was made from the Advanced R.E.Dump in N.E. corner of Aveluy Wood to the R.Ancre at Authuille Mill and a landing stage for loading stores into six pontoons which had been placed in the R.Ancre to push forward R.E.stores, T.M. bombs, etc.

REPAIR OF RIVER BANK AND CLEARING DEBRIS. A bad leak was repaired at the site of the Magenta bridge by removing an old tree root, protecting bank with corrugated iron and filling in behind it. Other minor repairs were also carried out. Trees which fell across river, and debris floating in river were removed to allow of free-way for pontoons.

BROAD-GAUGE RAILWAY. The rails were removed on both tracks near McMahon's Post to prevent their use by enemy for conveying messages, and later, where the front line trenches crossed the railway.

The northern track was repaired from about 100 yards south of McMahon's Post to within 80 yards of front trenches, to take trollies for sending forward R.E.stores, bombs.S.A.A. etc., and where it passed over the old French dug-outs in the railway embankment. The rails were propped up. Eight trollies were obtained for running on this line.

TRENCH TRAMWAY. The Martinsart end of the line was extended from the top of the hill, down the hill and steep bank where the line was shored up in places, and a siding of about 100 yards in length made in front of the divisional bomb and S.A.A. stores, and the metre gauge railway, alongside which was the C.R.E's Dump.

The line was laid along the Hamel - Albert road to connect up the two separate sections. Several hundred yards of the existing line were ballasted.

The ramped viaduct at R.Ancre near Authuille was completed and the line extended up it and through the village, along the lower road to Paisley Dump, where it joined the rails already laid parallel to Paisley Avenue; and wooden rails were laid from S.E.corner of Thiepval Wood to Johnston's Post. A branch was laid to the Collecting Station in the N.E.corner of Aveluy Wood, and two other sidings put in. Later on, when rails were available, it was extended from Paisley Dump up to and along Speyside.

Some hundreds of yards of Trench Tramway were laid for the formation of the Causeways.

Stores for repair of viaduct were collected near it.

Wheels and axles for forty trollies were obtained and bodies made for them suitable for carrying wounded in two tiers. Approximately twenty trollies were told far off for the wounded only, but numbers vary, and approximately twenty others carried up ammunition, stores, etc, and brought back wounded on the return journeys.

ROADS, TRACKS, RAMPS, LEVEL CROSSINGS. The defensive obstructions such as barricades etc, were removed from across the southern road in Hamel and replaced by screens. Trenches were bridged by bridges capable of taking Field Artillery, and where necessary trenches under them deepened. This was done right up to the front trench near the level crossing over which a bridge was placed, leaving only earth to be shovelled away, when required for use.

A track was marked out from Hedauville via Martinsart to the causeways, gaps made in fences, banks levelled etc., part of the way was along the broad gauge railway, trenches filled in, wire removed.

Two ramps, one up and one down, were made over the broad gauge railway between the two causeways.

A level crossing was made on the broad gauge railway at north end of Mound Keep, where it ran along the railway, to allow of which one rail of the eastern set was removed, and off the railway again some 150 yards further north.

The Martinsart - Englebelmer road, including that portion in 29th Division area was repaired, and the majority of its length widened, so that motor lorries could pass without getting into the mud at the side. This entailed transport of a large amount of stone, which was no sooner laid than traffic passed over it. This work was done without stopping the exceptionally heavy traffic on the road.

The Martinsart - Mesnil road was also repaired.

The road from Martinsart to the C.R.E's dump was subjected to very heavy traffic, and needed much repair.

Much chalk was put into the track from C.R.E's Dump to the Stone Dump at the Halte.

Some bad holes in Pioneer Road were repaired and where trenches crossed the road stone was thrown in to fill up.

BOMBARDMENT TRENCHES. Were dug for 121st and 150th Fd.Coys RE., in Martinsart Village, and for one section of 122nd Fd. Co.RE, in Martinsart Wood.

HUTTING AND BUNKING CELLARS. Huts were erected for 1½ battalions in Martinsart Wood. Seven huts were erected in Martinsart Village. Bunks for over one thousand men were put up in Martinsart Village and billets generally repaired. Three large cellars were bomb-proofed in Martinsart Village.

COMMUNICATION TRENCHES. Enniskilling, Sandy, and Cromarty Avenues were dug by 16th R.I.R.(P), and trench ladders recessed into the sides at intervals as a means of exit.

Ulster Av. was dug, and much labour was spent in keeping Jacob's Ladder in repair.

Brock's Benefit, approx. a mile in length was dug by working parties of the R.A., Charles Av. was improved. The trench leading to Hamel along the Hamel-Albert road was widened by working parties of R.A.M.C. to take stretchers. New trenches in Hamel were dug leading up to the Regtl.Aid Post others improved by RAMC. to take stretchers.

EXITS FOR ATTACK. Exits to take infantry in fours were cleared and taped out in Thiepval Wood at 50 yards intervals, sandbag buttresses made for spanning trenches with trench gratings.

DIVISIONAL REPORT CENTRE. Consisted of 8 compartments, 2 of which were of corrugated steel 11 ft. x 8 ft. and 2 of steel roofs supported on props and 4 of steel and timber roofs supported on props all 8 ft. x 12 ft. and 6 ft. 6 ins. clear in height, sides revetted.

They were all connected up by passages with 4 exits.

On top of roof joists, of those not of corrugated steel was laid corrugated iron sheets, then logs of timber laid transversely, then chalk in sandbags was carefully packed for three layers, then chalk was filled in, on top of this was road metalling in sandbags, and on top of all 240 steel rolled joists, making a total covering varying from 14 ft. to 12 ft. in depth. Three sleeping places of corrugated steel and shrapnel proof, each 8 ft. x 6 ft. were provided in a second tier, also a similar shelter 18 ft. x 8 ft. for orderlies, 3 latrines for officers, and a shrapnel proof cookhouse, and storeroom for water etc, were made, tables and benches were provided in the offices.

BRIGADE REPORT CENTRES. (a) In a ravine off the Hamel - Albert road at 0.24.d.2.5. were mined 4 compartments each 8 ft. x 12 f' all connected underground by a passage and outside by a well revetted trench. Construction was steel joist roof supported on props, average overhead cover 10 ft. x 12 ft. of virgin chalk. A shrapnel proof latrine was provided.
(b) At junction of Paisley and Elgin Avenue 3 pits to take corrugated steel shelters were dug and another one mined, overhead cover with bursting layer of flints about 10 ft.
(c) Consisted of a colonade 8 ft. wide with steel rails as roof joists supported on pit props, divided into 3 compartments.

BATTALION H.Q. In Thiepval Wood 6 H.Q. were formed by enlarging existing dug-outs, and providing second emergency exits. Two were dug in Hamel Sector to take corrugated steel shelters and a large shelter 8 ft. wide x 30 ft. long to accommodate orderlies.

The whole were connected up by trenches and included a bomb-proof cookhouse.

OBSERVATION POSTS. A survey observation post for the Army, a Divisional O.P. and another O.P. were made in Brock's Benefit. The steel cupulas for the Divnl.O.P. was made at the Camouflage works in Amiens. The Post was mined down and had about 15 ft. of overhead cover.

BOMB, S.A.A., GRENADE AND RATION STORES. The Divisional bomb and ration store was at the Martinsart end terminus of the trench tramway, and consisted of two compartments mined into the chalk bank, and of 6 compartments dug into the chalk bank, and covered with about 3 ft. of chalk, sides revetted.

The divnl.bomb store in Q.29.d. consisted of 2 mined shelters in the bank of the Hamel - Albert road, each of which had 2 entrances.

Brigade Bomb Store.
(a) At Speyside consisted of 3 mined shelters each with a entrances.
(b) Near Ross Castle off Forres Street of 8 compartments dug out of the chalk, and 4 of which were provided with shrapnel proof head cover; all were connected by a trench.
(c) In Hamel in strengthened cellars.

Brigade Ration Stores.
That in Hamel consisted of 2 shrapnel proof shelters dug into the bank at Q.23.a.9.2. There were 2 in Thiepval Wood.

Battalion Ration Stores.
One in Aveluy Wood dug by 16/R.I.R. (P) and 2 were dug in Thiepval Wood, and one in cellars in Hamel.

REGIMENTAL AID POSTS.

That at Ross Street was doubled in size, and connected by trenches to Sandy Avenue. A new one of corrugated steel was dug into hillside at Speyside.

The Swallows Nest (2 compartments) in bluff north of Authuille Village was made. That in the Railway Station at Mesnil was strengthened and bomb-proofing improved.

Two cellars in Hamel were strengthened and bomb-proofed. The dug-out of the old dressing station was improved and strengthened, gas curtains were fitted.

COLLECTING STATIONS. At north-east corner of Aveluy Wood consisted of 4½ corrugated steel shelters.

At Paisley Av. 2 new corrugated steel shelters were dug in and connected with an existed one which was also enlarged by underground passages, these again were connected underground to the "Colonade" which was first occupied by troops and then used for wounded. Gas curtains were fitted.

WATER SUPPLY. In Martinsart Village the existing pump house and engine house, and long length of shafting were bomb-proofed on top and sides.

A deep well pump was installed in a well near the Church, tanks erected and whole bomb-proofed, and arrangements made for filling water carts off the main road.

A pipe-line was laid to horse-troughs which were made

and erected in Martinsart Wood, and the pipe-line continued down to the huts in Martinsart Wood.

New horse troughs were made and erected at W.end of Martinsart Village, and connected up by pipe. The old arrangements for watering horses and filling water carts on the main road was dismantled.

Pump was installed in a new well near Northumberland Av., tanks erected and a pipe-line laid to Mesnil Cemetery with stand-pipes for filling water-carts.

Speyside. Improved bomb-proofing of existing pumphouse. Protected tanks at Ross Street and Sauchiehall Street, inclosed a spring and erected tanks in bank, and connected up with force pump.

Laid on water to collecting station at Paisley. Three water supply pumps were kept running and in working order.

Hamel. Erected sandbag breastwork at springs to protect men drawing water. Ran a pipe-line from Spring to Railway Embankment which provided a safer site for filling dixies. Installed a pump in a well and laid pipe to Regtl. Aid Post.

Mesnil. Repaired the windlasses of the well and fixed up new buckets.

R.E DUMPS. The main C.R.E.Dump was wired in, and sleeping accommodation for permanent loading parties made near Metre Gauge Railway. Road and trench tramway terminus near Martinsart. Advanced R.E. Dump was wired in at N.E. corner of Aveluy Wood along to Hamel-Albert road and trench tramway and close to Broad Gauge railway. Two dug-outs were made for Staff and officers and bombardment trenches for the permanent working parties of about 140 men.

Two brigade dumps were wired in in Thiepval Wood and one at Hamel near foot of Jacob's Ladder.

An average of 300 men a day for a week were required to fill the brigade dumps.

TIMBER CUTTING. Trees were cut at Acheux, Forceville, and Varennes.

STORES. Stores were drawn daily on No.6 and 7.R.E.Parks, and the Corps Dump at Varennes, and a great many, including steel girders were bought in Amiens. The transport of stores was a large undertaking.

PORTABLE BRIDGES. Two specimen bridges were made and experimented with by the G.O.C.,R.A. with a view to ascertaining their suitability for transporting on the limber wagon. Twelve portable bridges were prepared for the offensive, besides one used over a trench N.W. of Mesnil, and another left ready for use near top of Jacob's Ladder.

ULSTER TORPEDOES. Some 200 tubes, two metres long, of standarized type were made. Each tube was a complete charge in itself and any reasonable number of lengths could be joined together for use.

Canvas bags containing ammonal and petrol tins containing ammonal were prepared for use on raids.

PERISCOPES. Four large periscopes were made for the R.A.

DISCS. 300 distinguishing discs were made, and painted for the brigades.

CONCERTINAS BARBED WIRE. 500 were made.

LADDERS TRENCH. 120 were made.

BOMB PROOF SHELTERS. Seven with two entrances each and made of corrugated steel were dug into Belfast City, four would hold 20 men each, and 3 about 27 men each.

A long colonade about 200 ft. long and 8 ft. wide was dug in at Paisley, and roofed with short rails supported on props with 8 ft. of overhead cover and flint shell burster.

A similar colanade was dug, but time did not permit of its completion.

At Speyside a shelter was made for a section of R.E. and a tunnelled dug-out for an officer.

Shrapnel-proof shelters to accommodate one company were made in the hillside above Speyside.

Four boiler-plate dug-outs near the cookers on Hamel - Albert road were cleaned out and re-floored. They were used during the offensive as a Regtl.Aid Post. Shrapnel proof shelters were made to accomodate 500 officers and men of the R.A. along the Mesnil valley. The shelters were made in sections at 122nd Fd.Co.RE.H.Q's at Forceville, complete with bunks, conveyed to site on pontoon wagons and dropped into the pits dug for them, and then covered over with one foot of earth.

SAPS. Six saps were deepened to a depth of 6' - 6" to 7' by 16/R.I.R.(P).

TRENCH MORTAR BATTERIES HEAVY. Two emplacements were dug each with a bomb-proof shelter for men and magazine; one east and one west of Devial Avenue in Hamel.

Four emplacements were dug at northern extremity of Speyside with magazine and accommodation for men, old tunnels being made use of and enlarged.

Two emplacements were begun on east of Elgin Street and behind Whitchurch Street, but only one emplacement with a magazine and shelter was fully completed.

do. do **MEDIUM.** Six 4 gun batteries with magazines and accommodation for gun crews were dug.

(a) off west side of Thurso Street.
(b) off Whitchurch Street, east of Thurso Street.
(c) off West side of Elgin Avenue.
(d) between Tyrone and Inverness Street.
(e) between Inverness Street and Creeping Trench.
(f) astride of Inverness Street.

MACHINE GUN EMPLACEMENTS. One emplacement was put in in Jacob's Ladder, one in eastern defences of Mesnil, others in Thiepval, and Hamel sectors under Brigade arrangements. One of those put in Hamel in the course of a night stopped a direct hit from a 4.2 shell.

STOKES BATTERIES. All the work in connection with these batteries was done by 179th Tunnelling Co.R.E., except that the division supplies large carrying parties.

ASSEMBLY TRENCHES. Those in Thiepval Wood were pegged out by the RE., but were dug under regimental arrangements, as also the paths cut through the brushwood.

SCREENING. Screens were erected across Bridge at McMahon's Post, and at bend of Hamel - Albert road near Railway View, across the south Causeway, and in places the brushwood was drawn together over the trench tramway.

CAMOUFLAGE AND DYE. Some hundreds of rolls of rabbit wire were covered with grass. DYE was only obtainable in small quantities and green paint was available in small quantities only. But several hundred of sandbags and a few rolls of canvas were dyed green.

WORK UNDER BRIGADE ARRANGEMENTS. Much work was done in keeping existing lines in repair, such as deepening trenches in the Hamel sector, provision of deep dug-outs in Hamel sector, 2 new saps and a new trench in advance of front line trench. The R.E. also took part in the raid on Railway Sap.

In the Thiepval Sector making Whitchurch Street into a defensible line, digging Jack Street and Creeping Trench, restoration of George Street, traversing Elgin Avenue, deepening Ross Street and Forres Street, joining up Gordon Castle and Belfast City with a trench.

- - - - -

COPY.

H.Q. 36th Division "Q"

Reference your enquiry re trollies the following is the work for which they were used.

The 40 trollies were kept incessantly employed night and day during the bombardment and assault taking up materials for :-

(1) T.M.Batteries or new guns.
(2) Divisional bombs, Grenades, smoke bombs, S.A.A.
(3) Special Brigade RE sent up cylinders etc.
(4) Materials for repair of trench tramway.
(5) R.E.stores of all sorts and descriptions.

Examples of truck loads. It took at least 4 men, sometimes 5 to push a truck of :-

(1) 50 screw pickets.
(2) 24 coils barbed wire
(3) 10 coils French concertina wire.
(4) about 20 boxes of SAA.
(5) about 10 Heavy T.M.bombs.
(6) 100 picks or 100 shovels.
(7) 10 trench ladders.

Every truck in addition took up a trench bridge until they had all gone up.

Loading party, 60 men of 16/R.I.R. (P).

Pushing party, 50 men of 6/R.Scots.

Rly.Maintenance, 25 men of 16/R.I.R.(P).

Martinsart Dump, 8 men   ditto.

Stores at Hamel were sent up by G.S.wagons of Reserve Park, working during bombardment from dark to dawn. They managed 3 trips per night.

(sgd) P.T.Denis de Vitré.
Lt.-Colonel
C.R.E. 36th Division.

19.7.16.

COPY.

A.D.M.S. No.663.
d/19.7.16
(36th Division).

C.R.E.

About 725 lying and 1454 sitting cases came through from Aveluy Wood collecting Post. These figures include cases coming down from Hamel. It is impossible to say exactly how many cases came down by the trench tramway, but I think it is safe to say not less than 800.

(sgd) E.Marshall.
Capt.RAMC.
D.A.D.M.S. for
A.D.M.S.

19.7.16.

H.Q. 36th Division. Q.

For your information please.

Lt.-Col. RE.
C.R.E. 36th(Ulster) Divn.

19.7.16.

36th Divisional Engineers

C. R. E.

36th DIVISION.

JULY 1916

Engineer arrangements for the offensive.

RE 36th (ULSTER) DIVISION

CONFIDENTIAL

Army Form C. 2118.

Original

WAR DIARY
or
INTELLIGENCE SUMMARY.
(Erase heading not required.)

Place	Date	Hour	Summary of Events and Information	Remarks and references to Appendices
DIVISIONAL REPORT CENTRE at Q.31.B.10.9.	1.7.16		122nd Field Company R.E. To the attack this Field Coy, Nt (less 2 Sections, Utd off to 108th Brigade) covered Divisional Frontage at MOONDKEEP in shelling along side the Railway with an average between Jnty 18's T Trench head cover. No 3 Section Lt YOUNG RE was attached to 108th Brigade, left beds in HAMEL; this Section left MOONDKEEP on Y2 night at 9.0 hrs + constructed a shaped parapet on the HEDGEROWS HAMEL. on 2 day tasked to return until N.O. ceased there O.C. 9 R.I. Fus asked Lt YOUNG RE to make the Trenches less before the Section rest to, and 9th I/S R.I.F (P) cause air. Lt YOUNG RE then N.O. was from O.C. 9 R.I. Fus to collect and clear wounded. from the Company began the rest about 11.30 am to go from #8. The Section began again at trenches to work on 80 acre until the 2 day were wounded. His wie in to go on one C. By g.o.hr. Section had with drawn with heavy were cleared. 3. 0 p.m. This Section then there with drawn into MARTINSART. In attaching 7 mis, Task with own ammend late early 1 Infantry labour to the leading Platoon J Bn of 7r Section attaching Columns. After 300 wounded + 2 missing No 2 Section, Lt BENSON RE was attached to 108th Brigade on Thursday noon on RIGHT CENTRE SECTION. This Section Left MOOND KEEP at 10.0 hrs on Y2 night. Y2 night lived taped to the above SPEYSIDE on Y2 night.	A. page 1 D. page 6 H 8 D/page 6

WAR DIARY or INTELLIGENCE SUMMARY

Army Form C. 2118.

(2)

Place	Date	Hour	Summary of Events and Information	Remarks and references to Appendices

8 US seeker 4 men were last with by accurred into forces belongs to the leading platoon of attacking inf. 1 NCO & men 2 me missing. About 150 are 2nd Lt BENSON, R.E. got orders from O.C. 13. R.I.R. to man the front line wire of THIEPVAL N.M.S. in Right-Sector Section — He Section war Lieut Kell S.O. line

New position & recovered THIEPVAL N.M.S. to the two officers, one being 2nd Lt Kling received by O.C. 13.R.I.R. who carried no orders but written word not returned. 6 killed with mine SPENCER. Only the men were slightly wounded.

This officer had a scale German offic. Kaiserman 9 met with what looked about 3 of the men. One in the Allied & lightning stones 3 or 4 gas capsules 4 m.c. After a N days of 4 to 10 minds. He latter carried LT 3 officer on Allied. When it was returned to AVELUY N.M.D. & later on to MARTINSART.

No4 seeker Lt PARGITER R.E. & No1 seeker under Lt C.N.M. furnished Luttich A No5 seeker between Strucks & finished off No 7 seeker Infantry Patrol. After the was clear of seekers & murdered wrecks on its CAUSEWAYS, & assisted at 8.10 a.m. 2 days received telegram message H.L.

IN DIVISION at 2558 N.V.S.

9.
H.

Place	Date	Hour	Summary of Events and Information	Remarks and references to Appendices
			As O.C. 172 had previously myself the section started at 8.20 a.m., heading for [Valley] of [trees]. Lt. [illegible] Lt. PAGHER R.E. found a [large] across the line near HAMEL. He left hastily & went straight back & received orders from O.C. 172. On receipt of order that RAILWAY line was held, to withdraw the leading HAMER [bridge] [train] to O.C. 9 R.I.F. and not to proceed with [crowd] of [leaving] to N.G., until he had definite information that RAILWAY line was free of [enemy]. Pending the development O.C. 9 R.I.F. ordered Lt. [Carter] to [stop] at the [bridge] — & not to [work] till [he] had been [employed]. Lt. FARTHER joined Lt. YOUNG's section in clearing the [removed] [tank] about 6.0. [ft]., where the section was withdrawn to MONDICOURT, when it remained [until] by was [drawn] out on afternoon of May.	H1, H2. H3, H4, H5. H6, H7
			No.1 section under C.S.M. RUSSELL R.E. was ordered at 2 a.g. to [obtain] [rivets] & [beams]. It went out about 12.30 a.m. & got back about 4.30 a.m. without casualties. They went up EGGIN rd. MAMOURAH—ROSS ST. MAMOURAH—ROSS ST. & CROMARTY AD. but found no [incidents]	H8 H9, H11. H12, H13

WAR DIARY
or
INTELLIGENCE SUMMARY.
(Erase heading not required.)

Army Form C. 2118.

Place	Date	Hour	Summary of Events and Information	Remarks and references to Appendices
			About 1.0 p.m. Army No 1 Section under Capt. McIldowie R.E. went out to link up to 107. Bgy THIEPVAL WOOD. He received orders to put the tunnelled shelter at SOUTH END of SPEYSIDE + evacuate other — start 2 N2 also received orders to meet to start a new scars NO MANS LAND to B' line — beginning from the S end of SPEYSIDE AV.. On wheeling out here the tunnel late the return was cancelled. The section was transferred to a carrying party for ammunition. Its position held by Infantry Bgys 107, "B" Bgy's. The Mulebank was ordered + evacuated of to WHITCHURCH ST + there shellpit conflicted Capt McIldowie to have men in at Esson Au + to send on to find them to investigate. He found the infantry again west down no one could get back to NORTHAMPTON. The loos being brought up. West man, take nearly two's, + keen tried to get into touch with Bgy etc. between section two — SANDY ROW attached to Brigade, his other men two up extend but courage lifted. he sent 2 + only had 12 men left at 8.32. In getting the 12 Brigade + to was then forth entrances to be evac'd the two life. Good for spending gradually, Withdrew to HAMILTON T.	DIVISIONAL ORDER #12.a. A.13. A.13.a. A.14 A.15 A.16

WAR DIARY or INTELLIGENCE SUMMARY

Army Form C. 2118.

(Erase heading not required.)

Place	Date	Hour	Summary of Events and Information	Remarks and references to Appendices
			150 F. Sections. The whole Office (Sec Hewitt) went into the Ulrede Dug out at PAISLEY AV. at THIEPVAL WOOD on 23.6.16. while the Company occupied the maintenance of the Trenches and Communications — and subsequently — and employed the Infilements of a Heavy Trench Mortar Battery. This was undertaken under considerable shelling during the Bombardment. On 24.3.16, 2 N.C.O.s & Sappers for a working party with 9. R. Inf. Minsters, were left; it by also moved forward a large supply of the stores at McBryan Dump (109 E) to INVERNESS STREET.	L
			On 1.7.16 Sections No1. Lt. PEACOCK R.E. and No3. Lt. LONG. R.E. were attached to the 109th Bde. No1 Section was detailed to assist in consolidating the CRUCIFIX. I went over the ground with Mr PEACOCK R.E. and got into the Luckies Road. where Lt. PEACOCK R.E was killed. It is reported that a few Sappers reached the Redoubt but were returned; all the N.C.Os were lost except one. Including medals returning wounded, employed who did not go on to Thiepval. The Section Numbers 14.	I₁ I₃ I₄
			No3. Section was in Bryset Avenue, which was used in intimacy between three Keeping line open to recent renewal, and other miscellaneous jobs in rear; and providing parties for Intelligence carrying stores of (Hy. Morts sine). The casualties were slight. This Section was later partly employed at extending Mixed Ramsey. The remainder of the Company were in the Divisional Reserve.	
			No2. Section Lt. WISE. R.E. organised the Guards who had taken the last Hy. Morts position with carrying parties to take the R.E. stores. — It was partly employed on extention of Mixed Ramsey — Casual wounded. Lt. SMYTH. R.E. and one party he refused to take regretfully awarded upon the tank of the Late Ent hight harassing, and improving a	I₁ I₃ I₄
			No4. Section Mr. JAMESON R.E. did most of the work of the extending preliminary hostilities, & 2 section in No 4 were adopted. Casualties in No 4 were slight.	

2333 Wt. W2544/1454 700,000 5/15 D.D.&L. A.D.S.S./Forms/C.2118.

WAR DIARY
or
INTELLIGENCE SUMMARY.

Army Form C. 2118.

Place	Date	Hour	Summary of Events and Information	Remarks and references to Appendices
			at 6 ashes a 2 day the remainder of the by was placed at disposal of 109 N.Brig. & carried on with what they were doing.	I.5.
			The water supply retaining fairly well. Lt SMYTH R.E. and Pochlust work as sappers keeping	I.6. I.7.
			the water supplies going on repairs under Intinmense shellfire. They repaired the Reservoir high level and put in about 10 lengths new pipe line at different places. Pte 27 6.J. Smith Party lost 2 transport [...] of no Inf but it never ceased digging. Lt SMYTH R.E. was unable once by a shell but continued on with his work. On one occasion Lt SMYTH R.E. found a man trying to break a hole in the water pipe to fill 2 petrol tins with water, which he must have obtained from the biyug back supply.	
			at about 5.0 p.m. A.A day the Company was withdrawn to MARTINSART.	

WAR DIARY or INTELLIGENCE SUMMARY

Army Form C. 2118.

Place	Date	Hour	Summary of Events and Information	Remarks and references to Appendices
	1.7.16		121st Field Company, R.E. was in Divisional Reserve in huts in N.E. corner of AVELUY WOOD under Major Curtin. Lt. FAWCETT R.E. attached to 107th Brigade. By 5.0.a.m. 2 manning the huts had left AVELUY WOOD and got into a trench adjoining S. END of J SPEY 110 C. Later started up opposite B.M. and Intelligence Officer of 107th Bde (Captain Smith) Some officers & other information came in they kept us from time to time. Lt Fawcett was sent back but they said — Lt FAWCETT RE act/would — We about 2 minuted then until 11.00 mentioned 107 K.O.R.L were not present as at 4.0.a.m. D continued at this and then a.l.p 7-O.flow or a day by shell since they had closed the hutches juxtaposed about 7.30 per the Sheltered withdrawn 16 MART/WS/RT. Howsever 121st Field Coy MC in Divisional reserve were not used but relieved 122 Field Cy at MOUND kept at 9.5 a.m. A day.	E.L. Iq. I10. H.M.

WAR DIARY
or
INTELLIGENCE SUMMARY.

Army Form C. 2118.

Place	Date	Hour	Summary of Events and Information	Remarks and references to Appendices
16 R.I.R.(P.) in N.E. corner of AVELUY WOOD.			The Battalion was in Divisional Reserve. The following parties were [on] fat.[?] of French workers:	L
			C.R.E: & supervised by the asst. adjt. R.E.	
			(1) Loading party at C.R.E Dump at MARTINSART. 8 men. (2) Trench tramway repair and maintenance party, 25 - (3) Destroyers, 60 (N. Sloan 2nd Lt. D. Coe, 16 R.I.R/P)	R.N.
			Three were also a Covering party of 30 men of 3rd Royal Irish Rifles rocket suppliers.	
			About 1.6.40 a.m. 9.Z. day our Company were sent off for the Communication trench across NO MANS LAND with the THIEPVAL WOOD SECTOR. 4 men by it clearly repair the trench of ST PIERRE-DIVION.	K.2. 24.
			At 12 we[?] our men were sent to reconnoitre a new site for a Communication trench the men returned unmolested.	R3.
			The 2 Cos. detailed above were held up by fire	K.4. 26.
			at 6 AM. for orders. the Company relieved Rifles. Lt. Paul. Brown. to HAMEL trenches	
			the communication trench from Trench 103 was shelled.	R.S.
			At 6 was when the remainder of the Pioneer Battalion were placed in Bulgar of Trench 107 Troyen,	
			the communication trench stopping temporarily at 3.45 am in AVeny.	R.H.
			The R.E. that were divided amongst (1) C.R.E DUMP at MARTINSART. Environs of Steel Pioneers	
			(2) Divisional advanced dump at N.E Corner of AVELUY WOOD	
			(3) 2 Brigade dumps in THIEPVAL WOOD near GORDON CASTLE	
			(4) 1 Brigade Dump at Johnny JACOBS L9 D DER in HAMEL.	

WAR DIARY
or
INTELLIGENCE SUMMARY

Army Form C. 2118.

Place	Date	Hour	Summary of Events and Information	Remarks and references to Appendices

Col R.N. BOAN R.E. Applicant was i/c R.E. This sent the alternative methods of securing

Rear Tunnel (1) By ALBERT-MIRAUMONT ROAD for which 6 trenches began were detailed.

(2) By bridges on the Road/gauge Railway.

(3) By 6 tunnels on Divi. DH.R.E., to those on which were made.

Reg R Tunnel & small/ tunnels passing under later.

(4) By the Miraumont - Railway.

He suited storming parties for getting up this - 100 specialists for M.M.

anything above trenched.

The Division being withdrawn from the Line there arrangements were to

Officers & were washing it - (Majr R.E) were handed over as a guide

On now GCC 49th Division, Lt 2/Lt D COLE (18.R.I.R.I.P) was killed.

Stores were taken out by Pioneers & ..... by Jugglers & Z/A nights. M3

Work beginning of the Retreat all DUMPS were thrown over Fell hops.

BANGALORE TORPEDOES.
109th Brigade was supplied with 52 - Bgh lengths.
108 " .... 72 "
107 " .... 40 "

Army Form C. 2118.

WAR DIARY
or
INTELLIGENCE SUMMARY.
(Erase heading not required.)

Instructions regarding War Diaries and Intelligence Summaries are contained in F. S. Regs., Part II. and the Staff Manual respectively. Title pages will be prepared in manuscript.

Place	Date	Hour	Summary of Events and Information	Remarks and references to Appendices
Div. Rshd. CENTRE	2.7.16		Handed over to CRE 49 Div. cars in addition handed over to 49th Div. 121st Field Coy. RE (less 1 section) — 1 section of 122 Field Coy RE — also 2 Companies of Pioneers, with the parties employed on parties of maintenance & loading of tramway, Aveluy, Bde. the 122" & 150" Coys. withdrawn to MARTINSART also 1 section 9/2D.	N O
MARTINSART	3.7.16		The 132 (less 1 section) also 8 Coy RE & 1 section of 121 RE moved to MARTINSART. Received orders re WATER SUPPLY.	P
MARTINSART	4.7.16		Received intimation that a field Coy wd be required before 12.4.16.	
	5.7.16	10.30 am	Received orders of 150 Field Coy to join 12.4.16.	Q
		12.30pm 3.45pm 8.0pm	" " to move to RUBEMPRE on 6/7/16 — 122nd Field Coy RE to proceed to FREVILLE 150 Coy RE marched off to join 12 Div. at AVELUY. Lt FAWCETT section 9/21 RE relieved Lt FORRESTERS section 9/22 RE at MOUND KEEP. 2/1 Field Coy RE 49 Div relieved Lt section of Humphrey Engineers commanded by 121 Coy RE.	S
ON MARCH	6.7.16	10.6 am	Div. H.Q. moved to RUBEMPRE.	
		8.0 pm	Received orders to hold ready in readiness for move at 3½ hours notice after 8.0 am 7/7/16. Warned OC 122 RE accordingly.	R R1
		10.0 pm	Received orders from Capt. A.N. BURD — ADJUTANT RE to proceed to take command of 123rd Field Coy RE 8th Div.	
RUBEMPRE	7.7.16		Waiting ready to move at 3½ hours notice.	

Army Form C. 2118.

WAR DIARY
or
INTELLIGENCE SUMMARY.
(Erase heading not required.)

Instructions regarding War Diaries and Intelligence Summaries are contained in F. S. Regs., Part II. and the Staff Manual respectively. Title pages will be prepared in manuscript.

Place	Date	Hour	Summary of Events and Information	Remarks and references to Appendices
RUBEMPRÉ	8.7.16		121 Coy. R.E. withdrawn from A.g.H.Qrs. & marched to HARPONVILLE arriving 12.30 a.m on 9.7.16	Snew movement. T. T, U. O,
	9.7.16	10.15 a.m	150 Coy R.E. + 122 R.E.S. marched to HARPONVILLE. Received instructions for 122 Coy R.E. to k'day to PUCHEVILLERS.	
BERNAVILLE	10.7.16		All R.E. moved to BERNAVILLE. 124 & 150 Fields by rest to BEAUVAL & 122 F GEZAINCOURT.	
	11.7.16	2.0 p.m	H.Q.R.E moved off to billets for BARLINGHEM & the 3 Field Coys for CAMPAGNE.	
BARLINGHEM	12.7.16		H.Q.R.E at BARLINGHEM.	
SERQUES	13.7.16	6.45 p.m	H.Q.R.E & 3 Field Coys marched to SERQUES - A clean village with good billets.	
" "	14.7.16		Picture to DRANOUTRE & R.G work Scheme.	
" "	15.7.16		Inspection of billets - brought corner at WATTEN.	
" "	16.7.16		SUNDAY - Church parade 2.0 p.m.	
" "	17.7.16		Material received to beautere wicks for incinerators & stakes for latrine screens.	
" "	18.7.16		Road rollers in FOREST of EPERLECQUES.	
" "	19.7.16		Received warning to proceed next N.	
" "	20.7.16		Packing up.	

Army Form C. 2118.

WAR DIARY
or
INTELLIGENCE SUMMARY.
(Erase heading not required.)

Instructions regarding War Diaries and Intelligence Summaries are contained in F.S. Regs., Part II. and the Staff Manual respectively. Title pages will be prepared in manuscript.

Place	Date	Hour	Summary of Events and Information	Remarks and references to Appendices
SERQUES	21/7	8.30 a.m	H.Q. R.E. moved to ESQUELBECQ. 121. & 122. Field Coys moved to LEDRINGHEM.	
ESQUELBECQ	22/7	9.0a	122. Field Coy moved to ~~Hondeghem~~ WATOU hutt 1 long arch east road.	
			150 " " LEDRINGHEM.	
			121 " " ST MARIE CAPPEL.	
ESQUELBECQ	23/7		122 Field Coy remained at WATOU	
			150 " " marched to ABEELE.	
			121 " " " STEEN. WERCK.	
			H.Q. R.E marched to MONT NOIR. Took over some info from C.R.E 20.4.Div. who let me absolutely no unit was going on in the Sector we were taking over.	
MONT NOIR	24/7	—	122 & 150 Coys marched to CROIX POPERINGHE. Cancelled. 121 " " " letting over little from heavy.	
MONT NOIR	25/7	.	122 Fd Co marched to "BULFORD CAMPS" on NEUVE EGLISE — STEENWERCK RD. 150 Fd Co arrived to LE DON ½ mile E of ROMARIN.	
MONT NOIR	26/7	—	121 ordered to visit oredir Corps. & to move to CLYTTE. Inspected site for machine guns w/ G.S.O.	
" "	27/7	—	10 a.m Division cancelled. Inspected W/shops machine guns with G.S.O. No 2, 3 & 4 Section	
" "	28/7	—	122. F.O. moved into dug outs at RED LODGE + H.Q. R² by visited into ALDERSHOT H/Qrs. Saw C.E. V. Corps re latting charge of ANZAC DUMP.	
" "	29/7	—	121 & 26. R.E. moved Into billets ½ mile NE of ROMARIN. — Inspected HILL 63 w/ G.S.O. 1.	

Army Form C. 2118.

WAR DIARY
or
INTELLIGENCE SUMMARY.

(Erase heading not required.)

Instructions regarding War Diaries and Intelligence
Summaries are contained in F. S. Regs., Part II.
and the Staff Manual respectively. Title pages
will be prepared in manuscript.

Place	Date	Hour	Summary of Events and Information	Remarks and references to Appendices
	30/7/16	—	Sunday. Revnt Church at K.m.	
	31/7/16	—	Visited Kemford DETJDUS. Made arrangement to take it over. — also visited G.T. moments Rep to Divarge for their to take over the dump in LOCRE farm area. Arranged to hand over records on 2/8/16.	

T. Mungabli
W.W.W. 36 Div

SECRET

C. R. E's ORDER No. 2

A

(1) INFORMATION.

(a) The Fourth Army will take the offensive along its whole front at a date which will be notified later.

(b) The 36th Division will be on the left of the 10th Corps front of attack, and will have the 32nd Division on its right, and the 29th Division (8th Corps) on its left.

(2) INTENTION.

The 36th Division will attack on both sides of the River ANCRE. Coloured portion of map is position of the 36th Division.

(3) OBJECTIVES.

(a) On the left bank of the River ANCRE.

German "D" line, (coloured dark red).

(b) On the right bank of the River ANCRE.

The objective is the triangle of trenches enclosed between the left boundary line of the attack and the ANCRE and BEAUCOURT STATION.

(4) SUB-DIVISION OF FRONT.

(a) Right Section   Brown) 109th Brigade and 2
) Sections 150 Coy, R.E.

(b) Right Centre Section   Green)
) 108th Brigade and 2
(c) Left Centre Section   Red   ) Sections 122 Coy, R.E.
)
(d) Left Section   Blue   )

less 1 Section
121 Fld. Coy, R.E. will be in Divisional Reserve.

H.Q.& 2 Sections 122nd Coy, R.E.   ditto.

H.Q.& 2 Sections 150th Coy, R.E.   ditto.

Headquarters of Brigades concerned will arrange for the allotment of trenches in their Assembly Area to these R.E. Sections.

~~The remainder of the R.E. Field Companies will be in Divisional Reserve.~~

(5) POSITIONS OF ASSEMBLY.

See Charts.

(6) PLAN OF ATTACK.

Right Section.

Leading Battalion 109th Brigade, will attack, take and consolidate line C8 (CRUCIFIX), B 16 (DUNGANNON), C 9 (OMAGH) (exclusive) coloured blue line.

(1).

Right Centre Section.

Leading Battalion 108th Brigade will attack, take and consolidate Salient C 9 (OMAGH), C 10 (STRABANE), C 11 (ENNISKILLEN) blue line.

Flank Guard. A special detachment from troops allotted to Right Centre Section will clear the communication trench from B 19 (LURGAN) to C 12 (PORTADOWN), to hold PORTADOWN as a defensive post, sending detachments to the right to establish touch with their own troops, and towards C 13 (COLERAINE) to ensure observation and fire on the GRANDCOURT - ST PIERRE DIVION road.

Twoe Officer's patrols, each of one platoon and a Lewis gun, will be detailed by the 108th Brigade to reconniotre and clear out the trenches on the left of the Right Centre attack.

Left Centre Section.

No troops except flank guards mentioned above will be alloted to attack in this Section, unless they are unable to perform their task.

Left Section.

~~Two Battalions~~ will clear trenches and occupy BEAUCOURT STATION, the trench North of the Station along the Station - BEAUMONT - HAMEL road, Mill at R.13.a.2.6., and houses at R.13.a.1.7. and consolidate.

[margin note: See page 9]

(7) **THE INFANTRY ATTACK.**

The Infantry attack takes place at Zero time on 'Z' day.

All movements on "Z" day from the moment of assault are timed from Zero. The clock time of Zero will be notified in due course.

Prior to the hour of assault, the leading Battalions in the attack will leave their trenches under cover of the bombardment and lie down in front in the formations in which they are about to advance.

The supporting Battalions of the attack will move into the front line trenches and assembly trenches vacated by the leading Battalions.

The Battalions of 107th Brigade in Divisional Reserve will begin to move at the same time from AVELUY WOOD into THIEPVAL WOOD.

Each section of the attack will time its advance so that the first line of the attacking troops is within 150 yds of the "A" trenches at Zero time.

All ranks must understand that there should be no halt in any captured trenches until the "C" line has been reached.

If the "C" line is held and the leading line of the attack is unable to get forward without reinforcements, the attack will proceed as in normal open warfare, by short rushes.

(8) ARTILLERY TIME TABLE.

The Artillery time table of lifts is as follows:-

At 0.   From front trenches to support trenches of
             the 'A' line.

" 0.3   To the 'B' line.

" 0.18   "   " 'C' line.

" 1.18   "   " 'D' line.

" 2.38   Forms barrage behind 'D' line.

On the right bank of the ANCRE the Artillery lifts have to be slightly altered to conform with the lifts of the Vlllth Corps Artillery on our left and they will be as follows:-

0.0.   From front line on to support trenches.

0.3.   On to the 'B' line (B.21, B.23, B.25).

0.8.   On to the line B.22, B.24, B.26.

0.13.   On to BEAUCOURT STATION and on the trench North
             of it (Q.18.B.07. to Q.18.B.8.6.)

0.33.   Barrage in rear of BEAUCOURT STATION and on the
             trench running due North from Q.12.d.6.0.

It is possible that the leading line of the attack may be in advance of the time table on the 'B' and 'C' lines.

This will not affect the commencement of the advance from the preceding line, but the leading troops will in this case halt and lie down 150 to 200 yds from the objective and rush in as soon as the Artillery lifts off it.

Attack on 'D' Line.

The assault of the 'D' line will be carried out by the three battalions of the 107th Brigade in Divisional Reserve.

The 107th Brigade will advance from THIEPVAL WOOD, following the 109th Brigade. It will attack the 'D' line from 'D'8 to D. 9 (both inclusive), passing through the leading Brigades at the 'C' line and making its assault on the 'D' line when the Artillery barrage lifts.

(4).

(9). CONSOLIDATION OF CAPTURED TRENCHES.

The consolidation of captured trenches will be begun immediately they are occupied by the troops alloted to them.

Strong points, for a garrison of a platoon (not less than 30 men) will be constructed at the following places:-

by 107th Brigade   D 8. D 9. D 10. DERRY CITY.

" 108th   "   and 2 Sections of 122nd Coy, R.E.

        C 9 (OMAGH), C 10 (STRABANE), C 11

        (ENNISKILLEN), C 12 (PORTADOWN), B 19.

        B 17.
        (LURGAN), and on right bank of River

        ANCRE B 26 (GOBBINS), B 24 (LARNE),

        B 21 and BEAUCOURT STATION.

by 109th Brigade and 2 Sections 150th Coy, R.E.

        B 13 (CRUCIFIX), C 8 (LISNASKEA), B 16

        (DUNGANNON).

(10) MACHINE GUNS.

Machine guns will be alloted to strong points as under :-

CRUCIFIX	B 13	2 guns	)	
DUNGANNON	B 16	2 "	)	Right Section.
LISNASKEA	C 8	2 "	)	
	B 17	2 guns	)	
OMAGH	C 9	1 "	)	Right Centre Section.
STRABANE	C 10	2 "	)	
ENNISKILLEN	C 11	1 "	)	
LURGAN	B 19	1 "	)	Left Centre Section.
PORTADOWN	C 12	1 "	)	

(11) R.E. STORES.

These will be stored in 3 Brigade Dumps, marked on map.

A list of the main Stores available was attached to 36th Divisional Order No 30 of the 11/6/16.

An N.C.O. will be placed in charge of each of these Dumps, 2 by O.C. 122nd Coy, R.E., and 1 by O.C. 150th Coy, R.E. respectively, and will issue them.

(5).

The rear platoon of each Company in the leading Battalions and the two rear platoons of each Coy, in the Supporting Battalions and in the Reserve Brigade will carry forward R.E. Stores in addition to their ordinary equipment.

During the preliminary bombardment, the Battalion holding the line in each Section will, under orders from its Brigade Headquarters, draw such R.E. Stores as are requisite from the Brigade Dumps and place them along the assembly trenches of the rear platoons, so that these platoons directly they emerge from the trenches will take up their stores and carry them forward.

Brigade Commanders will therefore arrange that the trenches occupied by the rear platoons of each Coy. are clearly marked and that the Battalion of their Brigade in the line receives a list of the stores which each platoon is to carry forward. The wire round these Dumps to be removed before assault.

(12) EQUIPMENT.

Packs and greatcoats will not be taken to the assembly trenches but will be labelled and left under guard in selected houses, dug-outs etc.

Each Sapper will carry Waterproof sheet, woollen waistecoat, rifle and equipment; (less pack), ammunition,
Two sandbags in belt, one iron ration and unexpired portion of days ration, two smoke helmets and goggles; and in addition the following tools divided among them:-

    Wire cutters.
    Crowbars
    Hand axes
    Hedging gloves
    Plain wire
    Hand saws
    Masons chisels
    Masons hammers
    Picks
    Shovels
    Felling Axes
    One lashing
    Bastard cross-cut saws
    6 hammers
    4 tracing tapes

or as may be varied by O.C. Field Coys'.

(13) TRENCH TRAFFIC ARRANGEMENT.

Communication trenches will be reserved for up and down traffic as follows :-

(a) Right Section.

ENNISKILLEN AVENUE.	UP.
ELGIN AVENUE.	DOWN.

(b) Right Centre Section.

SANDY AVENUE.	DOWN.
CROMARTY AVENUE.	UP.

(c) Left Section.

CHARLES AVENUE & PROSPECT ROW.	UP.

JACOBS LADDER.   UP.

HAMEL-AVELUY ROAD.   DOWN.

O.C. 121st will label Left Section and O.C. 150th will label THIEPVAL WOOD.

Brigades concerned will place a sentry at the exit end of these trenches to prevent their being used for traffic in the contrary direction.

(14) DISTINGUISHING FLAGS.

Flags of 107th Brigade = Yellow with 1 black vertical stripe.
"   "   108th   "   =   "   "   2   "   "   "
"   "   109th   "   =   "   "   3   "   "   "

Distinguishing flags or discs are not to be planted in enemy parapet, and left where they can fall into his hands. They must be carried and waved by hand.

(15) TRANSPORT.

All first line transport (R.E. transport is all first line) will move into bivouac by noon on date   and will be under an Officer detailed by O.C. 16th R.I.R. (P) and will be controlled by Divisional Headquarters in the first stages of the offensive.

Pontoon wagons will remain at bivouac till ordered up.

(16) WATER.

In addition to arrangements detailed in Administrative Instructions, I am trying to get a supply of Petrol tins from D.A.D.O.S.

(17) RATIONS.

For day following 'Z' day rations will be sent up with first line transport if the situation permits of transport being employed.

A guide from each Field Coy, to meet transport at the Mill on HAMEL-THIEPVAL road.

If situation does not permit, the transport being sent up on night of "Z/A" the companies will draw from the nearest Dump.

Sufficient sandbags have been placed in each Brigade Dump to enable all the rations in each Dump to be carried up, if 8 rations are placed in one bag.

(18) MEDICAL.

Posts will be established at the following positions:-

REGIMENTAL AID POSTS.

Left Section.

H A M E L.	Q.23.d.5.8.	(Present Post)
	Q.23.a.9.2.	(New Post)
	Q.23.b.3.2.	(Reserve Post)
Right & Centre Sections.	Q.30.b.1.8.	(Speyside St - New Post)
	Q.30.b.5.2.	(Present Post).

(7).

COLLECTING POSTS (Field Ambulances).

(1) Railway bank S. of HAMEL on HAMEL-ALBERT road, Q.29.b.5.3.

(2) THIEPVAL WOOD (3 shell proof shelters) Q.30.c.9.4. (all communication trenches N. of this WOOD converge on this point).

(3) East bank of River N. of AUTHUILLE (2 shell proof shelters) Q.36.c.7.6.

(4) AVELUY WOOD (5 shell proof shelters) Q.35.d.1.9.

(5) MESNIL Light Railway Station (Cellars and shell-proof shelters on road opposite Station) Q.28.c.3.7.

Casualities able to walk will be directed from the Collecting Post in AVELUY WOOD- Q.35.d.1.9. to MARTINSART by a pathway which will be marked by directing Posts.

ADVANCED DRESSING STATION - MARTINSART - W.3.a.9.8 and Chateau Stable- W.3.a.9.8.

MAIN DRESSING STATIONS. FORCEVILLE & CLAIRFAYE.

(19) VETERINARY.

An advanced Veterinary Dressing Station will be established at P.36.b.8.8 before the bombardment commences.

(20) DRESS.

During the progress of operations, Regimental Officers will wear trousers and puttees and the same equipment as the their men.

The chin straps of Steel Helmets must be worn down.

(21) INFORMATION TO THE ENEMY.

No papers or orders of any kind which might give information to the enemy will be carried on either Officers or men. Compliance with this order will be verified by inspection prior to going into the assembly trenches.

All ranks are to be warned that if taken prisoner they are only bound to give their name and rank and should refuse to answer any other question.

(22) MAPS.

All Officers will carry 1/20,000 57.D.S.E. and 57.C.S.W. and the special Corps map. These maps will be referred to in orders, reports and messages. Maps showing our trenches are not to be carried.

(23) REPORT CENTRE.

Divisional Headquarters will remain at HEDAUVILLE up till 9p,m, on the Y/Z night, at which hour it will open at the Advanced Divisional Report Centre, Q.25.d.2.0.

(24) **SIGNAL WIRES.**

Lines found in hostile trenches are **NOT** to be cut, but dealt with by Signal Coy.

Should it be necessary to retire CUT all wires possible

(25) **CODE.**

The amended list of Code Calls issued under G.91/5/7 of June 12th 1916, will be used for all messages by visual, aeroplane, balloon, wireless, or pigeon or by forward Telephone lines.

The Code call will be used as a Station Call and also as a Code name to denote a unit in the "addressto" "text" or "address from" of a message.

These Code Calls will not be used in messages transmitted above Divisional or Heavy Artillery Headquarters, but will be decoded at the Signal Office.

The Writer of any message emanating from or passing into the forward area and also of any message to be sent by visual, wireless or pigeon will be responsible for inserting the code name in his message.

(26) **MESSENGERS & MESSAGES.**

Each O.C. of Coys will detail a messenger to C.R.E., to report to him on Y'day at 9a.m, at C.R.E's Office.

Messengers from the Companies to C.R.E., will proceed on foot to MARTINSART and call at No.   where bicycles will be stored, obtain a bicycle and proceed to C.R.E. Divisional Headquarters, Report Centre.

On his return he will hand in bicycle to store and proceed to the Coy. on foot.

All messages sent through Signals must be Coded.

(27) **ROADS.** On capture of enemy position the following roads will be available to 36th Division:-

AVELUY - HAMEL - ST.PIERRE DIVION ROAD.

AUTHUILLE- THIEPVAL ROAD is alloted to 32nd Division.

The C.E. Xth Corps will, as soon as situation permits of work being started, improve the road alloted to 36th Div. as far as Mill in Q.24.

(28) **TOOLS.** The Companies will probably be able to make good use of their pack animals for getting up tools.

(29) **GERMAN ARTILLERY SCREENS.** It is important not to move German Screens which are a signal to their Artillery.

Left Section.

The tasks allotted to the two battalions of the 108th Brigade in the Left Section are :-

- (a) Assault of the Salient in the German 'A' line between Q.17.b.2010 and Q.17.b.1030.

- (b) To clear the German trenches, East of the Salient, down to ALBERT-HAMEL Railway.

- (c) To establish strong points at B.26 (GOBBINS), B.24 (LARNE) and B.21 (BUSHMILLS).

- (d) To occupy BEAUCOURT STATION AND THE TRENCHES immediately behind the Station, and afterwards to occupy the MILL in R.QE.a. and the two houses about 250 yards beyond the Station, between the Railway road and the Railway.

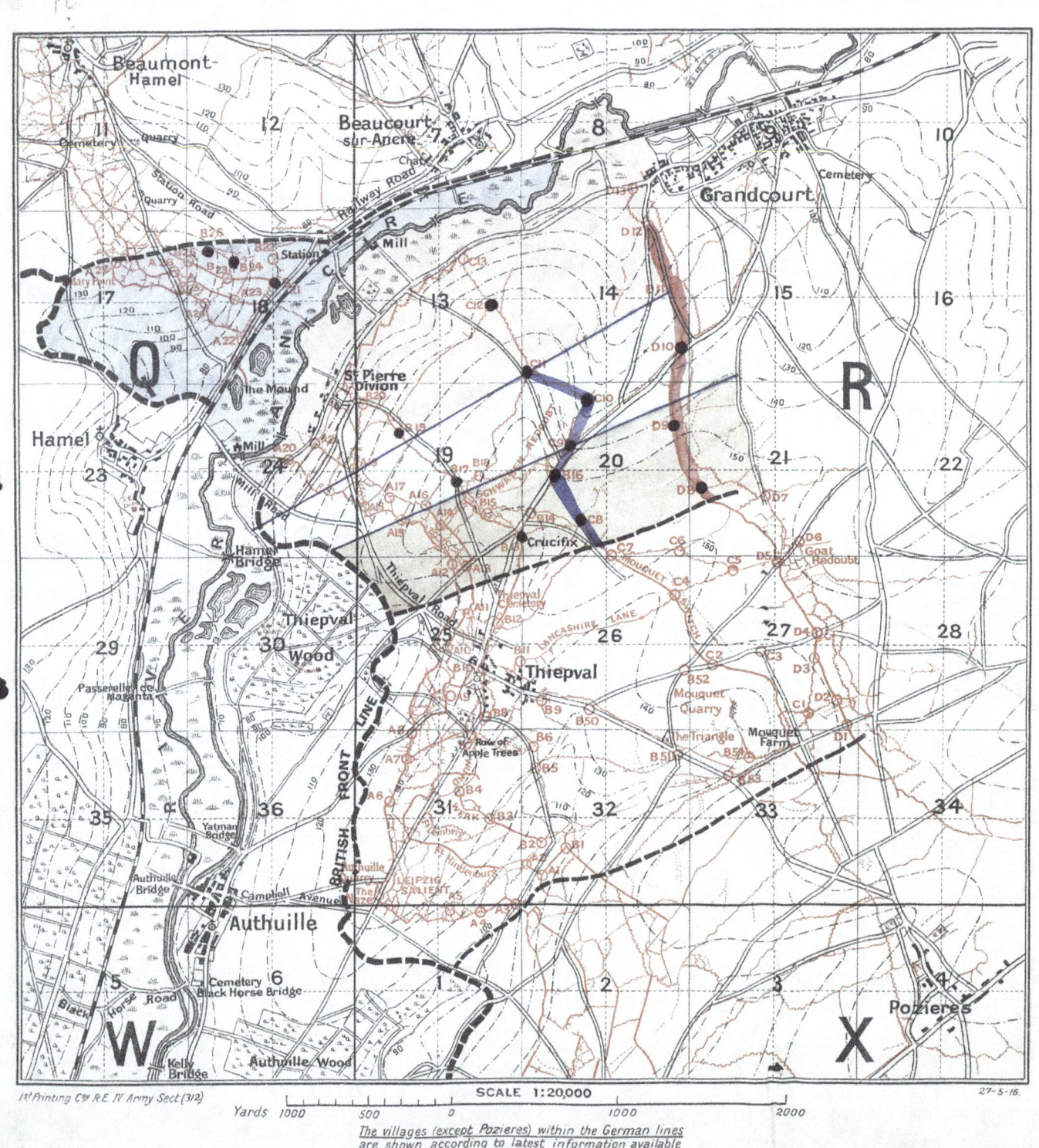

MOVEMENT ORDER

by

Lt. Col. P. T. Denis de Vitre.

C. R. E. 36th Division.
****

B

15. 6. 16.

On 19. 6. 16 the following moves will take place.

The 122nd Field Coy, R.E. less its mounted portion will move into MOUND KEEP.

The 150th Field Coy, R.E. less its mointed portion will move into THIEPVAL WOOD, into the Colonnade at PAISLEY.

First line transport of 121, 122 and 150 will move as directed in Administrative Instructions Supplementary to 36th Div. Order No. 30 dated 11. 6. 16., and be at P.36.B.7.0. by 12 noon and report to an Officer to be detailed by O.C. 121 R.E. to remain in charge of the transport of the 3 Field Companies, R.E.

The general idea is that as far as possible transport of uni should be intact behibd so that in case of an advance it will be ready to come up to them, and that during the first phases of the attack they should use trench stores as far as possible, but Field Coy Commanders will probably find it necessary to take certain tools and explosives with them into MOUND KEEP & THIEPVAL, for which they will make their own arrangements, provided the transport is parked as above by 12 noon, it is suggested that pack horses could take all that is required.

TRAIN TRANSPORT - BAGGAGE WAGONS. In case of Field Coys, this refers to limbered R.E. wagons, and H.Q. G.S. wagons and cooks G.S. wagons, these will not be left behind, but accompany the first line transport, as they include technical stores.

All Surplus Stores and Kit.

O.C.121 & 122 will collect into MARTINSART VILLAGE DUMP, and O.C. 150 Coy into FORCEVILLE DUMP, in accordance with above referred to Administrative Instructions. Each Coy will leave 1 man in charge.

Great Coats and Packs.

All ranks going to the first line transport rendezvous will take theirs with them.

All ranks going to THIEPVAL & MOUND KEEP WILL TAKE THEM
these will be collected and labelled before assault, and one
man per Coy left in charge of them.

O.C. 121 will do likewise and leave them in MARTINSART.

Rations.

Vide. above referred to Administrative Instructions, all
ranks must carry ½ the Emergency Ration.

Coke. Ditto

Water. Ditto.

Bucket and 50ft of rope. Ditto, draw and fix on to water cart.

Ordnance. Ditto. Note the first two lines.

The 121st Coy will, except as stated above, concentrate at
Martinsart, and be accommodated in Cellars.

O.C. 121 Coy will leave men at Pumping Engines in THIEPVAL
& MARTINSART until relieved.

Those in THIEPVAL WILL BE RATIONED BY O.C. 150th Coy.

These men will be left fully equipped.

Particular attention is to be paid to not overloading wagons.

Medical Officer R.E.

The Maltese cart with Medical Companion and Medical Orderly
will rejoin H.Q. R.E. at HEDAUVILLE.

The M.O. takes up other duties under A.D.M.S.

LT.COL?
C.R.E. 36th Division.

OPERATION ORDER BY C.R.E. NO.3.

Those portions of the 121st, 122nd and 150th Field Coy R.E. which are in Divisional Reserve will parade, so as to be ready to move off at 7.30a.m. on 29. 6. 16.

After inspection O.C's of Units will allow these men to fall out, but they must be ready to fall in and move off at a moments notice.

Zero time is 7.30a.m. on 29. 6. 16.

R.E. Transport in Divisional Bivouac.

At 7.30 a.m. on 29. 6. 16, all R.E. Transport is to be hooked in, in marching order. Dismounted men paraded in marching order.

The whole to be carefully inspected for which purpose the senior N.C.O. of each unit will help the transport officer to see that men are carrying their gas helmets, iron rations, ammunition, etc., etc. After the inspection the horses will be unhooked, girths slackened and men allowed to fall out. No one allowed to leave the Bivouac except on duty, but all ranks will be ready to hook in and move at short notice.

28. 6. 16.

Lt.Col.
C.R.E. 36th Division.

SECRET.

108th INFANTRY BRIGADE
No 548
JUN 25 1916

Copy No 4

D

108TH INFANTRY BRIGADE OPERATION ORDER NO 1.

23rd June 1916.

1. **INFORMATION.**

The Fourth Army is taking the offensive along its whole front at a date which will be notified later.

The 36th Division is to attack on both sides of the ANCRE and will have the 32nd Division on its right and the 29th Division on its left.

The right boundary of attack, which coincides with the left boundary of the 32nd Division attack, will be a line drawn from the N.E. corner of THIEPVAL WOOD to a point (R.21.C.20.65.) 100 yards S.of D.8.

The left boundary will be a line from the extreme point of MARY REDAN Q.17.a.6/3½ in a straight line to the two houses in R.7.c.20. (inclusive to Xth Corps), thence S.E. to the river at R.13.a.48.thence along the river ANCRE to the point where it crosses the railway at R.8.c.4½/6, thence along the railway.

The objectives of the 36th Division are:-
 (a) On the left bank of the ANCRE.
    The German "D" line from D.8. to D.12., both inclusive.

 (b) On the right bank of the ANCRE.
    The triangle of trenches enclosed between the left boundary of the attack and the ANCRE and BEAUCOURT STATION.

2. **INTENTION.** The 108th Infantry Brigade will attack on both sides of the ANCRE.
Right boundary of attack. will be:- a line drawn from our trenches at Q.24.1/2, just S. of C.9. (OMAGH) to R.21.a.10/90.
Left boundary of attack.will be:- Left boundary of the Divisional Attack.

3. **OBJECTIVES.**
 (a) On the left bank of the ANCRE.
    The German "C" line between C.9. (OMAGH) inclusive, to the river ANCRE.

 (b) On the right bank of the ANCRE.
    The triangle of trenches enclosed between the left boundary of the attack and the ANCRE and BEAUCOURT STATION.

4. **SUB-DIVISION OF DIVISIONAL FRONT.**

For the purpose of the attack the front of the Division will be divided into four sections:-
 (a) Right Section.
    Right boundary of the attack to a line drawn from our trenches at Q.24.1/2 just South of C.9. (OMAGH) to R.21.A.10.90.
 (b) Right Centre Section.
    From left boundary of right section to a line drawn from N. corner of THIEPVAL WOOD (Q24.12.) by B.19.(LURGAN), C.11. (ENNISKILLEN) to D.11.(BUNDORAN) all inclusive.
 (c) Left Centre Section. North of right centre section to the ANCRE.
 (d) Left Section. From the ANCRE to the left boundary of the Divisional attack.

5. ALLOTMENT OF TROOPS.

Right Section. 109th Infantry Brigade.
Right Centre Section. 11th R.Ir.Rif. & 13th R.Ir.Rif. and the 15th R.Ir.Rif. (107th Infantry Brigade attached), all under the Command of the G.O.C. 108th Infantry Brigade.
Left Centre Section. This section is not being directly attacked.
Left Section. 9th R.Ir.Fus. and 12th R.Ir.Rif.
Divisional Reserve. 107th Infantry Brigade (less 15th Royal Ir. Rifles).

Three Field Companies, R.E. (less the sections detailed to accompany the attacking Brigades).
16th. Battn. Royal Irish Rifles (P).

6. POSITIONS OF ASSEMBLY.

LEFT BANK OF THE ANCRE.
Right Centre Section.
Portion of THIEPVAL WOOD bounded on the right, by a line drawn from Q.24.1/2. to the junction of WHITCHURCH STREET and ELGIN AVENUE - thence by ELGIN AVENUE exclusive.

RIGHT BANK OF THE ANCRE.
Left Section.
9th Royal Ir. Fusiliers:- HEDGEROWS TRENCH and trenches in front of it.
12th Royal Ir. Rifles :- Front and Support line trenches from WINCHESTER STREET to the left of the section and ROYAL AVENUE. Also Cellars and trenches in HAMEL.

7. BOMBARDMENT.
There will be 5 days preliminary bombardment, known as U,V,W,X and Y days. There will be an intense bombardment previous to launching the Infantry attack, on Z day.

8. PLAN OF ATTACK.

LEFT BANK OF ANCRE.
RIGHT CENTRE ATTACK.
Boundaries as stated in para 4 (b).
The task of the troops allotted is to clear the A and B lines within the section and to advance as far as C line, where they will halt and consolidate on the salient C.9, C.10, C.11.

The 11th Royal Ir. Rifles will be on the right.
The 13th Royal Ir. Rifles " " left.
The 15th Royal Ir. Rifles will be in support.

Dividing line between the leading Battalions will be a straight line drawn from our trench through a point 50 yards N.W. of A.18. - through junction of communication trench with "A" line 100 yards N.W. of A.17. - to 100 yards N.W. of C.10. (STRABANE) in "C" line.

The leading Battalions will each attack with two Companies in line, these Companies being each on a frontage of 1 platoon extended, i.e. 4 waves. Supporting Companies will be in the same formation except that platoons will move in column until compelled to deploy.

The 13th Royal Ir. Rifles will furnish four special detachments:-

"A" (Flankguard), B, C, and D, each under an Officer.
"A" DETACHMENT. Consisting of 1 Company, (less 1 platoon), 1 Stokes mortar, 1 machine Gun, and 1 Lewis Gun will leave parties to block the German "Front" and "A" line trenches on the left of our advance, and will then clear communication trenches from A.19. - N. of B.19. to C.12 (PORTADOWN), whence it will send detachments:-

(a) To the right, to gain touch with our troops at C.11.
(b) To the left, to ensure observation and fire on the ST. PIERRE DIVION - GRANDCOURT Road.

8. PLAN OF ATTACK (CONTINUED).

"B" DETACHMENT. Consisting of 1 platoon and 1 Lewis Gun of the above mentioned Company, will reconnoitre the left of the "A" lines down to the river ANCRE, and thence along the marsh to C.13. (COLERAINE) keeping touch with "D" Detachment from ST.PIERRE DIVION onwards.

On arrival at C.13. (COLERAINE) this party will establish posts to watch the marsh from the road at C.13.(COLERAINE) exclusive to the bridge over the ANCRE at R.13.b.00.90.

"C" Detachment. Consisting of 1 platoon and 1 Lewis Gun will clear the communication trenches from A.19. to B.20., and from Q.24.b.85.05. to trench junction R.19.a.00.40. to the church at ST.PIERRE DIVION afterwards establishing themselves in ST.PIERRE DIVION covering the approaches from the right bank of the river.

"D" DETACHMENT. Composition as for "C" will follow "A" Detachment (Flankguard) to B.19. and then clear the left of "B" line and ST.PIERRE DIVION. From here it will clear the communication trench to C.13. (COLERAINE) and the road running parallel to it and get touch with the party of our troops at C.12. (PORTADOWN). From ST.PIERRE DIVION to COLERAINE it will keep touch with "B" Detachment.

These parties should be specially warned of the importance of sending in early information as to the presence or absence of hostile troops in the area to be reconnoitred by them.

SUPPORTING BATTALION. When the rear lines of the leading Battalions reach the German front lines, the Supporting Battalion (15th Royal Irish Rifles) will advance.

LEFT CENTRE ATTACK. No troops allotted other than those mentioned above.

RIGHT BANK OF ANCRE.

LEFT ATTACK.
Boundaries as stated in para 4 (b).
The task of the troops allotted are:-
(a) To clear the 1st, 2nd, and 3rd lines of German trenches within their section.
(b) To establish strong points at B.21.(BUSHMILLS), B.24. (LARNE), and B.26. (GOBBINS).
(c) To occupy BEAUCOURT STATION and the trenches immediately behind the station and afterwards to occupy the MILL in R.13.(a), and the two houses about 250 yards behind the station between the railway road and the railway.

As soon as the task of these two battalions is completed, the 12th R.Ir.Rif. will be withdrawn into NO MAN'S LAND and held in readiness to move across the river; the 9th R.Ir.Fusiliers taking over positions evacuated by the 12th Royal Irish Rifles.

The dividing line between the 9th R.Ir.Fus. on the right and the 12th R.Ir.Rif. on the left will be A.25.(exclusive to the 9th R.Ir.Fus.), to B.26.(GOBBINS), (inclusive to the 9th R.Ir.Fus.).

The 9th R.Ir.Fus. will enter enemy's lines between the railway and Q.17.b.95.00. Tasks (a), (b), and (c) as stated above, on right of dividing line, fall to this battalion.

FORMATION.
Four companies in lines of platoons, each company in four waves.

--- 4 ---

8. PLAN OF ATTACK (CONTINUED).

12th Royal Irish Rifles. One Company will enter the enemy's trenches about Q.17.b.8/1. on the left of the 9th Royal Irish Fusiliers, and will clear enemy's 1st, 2nd, and 3rd line trenches North Westwards.

No 2 Company 12th Royal Ir. Rifles supported by No 3 Company will assault the enemy's salient between Q.17.b.20.10 and Q.17.b.19.30. and will occupy their 1st and support trenches and clear these trenches Eastwards to get touch with their No 1. Company.

They will block trenches to their left and will send bombing patrols to establish communication with the 29th Division.

No 4 Company 12th Royal Irish Rifles will detail 1 platoon under an Officer with a Lewis Gun to enter enemy trench (RAILWAY SAP) about Q.18.c.6/2 and clear it North Eastwards to Q.18.c.76/75. This platoon will afterwards reconnoitre the ground along the railway line towards BEAUCOURT STATION on the right of the 9th Royal Irish Fusiliers.

A second platoon from this company under an officer with a Lewis Gun will reconnoitre the marsh on the right bank of the ANCRE up to BEAUCOURT STATION.

The remaining ½ company 12th Royal Irish Rifles will support the 9th Royal Irish Fusiliers, moving out from our front line trenches as the rear wave of the 9th Royal Irish Fusiliers enters the enemy's front trench. Companies will move in waves on a front of 1 platoon.

9. INFANTRY ATTACK.

The Infantry attack takes place at Zero time on "Z" day.

All movements on "Z" day from the moment of assault are timed from Zero.

The clock time of Zero will be notified in due course.

Prior to the hour of assault, the leading battalions in the attack will leave their trenches under cover of the bombardment and lie down in front in the formations in which they are about to advance.

The supporting battalions of the attack will move into the front line trenches and assembly trenches vacated by the leading battalions.

Each section of the attack will time its advance so that the 1st line of the attacking troops is within 150 yards of the "A" trenches at Zero time.

The Artillery Time Table of lifts is as follows:-

LEFT BANK OF ANCRE.

Time	
At 00	From front trenches to support trenches of the "A" line.
" 03	To the "B" line.
" 0.18	To the "C" line.
" 1.18	To the "D" line.
" 2.36	Forms barrage behind "D" line.

RIGHT BANK OF THE ANCRE.

Time	
At 00	From front line on to Support Trenches.
" 03	On to the "B" line (B.21. B.23. B.25.).
" 08	On to the line B.22. B.24. B.26.
" 0.13	On to BEAUCOURT STATION and on the trench North of it (Q.18.b.07. to Q.18.b.8.6.).
" 0.33	Barrage in rear of BEAUCOURT STATION and on the trench running due North from Q.12.d.6.0.

It is possible that the leading line of the attack on left bank of the ANCRE may be in advance of the time table on the "B" and "C" lines.

This will not effect the commencement of the advance from the preceding line, but the leading troops will in this case halt and lie down 150 to 200 yards from the objective and rush in as soon as the Artillery lifts off it.

9. INFANTRY ATTACK (CONTINUED).

All ranks must understand that there should be no halt in any captured trenches until the "C" line has been reached.

If the "C" line is held and the leading line of the attack is unable to get forward without reinforcement, the attack will proceed as in normal open warfare, by short rushes.

During the progress of the advance, as each line of hostile trench is captured, contact must be established between neighbouring Battalions and Brigades all along the line, and this should be done in conjunction with the work of clearing up the trenches.

In order to cover the advance of the attacking troops on either side of the ANCRE from hostile view and fire from the high ground on the other side, a smoke barrage will be created up the valley of the ANCRE.

10. CONSOLIDATION OF CAPTURED TRENCHES.

The consolidation of captured trenches will be begun immediately they are occupied by the troops allotted to them.

Strong points, for a garrison of a platoon (not less than 30 men) will be constructed at the following places by the troops as shewn hereunder:-

LEFT BANK OF THE ANCRE.
B.17 (CLONES), B.19 (LURGAN) by 15th R.Ir.Rif.
C.9.(OMAGH), C.10 (STRABANE) by 11th R.Ir.Rif.
C.11 (ENNISKILLEN), C.12 (PORTADOWN) by 13th R.Ir.Rif.
RIGHT BANK OF THE ANCRE.
B.21 (BUSHMILLS), B.24 (LARNE), B.26 (GOBBINS) and BEAUCOURT STATION by 9th Royal Irish Fusiliers.

Rear platoon of each Company of leading units will be told off as carrying and consolidating party.

Support Battalion will tell off 2 platoons per Company for similar duties.

11. MACHINE GUNS.

3 Machine Guns will accompany 11th R.Ir.Rif. and 9th R.Ir.Fus respectively.

2 Machine Guns will accompany 13th R.Ir.Rif. and 12th R.Ir.Rif. respectively.

These guns will eventually be placed in strong points as follows:-

LEFT BANK OF ANCRE.		RIGHT BANK OF ANCRE.	
OMAGH.	1	BEAUCOURT STATION.	2
STRABANE.	2	BUSHMILLS.	1
ENNISKILLEN.	1	LARNE.	1
PORTADOWN.	1	GOBBINS.	1

The remaining 6 machine guns of the 108th Brigade which will have been co-operating with Artillery bombardment during the previous nights will leave their positions on MESNIL ridge at 12 midnight on Y/Z night and proceed:-

4 Guns to Left bank of ANCRE.
2 Guns to Right bank of ANCRE, where they will report to the Senior Officer of the Right Centre Section and Left Section of the attack respectively.

These 6 guns will remain, at first, in reserve to cover attack, and meet emergencies. They will move forward under orders from the Senior Officer of their respective section of attack. Details of carrying parties for machine guns are shown in Appendix "E".

12. CLEARING PARTIES.

Clearing parties will be detailed from 3rd wave of leading units. Their task will be to search trenches for small parties of enemy who may have escaped the leading waves.

13. BLOCKING PARTIES.

Leading Units in the attack will be responsible for blocking all trenches to the flanks outside their zone of action, and all trenches leading towards the enemy in advance of the line held by them at the moment.

13. BLOCKING PARTIES (CONTINUED).

Blocking parties should be at least 40 yards to the front or flank of other troops. This subject will be carefully thought out in advance by Company Commanders.

14. CONNECTION WITH OTHER UNITS.

Officers Commanding Units will pay special attention to keeping touch with units on their right and left.

15. R.E.

Two Sections, 122nd Field Company, R.E. are allotted to the Brigade, one on each side of the ANCRE. Their duties will be to assist in consolidating strong points, after capture, and any other technical work required. They will obtain instructions from Senior Officer of their respective Section of attack.

16. STOKES MORTAR.

Stokes Trench Mortars will assist in the attack in accordance with instructions which will be issued later. 4 Mortars will advance on left bank of ANCRE, and two on right bank.

17. DISTINGUISHING FLAGS.

Yellow flags to mark position will be carried by each platoon, bombing party or patrol. Flags of the 107th Brigade will have a single vertical black stripe, the 108th Brigade two, and the 109th Brigade three such stripes.

18. FLARES.

Company Officers and N.C.O's, above rank of Lance Corporal, will carry three red flares each for use in accordance with instructions already issued.

19. TORPEDOES.

Each Battalion will carry 8 lengths of Bangalore Torpedo. An additional 8 lengths will be in possession of each R.E. section attached to the Brigade.

20. VERY LIGHTS.

Very Lights and Pistols will be carried by Units.

21. EQUIPMENT.

Packs and Greatcoats will not be taken to the assembly trenches on the night preceding the assault but will be labelled and left under guard of 1 man per Company in selected houses, dug-outs etc. Every Infantry man, except those detailed for such special employment as prevents it, will carry - Waterproof Sheet, Woollen Waistcoat, Rifle and Equipment (less pack), 170 rounds of ammunition, two Mills Grenades, two Sandbags in belt, one iron ration and unexpired portion of day's ration, two smoke helmets and goggles.

Regimental Officers will wear trousers and putties and the same equipment as their men. A thorough inspection will be made before Units move to their assembly positions to ensure that all ranks are fully equipped and that clothing and boots are in serviceable condition.

22. TRENCH TRAFFIC ARRANGEMENTS.

Communication trenches will be reserved for up and down traffic as follows:-

Right Centre Section.

SANDY AVENUE	.. ..	DOWN.
CROMARTY AVENUE	.. ..	UP.

Left Section.

CHARLES AVENUE & PROSPECT ROW.	.. ..	UP.
JACOB'S LADDER	.. ..	UP.
HAMEL - AVELUY WOOD	.. ..	DOWN.

11th R.Ir.Rif.) Will place sentries at exit ends of communication
9th R.Ir.Fus.) trenches in their respective sections to prevent them being used for traffic in contrary directions.

23. MEDICAL.
Posts will be established at the following positions:-

REGIMENTAL AID POSTS.
Left Section.	Q.23.D.5.8.	(Present post).
HAMEL.	Q.23.A.9.2.	(New post).
	Q.23.B.3.2.	(Reserve Post).
Right & Centre Sections.	Q.30.B.1.8.	(SPEYSIDE ST.-New Post).
	Q.30.B.5.2.	(Present Post).

COLLECTING POSTS. (FIELD AMBULANCES).
(1) Railway Bank S. of HAMEL on HAMEL - ALBERT ROAD. Q.29.B.5.3.

(2) THIEPVAL WOOD (3 shell proof shelters) Q.30.C.9.4. (all communication trenches N. and E. of this wood converge on this point).

(3) East bank of river N. of AUTHUILLE (two shell-proof shelters) Q.36.C.7.6.

(4) AVELUY WOOD (5 shell proof shelters) Q.35.D.1.9.

(5) MESNIL light Railway Station (cellars and shell-proof shelters on road opposite Station) Q.28.C.3.7.

Casualties able to walk will be directed from the Collecting Posts in AVELUY WOOD - Q.35.D.1.9. to MARTINSART by a pathway which will be marked by directing posts.

A Motor Ambulance Car Park will be established at W.9.B.7.5

ADVANCED DRESSING STATION - MARTINSART - W.3.A.9.8. and Chateau Stable - W.3.A.9.8.

MAIN DRESSING STATIONS. - FORCEVILLE and CLAIRFAYE.

24. INFORMATION TO ENEMY.
No papers or orders of any kind which might give information to the enemy will be carried on either officers or men.

Compliance with this order will be verified by inspection prior to going into assembly trenches.

All ranks are to be warned that if taken prisoner they are only bound to give their name and rank and should refuse to answer any other question.

25. MAPS.
All officers will carry 1/20,000 57d. S.E. and 57c.S.W. and the special Corps Map. These maps will be referred to in orders reports and messages. Maps showing our trenches are not to be carried.

26. SYNCHRONISATION OF WATCHES.
Watches will be synchronised at 9 a.m. "Y" day by signal and at 7 p.m. "Y" day personally at Brigade Headquarters by a representative from every unit of the Brigade.

27. TRANSPORT.
(a) **1st Line Transport.**
All 1st line transport of Infantry and R.E. Units will move into bivouac along the ENGLEBELMER - BOUZINCOURT ROAD before "Z" day.

All 1st line transport will be controlled by Divisional Headquarters in the first stages of the offensive.

— — — 8 — — — —

27. TRANSPORT. (CONTINUED).

(b) <u>Train Transport</u>. Baggage wagons of all units will be loaded in accordance with Mobilization Store Tables. Those of R.E. and Infantry Units will remain on the 1st line bivouac ground when the 1st line transport marches off and they will be picked up by the O.C. Divisional Train when he comes along.

Those of other units will remain at Headquarters of the Unit and in the event of a general advance of the Division taking place from the nearest zone all the latter train transport wagons will rendezvous on the football ground at HEDAUVILLE.

Care must be taken to see that wagons are not overloaded.

The O.C. Divisional Train will be empowered to jettison any baggage on the wagons which in his opinion is in excess of the authorised load.

28. SALVAGE.

The Divisional Ordnance Dump for collection of abandoned arms, equipment and other material of the battlefield will be established at P.36.b.10.4. which is close to the bivouac grounds of Infantry Battalions and on the direct line of empty wagons returning from MARTINSART.

All units and individuals should co-operate in collecting salvaged articles to this point by every means of transport.

29. WATER.

It will be necessary for Medical Officers of Units to test any sources of water within the present German area before they can be used by our troops, for fear of poisoning or pollution.

One well bucket and 50 feet of rope will be issued to each company of R.E. and Infantry Battalion by D.A.D.O.S. on demand. These should be taken forward with the water carts.

30. RATIONS.

Rations for consumption on the day following 'Z' day will be sent up in cookers with the remainder of the 1st line transport (ammunition, tools, water carts, etc.) if the situation permits of transport being used. It may be possible to work limbered wagons along the ST.PIERRE DIVION-GRANDCOURT road or failing that, to dump on the side of the sunken HAMEL -THIEPVAL ROAD which runs through the present "NO MAN'S LAND" in front of THIEPVAL WOOD.

An officer to act as guide for the transport of each unit should meet the transport at the MILL on the HAMEL-THIEPVAL Road.

If the situation does not permit of transport being sent up on the night of Z/A the troops must draw their rations from 'A' day from the Brigade Reserve Ration Dumps in THIEPVAL WOOD and HAMEL. In that event the 109th Infantry Brigade will draw from Brigade Dump in THIEPVAL right, 107th Brigade will draw from Brigade Dump in THIEPVAL left; 108th Brigade will draw from Brigade Dump in HAMEL, and other Units from the nearest Dump.

Sufficient sandbags have been placed in each Brigade Dump to enable all the rations in each Dump to be carried up, if 8 rations are placed in each bag.

31. BRIGADE REPORT CENTRE.

Brigade report centre will be at RAILWAY VIEW Q.29.d.3.5.

<u>MEMORANDA.</u> Not more than 20 officers will accompany battalions into action. A proportion of Warrant Officers and skilled N.C.O's and men will also be left behind in accordance with instructions issued. (Appendix "F").

MEMORANDA (CONTINUED).

Distance between waves of the attack will be 60 yards.
Instructions re tools and engineer stores to be carried forward are issued separately.
Appendices "A", "B", "C", "D" and "E" relating to Signal communication, prisoners of war, ammunition supply, Dumps and Stragglers Posts, and carrying parties are attached. Also Appendices "F", "G" and "H", and extracts from previous instructions

ACKNOWLEDGE.

[signature]

CAPTAIN.

Brigade Major,
108th Infantry Brigade.

Copies to:-

No 1. 36th Division. "G".
2. 36th Division. "Q".
3. C.R.A.
4. C.R.E.
5. 107th Infantry Brigade.
6. 109th Infantry Brigade.
7. 87th Infantry Brigade.
8. 122nd Field Company, R.E.
9. 11th Royal Ir. Rifles.
10. 12th Royal Ir. Rifles.
11. 13th Royal Ir. Rifles.
12. 9th Royal Ir. Fusiliers.
13. 15th Royal Ir. Rifles. (107th Brigade).
14. 108th Brigade Machine Gun Company.
15. 108th Trench Mortar Battery.
16. 146th Trench Mortar Battery.
17, 18 & 19. Office Copies.
20. War Diary.

APPENDIX "A".

SIGNAL COMMUNICATIONS.

1. CABLE LINES. Every Unit must go forward with its full establishment of Cable.

Cables laid out during and advance must be run outside communication trenches.

When lateral communication cannot be managed by arrangement, the onus of providing the same lies with the Southern Unit.

Places should be selected in the enemy's line where Signal Offices are to be established, and at least three alternative lines should be run to each.

It is better to have a few points connected by alternative lines than more points connected by only a single line.

Enemy's lines found in the hostile trenches should not be cut by Infantry; they should be left to be dealt with by Signallers.

Sign Posts to Signal Offices in hostile trenches should be erected as soon as possible.

When a Headquarters moves forward linemen must be left to hand over the lines to the formation in rear taking over.

Shoild it be necessary to retire from a position that has been reached, and cables that have been run forward to it must be cut.

2. VISUAL (GROUND). Divisional Reading Stations have been selected as follows:-

32nd Division.	W.15.b.6/3.	Landmark from front, two southern trees on MEULES ridge.
36th Division.	Q.22.d.8/8.	Landmark from front, single tree on MESNIL ridge.
49th Division.	Q.29.c.2/4.	Landmark MESNIL CHATEAU.

These Stations are primarily intended for their own Divisional front, but all must be prepared to take a message frommany station in front which is endeavouring to send.

Messages will only be sent back by visual; Stations in rear will not answer or acknowledge.

Only messages equivalent to priority should be sent and they should be limited to six words.

Codes as laid down for comminication between ground and aeroplanes may be used.

It is hoped that one big French Lamp per battalion and 7 per Signalling Company will be available.

Practically all the ground between our trenches and "D" line is visible from the visual reading station.

3. CONTACT AEROPLANE. The Xth Corps Aeroplane (type B.E.2c.) will have a broad black band under the right bottom plane.

Signals will be as follows:-

<u>From Advanced Infantry.</u> By flares denoting "We are here" and from flashing of mirrors. These flares will be used fired in a row at 3 or 4 paces interval between each ¼ minute between the firing of each flare.

3. CONTACT AEROPLANE (CONTINUED).

From Battalion or Brigade Headquarters. By panneau (ground signalling sheet) or lamp. The former will be used in preference to the latter whenever possible.

When wishing to signal, Brigades or Battalions will open ground sheet.

As soon as aeroplane is in position to receive, ground station sends its unit call, meaning "H.Q" "are here".

This may be followed by one of the following signals:-

NN. meaning "short of ammunition"
YY. " "short of grenades"
OO. " "Barrage required"
HH. " "Lengthen range"
XX. " "Held up by machine gun fire"
ZZ. " "Held up by wire"

Each message will be repeated continuously in its entirety.

If necessary, the signal may be followed by map location of point or line where barrage is wanted or range needs to be lengthened. No other signals will be used.

Aeroplane will acknowledge signals if possible but will not necessarily do so.

From Aeroplane. White light meaning "Where are you".

Messages received by aeroplane will be transmitted as received (adding time of receipt) by wireless. Simultaneously to Corps Headquarters and to the Artillery report centres of each Division in the line or by dropping message bag at Corps Headquarters.

In cases of great urgency messages may be dropped from a low altitude at Divisional, Brigade or Battalion Headquarterss.

4. BALLOON.

A Balloon will be employed to keep touch with the Infantry, and should be especially valuable at night. It may be connected by telephone with Corps Headquarters.

The Balloon will take lamp messages from Brigade Headquarters and acknowledge them.

The code laid down for use between Infantry and Aeroplane will normally be used, but messages may be sent in full if necessary.

Messages should only be sent to Aeroplane or Balloon when of great importance, as the number that can be received is necessarily very limited.

5. PIGEONS.

A loft will be established at Corps Headquarters. Each of the four leading Brigades will be furnished with 6 pigeons. A reserve of 8 birds will be with the Brigade in Divisional Reserve of 32nd and 36th Division.

The pigeons should be kept well forward and not at Brigade Headquarters.

Pigeons will only be used when all other means of communication have failed.

Messages must be properly addressed and show the unit from which despatched and time of despatch.

Pigeons cannot fly at night, and must therefore be released in time to reach Corps Headquarters before dark.

6. WIRELESS.

Two Trench wireless sets will be with each Division; their range is 2000 to 4000 yards.

Those of the 32nd and 36th Division will be with the leading Brigades packed up and ready to go forward.

The sets of the 49th Division will be set up by Brigade in Divisional Reserve of the 32nd and 36th Divisions respectively.

Three operators and four men for carrying for each of these latter sets will be provided by 49th Division.

The Corps parent set has a range of about 6000 yards; It will be set up South of MARTINSART WOOD and will be connected to Corps Headquarters by telephone. Dug-outs for working sets must be provided.

Messages sent by wireless will be in cipher unless unless distinctly marked "in clear" by the Staff Officer originating them.

Instructions for control of working will be issued by A.D.A.S.

----- 3 -----

7. ROCKETS. 3 red rockets in quick succession, repeated at short intervals until acted on, will continue to represent the S.O.S. Signal. Rockets will only be sent up at points where the enemy's Infantry is attacking.

8. CODE. The amended list of code calls issued under G.91/5/7 of June 12th 1916, will be used for all messages by visual, aeroplane, balloon, wireless or pigeon or by forward telephone lines.

The Code Call will be used as a Station Call and also as a code name to denote a Unit in the "address to" "text" or "address from" of a message.

These code calls will not be used in messages transmitted above Divisional or Heavy Artillery Headquarters, but will be decoded at the Signal Office.

The writer of any message emanating from or passing into the forward area and also of any message to be sent by visual, wireless or pigeon will be responsible for inserting the code name in his message.

9. INSTRUCTIONS FOR CO-OPERATION BETWEEN INFANTRY AND KITE BALLOONS.

(a) By day lamp cannot be read, helio can be read, light must be alinged on the basket and NOT on the balloon. The panel might also be read if placed against a steep bank.

(b) By night lamp can be easily read.

(c) Communication will be from Battalion and Brigade Headquarters.

(d) Infantry will recognise their own Corps Balloon.

By day - by its distinctive pennant 18' x 3' 30 feet below the basket.

	BY DAY.	BY NIGHT.
VIII Corps	Black & White chequered.	Light exposed for 10 seconds at intervals of 10 minutes.
X "	Half red & half white.	Succession of dots every 10 minutes.
III "	Plain white.	Succession of dots and dashes every 10 minutes.

(e) All messages will be "D D - D D" and Balloon will only answer:-

(i) With lamp "R D" (received) and "I M I" (repeat).

(ii) With pennant; when the unit calls up with its code calls the pennant will be hauled up to the basket.
As soon as the observer is ready to read the pennant will be lowered again. When the message has been received the pennant will be hauled up and down three times in succession.

(f) The following code signals will be used:-
Battalion or Brigade call letter and followed by map square.

```
         Headquarters are at......................
    NN   -   Short of ammunition.
    YY   -   Short of Grenades.
    OO   -   Barrage wanted.
    HH   -   Lengthen range.
    XX   -   Held up by Machine Gun fire.
    ZZ   -   Held up by wire.
```

Signals will be preceded by Battalion or Brigade Call Letter, or followed by map location of point or line where "barrage" is wanted, or range needs to be lengthened:

 e.g. (Bn. Call) NN. - Battn. Short of ammunition.

 OO. R.24.a.3/4   - Barrage wanted at R.24.a.3/4.

All messages will be repeated continuously in their entirety until acknowledged.

APPENDIX "B".

PRISONERS OF WAR.

Prisoners will be sent under Regimental Escort to the Divisional Prisoner Collecting Post on the ALBERT - HAMEL Railway at Q.35.b.5.0.

The escort will take due precautions to ensure that prisoners do not destroy any papers, and no conversation will be permitted among the prisoners or between prisoners and escort.

Officers and Warrant Officers should be marched separately and under a different escort.

A German speaking Officer and N.C.O. will be posted at the Divisional Prisoner Collecting Post.

Here the prisoners will be handed over by the Regimental escort to an escort furnished by the A.P.M.

Regimental escorts will return to their units after furnishing full information of the place and circumstances under which the capture was effected.

At the Divisional Collecting Post all documents will be taken and prisoners will be rapidly examined by the German speaking Officer or N.C.O. and then sent as quickly as possible to the Corps Collecting Post at W.15.b.1.9. where prisoners and papers will be handed over and the Divisional escort will then return to his post.

The strength of the escort will not exceed 15% of the number of prisoners.

APPENDIX 'C'

AMMUNITION SUPPLY AND ACCOUNTING FOR AMMUNITION.

During active operations it is essential that Divisional Headquarters should know at any time the approximate amount of ammunition, grenades etc. in the different echelons and dumps. A strict control will be kept on all issues and receipts by Units concerned, and all returns must be rendered punctually, as it is more important to have an approximate return at the right time than an accurate return late.

GRENADES, S.A.A. & T.M. AMMUNITION.

The Brigade and Divisional Dumps already established are intended to be sufficient to meet all requirements in the first phase of the Infantry Attack.

Should these dumps not prove to be sufficient their replenishment will proceed in the normal manner as during the present dumping period, 1st line transport of units being under the control of Divisional Headquarters for this purpose.

As soon as the situation permits of ammunition being sent forward on wheels Brigade Dumps for ammunition will be established in the same way as the Ration Dumps further forward.

All Grenades sent to Brigade Dumps will have been already charged with detonators under Divisional arrangements.

Empty ammunition wagons of infantry will refill at the Advanced Divisional Dump on ALBERT - HAMEL ROAD and when that is exhausted at the Main Divisional Dump near MARTINSART STATION.

The D.A.C. will be responsible for bringing the S.A.A. and Grenades etc. to the Main Divisional Dump near MARTINSART STATION, until the situation permits of a new Divisional Dump being established further forward.

APPENDIX "D".

108TH INFANTRY BRIGADE:

DUMPS AND STRAGGLERS POSTS WILL BE FOUND BY BATTALIONS AS FOLLOWS:-

DISCRIPTION.	MAP REFERENCE.	STRENGTH.	UNIT.	REMARKS.
Brigade Ration Dump THIEPVAL.	Q.30.b.2.9.	1 Officer. 1 N.C.O. 1 man.	13th R.Ir.Rif.	To be taken over on morning of "Y" day. Officers & men i/c of Brigade Ration Dumps to report to Staff Captain RAILWAY VIEW at 7 p.m. same evening.
- do -	HAMEL.	New HAMEL Church.	-do-	12th R.Ir.Rif.
Brigade Magazine THIEPVAL.	Q.30.b.1.7.	-do-	11th R.Ir.Rif.	Officers i/c Magazines to report to Brigade Grenade Officer at RAILWAY VIEW at 7 p.m. "Y" day. Magazines will be under the supervision of a Brigade Officer
- do -	HAMEL.	Q.23.d.4.5.	-do-	9th R.Ir.Fus.
Brigade R.E. Dump. THIEPVAL.	Q.30.a.8.0.	-do-	13th R.Ir.Rif.
- do -	HAMEL.	Q.23.d.4.5.	-do-	9th R.Ir.Fus.
Stragglers Post No.4.MOUND KEEP.	Q.35.b.4.5.	2 N.C.O's 4 men	1 N.C.O. 11th R.Ir.Rif.) 1 N.C.O. 4 men) Bde. Pioneers	Officers, N.C.O's & men to be selected from those not taking part in the attack, i.e. spare grooms, Lewis Gunners, C.S.M's etc.
- do - No.5.MESNIL.	Q.28.d.65.85.	-do-	1 N.C.O. 12th R.Ir.Rif.) 1 N.C.O. 4 men) Bde. Pioneers	
Water and Iron Rations.	MESNIL. Q.28.c.8.4.	1 man.	12th R.Ir.Rif.	
- do -	HAMEL. Q.23.d.4.5.	-do-	9th R.Ir.Fus.	

108TH INFANTRY BRIGADE.

APPENDIX "E"

	9th R.Ir.Fus.	11th R.Ir.Rif.	12th R.Ir.Rif.	13th R.Ir.Rif.	15th R.Ir.Rif.	TOTAL.	Report to.
GRENADES S.A.A. R.E. STORES.	20	15	20	15	20	90	Brigade Grenade Officer at Brigade Hd.Qrs. at 6 p.m. W/X night.
MACHINE GUN COY.	12	12	12	12	12	60	O.C. 108th M.G.Coy. at LANCASHIRE DUMP at 9-30 a.m. "Y" day.

(Extra carriers can be called for, from 15th R.Ir.Rif. when reserve Machine Guns move forward.)

The 90 men reporting to Brigade Grenade Officer on W/X night will be divided between the two sub-sectors and will be used for carrying forward grenades, S.A.A., R.E.Stores etc. under Brigade arrangements.

The 12 men reporting to O.C. Machine Gun Company must include any men trained in battalions in the Vickers Gun.

APPENDIX "F"
-:xxxxxxxxxxxxxxxxxxxxxxxxxxx:-

The following Officers N.C.O's and men should be left out of the fighting ranks in the event of Offensive Operations:-

	Off.	OR.
Regimental Transport.	1	25
Regimental Transport.(Loaders with Train).		3
Reserve Water Cart Drivers.		2
Grooms.		6
Cooks.		11
Quartermasters Store.	1	10
Orderly Room.		2
Police, Qr. Guard, etc.		4
Sanitary Squad.		5
Shoeing Smiths.		5
Average Sick, light duty.		9

Specialists:-
       (4 Company Sergt. Majors or their
         understudies.).
       (2 N.C.O's and 2 men Lewis Gun.)
       (1 Signalling Instructor.   )
       (1 Bombing Instructor.   )

Left behind i/c Stores.   All Tailors and Shoemakers.

Only 20 officers per battalion will take part in the attack.
The Officers and other ranks left behind will join the transport of their battalions on "W" day.

APPENDIX "G".

CARRIAGE OF TOOLS AND R.E. STORES.

The platoons detailed in Para 10 of Brigade Operation Order No 1, will carry the following:-

2 Coils (12 rolls) French expanding wire to be carried by	4 men
1 Coil of plain wire to be carried by	1 man
12 Coils of barbed wire to be carried by	12 men
40 screw iron stakes (4 each man)	10 men
Total.	27

In addition 8 picks and 12 shovels and 200 sandbags must be distributed amongst the platoon.

All other platoons will carry 8 picks and 8 shovels.

Battalions will make their own arrangements as to drawing of tools from Brigade R.E. Dumps for all platoons <u>except</u> consolidating platoons.

ON "Y" DAY.

<u>11th R.Ir.Rif.</u>. will draw all necessary stores for consolidating platoons of the 3 Battalions of Right Centre Section of attack, and will place them in the assembly positions, marked for these platoons, viz:-

Rear platoons of Companies of 11th R.Ir.Rif. and 13th R.Ir.Rif., and 3rd and 4th platoons of 15th. R.Ir.Rif.

These positions will be selected in conjunction with representatives of Units concerned.

<u>9th R.Ir.Fus.</u> will perform similar duties on behalf of themselves and 12th R.Ir.Rif. in conjunction with representative of 12th R.Ir.Rif.

APPENDIX "H".

3" STOKES TRENCH MORTARS.

The 3" Stokes Mortars in position for firing will open rapid fire on "Z" day previous to the assault from - 0.5. to Zero time.

They will not fire on previous occasions except in emergencyes: and for ranging purposes just prior to their bombardment.

Trench Mortars will advance with the attack as follows:-

LEFT BANK OF ANCRE.- 4 Trench Mortars (108th T.M.B.),
            (personnel of remaining 4 Mortars of this
            Battery acting as extra carriers):-
1 Mortar with Right leading Company 11th R.Ir.Rif. objective C.9.
            (OMAGH).
1 Mortar with left flankguard 13th R.Ir.Rif. (detach. "A"),
            objective C.12 (PORTADOWN).
1 Mortar follow 11th R.Ir.Rif. objective C.10 (STRABANE).
1 Mortar follow 13th R.Ir.Rif. objective C.11.(ENNISKILLEN).

RIGHT BANK OF ANCRE.- 2 Trench Mortars (108th T.M.B.),
    LEFT ATTACK.   (personnel of 2 other Mortars acting as extra
                     carriers):-
These will follow 9th R.Ir.Fus. objective B.24.(LARNE) and B.26
            (GOBBINS) respectively.

As soon as the attack has gone forward all 49th Division Stokes Mortars will assemble on the road opposite the NORTHERN CAUSEWAYm(Q.29.b.45.00).

APPENDIX "H" (CONTINUED).

DISTRIBUTION OF STOKES MORTARS - 108TH INFANTRY BRIGADE FRONTAGE.

	In position for firing.	In Reserve. Mortars.	Total Allotted Mortars.	Firing Positions.
LEFT BANK OF ANCRE. (RIGHT CENTRE SECTION OF ATTACK).	108th T.M.B. 6 Mortars. 143rd T.M.B. 4 "	2 -	8 4	Saps 7, 8, and 10.
RIGHT BANK OF ANCRE. (RIGHT SECTION OF ATTACK).	108th T.M.B. - 146th T.M.B. 8 Mortars.	4 -	4 8	(4 - about N. end of New Trench, { Q.17.c.5.7. (4 - in CROW'S NEST & LANCASHIRE POST

ADDENDA.

108TH INFANTRY BRIGADE OPERATION ORDER NO 1.

23rd June 1916.

Page 3 - Between paras SUPPORTING BATTALION and LEFT CENTRE ATTACK insert:-

ASSAULT OF THE "D" LINE

The assault of the "D" line will be carried out bt the three battalion of the 107th Brigade in Divisional Reserve.

The 107th Brigade will advance from THIEPVAL WOOD, following the 109th Brigade. It will attack the "D" line from D.8. to D.9. (both inclusive), passing through the leading Brigades at the "C" line and making its assault on the "D" line when the Artillery barrage lifts.

This assault will be supported by all the fire the Battalions holding the "C" line can bring to bear.

No opportunity should be neglected of getting Vickers and Lewis Guns out on the flanks of the line of attack of the 107th Brigade to assist in keeping down the fire of hostile machine guns or infantry, both on the front to be attached and on the flanks of it.

Shell holes and communication trenches leading to the front will make useful emplacements and should be utilised.

SECRET.

107TH INFANTRY BRIGADE OPERATION ORDER, No.1.

Copy No. 13

21st June, 1916.

1. INFORMATION.

The Fourth Army will take the offensive along its whole front at a date which will be notified later.

The 36th Division will attack on both sides of the ANCRE and will have the 32nd Division on its right and the 29th Division on its left.

The right boundary of the attack, which coincides with the left boundary of the 32nd Division attack, will be a line drawn from the N.E., corner of THIEPVAL WOOD to a point (R.21.c.20.65) 100 yards S. of D 8.

The left boundary will be a line from the extreme point of MARY REDAN, Q.17.a.6/3½ in a straight line to the two houses in R.7.c.20, (inclusive to Xth Corps, thence S.E. to the river at R.13.a.48 thence along the river ANCRE to the point where it crosses the Railway at R.8.c.4½/6, thence along the railway.

2. OBJECTIVES.

The objectives of the 36th Division are:-
(a) On the left bank of the ANCRE,
    the German "D" line from D.8 to D.12, both inclusive.
(b) On the right bank of the ANCRE,
    the triangle on trenches enclosed between the left boundary of the attack and the ANCRE and BEAUCOURT STATION.

3. SUB-DIVISION OF FRONT.

For the purpose of the attack the front of the Division will be divided into four sections:-
(a) Right Section. Right boundary of the attack to a line drawn from our trenches at Q.24 1/2, just S. of C.9 (OMAGH) to R.21.A.10.90.
(b) Right Centre Section. From left boundary of Right Section to a line drawn from N. corner of THIEPVAL WOOD (Q.24.12) by B.19 (LURGAN) C.11 (ENNISKILLEN) to D.11 (BUNDORAN) all inclusive.
(c) Left Centre Section. North of Right Centre Section to the ANCRE.
(d) Left Section. From the ANCRE to the left boundary of the Divisional attack.

4. ALLOTMENT OF TROOPS.

Right Section.   109th Infantry Brigade.
Right Centre Section. Two Battalions of the 108th Infantry Brigade and the 15th Bn. Royal Irish Rifles; all under the command of the G.O.C., 108th Infantry Brigade.
Left Centre Section. This section is not being directly attacked.
Left Section.   Two Battalions, 108th Infantry Brigade.
Divisional Reserve. 107th Infantry Brigade (less 15th Battalion Royal Irish Rifles).
Three Field Sections R.E., (less the sections detailed to accompany the attacking Brigades).
16th Battalion Royal Irish Rifles.

5. POSITIONS OF ASSEMBLY.

Right Section. In THIEPVAL WOOD.

Right Centre Section. In THIEPVAL WOOD; the 15th R. Irish Rifles being in the Assembly Trenches in Q.30.C. west of ELGIN AVENUE.

Divisional Reserve.   in AVELUY WOOD and MARTINSART.
The 8th, 9th and 10th Bns. Royal Irish Rifles and 107th Brigade Machine Gun Company (less 8 Guns) in Assembly Trenches in AVELUY WOOD at Q.35. A and C.
The 107th Stokes Mortar Batteries in AVELUY WOOD at Q 35 D 2.5.

Four Guns 107th Brigade Machine Gun Company in emplacements in HAMEL Sub-sector and four Guns in emplacements in THIEPVAL WOOD Sub-sector.

1 Section 121 Coy, R.E., in AVELUY WOOD.

6. **PLAN OF ATTACK.** The 109th Inf. Brigade have been ordered to attack the 'A' and 'B' Lines within their section and to advance as far as a line drawn from C 8 (LISNASKEA) - B 16 (DUNGANNON) to the GRANDCOURT - THIEPVAL Road at C9-(exclusive) and to halt and consolidate on this line.

The two Battalions of the 108th Inf. Brigade and the 15th R. Irish Rifles in the right centre Section have been ordered to clear the 'A' and 'B' lines within their section and to advance as far as the 'C' line where they will halt and consolidate on the Salient C 9 (OMAGH) C 10 (STRABANE) C 11 (ENNISKILLEN).

Detachments from the Right Centre Section have been detailed to clear the C.T. from B 19 to C 12, to hold C 12 as a defensive post, to establish touch between C 12 and C 11, and to proceed towards C 13 to ensure observation and fire on the GRANDCOURT - ST. PIERRE DIVON Road.

Patrols from the Right Centre Section have been detailed to reconnoitre and clear out the trenches on the left of the Right Centre attack, to establish themselves in ST. PIERRE DIVON, and to reconnoitre the C.T. along the river valley as far as C 13 and from there to communicate with the post established at C 12.

The two Battalions of the 108th Inf. Brigade in the Left Section have been ordered:-
- (a) To assault the Salient in the German 'A' Line between Q 17 b 20.10 and Q 17 b 10.30.
- (b) To clear the German trenches East of the Salient down to the ALBERT - HAMEL Railway.
- (c) To establish strong points at B 26, B 24 and B 21.
- (d) To occupy BEAUCOURT STATION and the trenches immediately behind the Station and afterwards to occupy the MILL in R 13 a and the two houses about 250 yards beyond the station, between the Railway Road and the Railway.

The assault of the 'D' line will be carried out by the three Battalions of the 107th Inf. Brigade in Divisional Reserve.

The 107th Inf. Brigade will advance from the THIEPVAL WOOD following the 109th Inf. Brigade and will attack the 'D' line from 'D' 8 to 'D' 9 (both inclusive) passing through the leading brigades at the 'C' line and making its assault on the 'D' line when the Artillery barrage lifts.

7. **ARTILLERY TIME TABLE OF LIFTS.**

At 0 From front trenches to support trenches of "A" line.

At 0.3 to the "B" line.
At 0.18 to the "C" line.
At 1.18 to the "D" line.
At 2.38 Forms barrage behind "D" line.

8. **THE INFANTRY ATTACK.**

The Infantry attack takes place at Zero time on "Z" day.
All movements on "Z" day from the moment of the assault are timed from Zero.

The clock time of Zero will be notified in due course.

At half an hour before Zero the troops of the 107th Infantry Brigade will start their march from AVELUY WOOD to front line trenches in THIEPVAL WOOD.

The 9th R. Irish Rifles will lead and will march by the AVELUY - HAMEL ROAD, Northern Causeway, S. of Assembly Trenches of the 15th R. Irish Rifles to ELGIN AVENUE, thence along the South Side of ELGIN AVENUE to their position in rear of the left supporting Battalion of the 109th Inf. Brigade from junction of trench Q 24 1/2 to junction of trenches R 25 20 and 21.

The 10th R. Irish Rifles will follow the 9th R. Irish Rifles and will march by the AVELUY - HAMEL ROAD, Southern Causeway, South of Brigade H.Q., thence along the South side of ENNISKILLEN AVENUE to their position in rear of the right supporting Battalion of the 109th Inf. Brigade from junction of trenches R.25.20 and 21 to junction of trenches R.25.15 and 16.

The 8th R. Irish Rifles will follow the 10th R. Irish Rifles and will march by the AVELUY - HAMEL ROAD, Northern Causeway, S. of Assembly Trenches of 15th R. Irish Rifles, to ELGIN AVENUE thence along South side of ELGIN AVENUE, and will form up behind the 9th R. Irish Rifles and 10th R. Irish Rifles in front of the trenches R 25.18 to R 25.21.

The 9th R. Irish Rifles and the 10th R. Irish Rifles will assault the "D" line from "D" 8 to "D" 9 and will be supported in their attack by the 8th R. Irish Rifles.

The 9th R. Irish Rifles and 10th R. Irish Rifles will follow the supporting Battalions of the 109th Inf. Brigade at a distance of 200 yards.

The 10th R. Irish Rifles will advance with their right on C 8 (LISNASKEA) and on D 8.

The 9th R. Irish Rifles will advance in line with and on the left of the 10th R. Irish Rifles and will assault the 'D' line with their left on D 9.

The O.C., 10th R. Irish Rifles will be responsible for giving the signal for the line to advance.

The 8th R. Irish Rifles will advance in rear of the 9th R. Irish Rifles and 10th R. Irish Rifles at a distance of 100 yards.

The O.C., 8th R. Irish Rifles will detail one Company to form a defensive flank from D 9 in the direction of C 10 (STRABANE); he will also detail one Platoon with two Lewis Guns to clear the trench running along the N. side of the THIEPVAL - GRANDCOURT Road as far as Point 2774 where they will establish a strong post.

Great care must be taken to avoid being absorbed into the attack of the 109th Inf. Brigade on the 'C' line unless it is quite clear that the 109th Inf. Brigade are unable to take 'C' line without assistance.

Immediately the barrage lifts from the 'C' line the advance will be continued through the 'C' line to within 200 yards of the 'D' line so as to be ready to assault that line as soon as the barrage lifts at 2.38.

No. 4 Section, 121 Field Coy, R.E., under Lieut. FAWCETT will be attached to the 10th R. Irish Rifles and will advance immediately behind this Battalion, and will be prepared to cut gaps with amonal torpedoes in enemy's wire in front of 'D' line should this wire not be demolished by our Artillery. After the capture of 'D' line they will assist in the consolidation of the strong points at D 8 and D 9.

9. BOMBING SQUADS.

Each Platoon bombing squad will accompany its own Platoon.

In addition, five men per Platoon will each carry one bucket, each Bucket containing 12 Mills Grenades.

In the advance from 'C' line to 'D' line the O.C., 9th R. Irish Rifles will detail one squad to bomb down the trench from B 16 (DUNGANNON) to D 9.

10. CONSOLIDATION OF CAPTURED TRENCHES.

The consolidation of captured trenches will be taken in hand from the moment of occupation by the troops allotted to them.

The 10th R. Irish Rifles will detail one Platoon with two Vickers Guns and two Lewis Guns to consolidate and hold the strong point D 8.

The 9th R. Irish Rifles will detail one Platoon with two Vickers Guns and two Lewis Guns to consolidate and hold the strong point D 9 and one Platoon and two Lewis Guns to clear the trench from D 9 to D 10 (DERRY CITY) and to consolidate and hold D 10 (DERRY CITY).

The 10th R. Irish Rifles will consolidate the captured trench from D 8 for 200 yards towards D 9 and the 9th R. Irish Rifles will consolidate from D 9 for 200 yards towards D 8.

The 8th R. Irish Rifles will assist in the consolidation at whatever parts of the trench they may find themselves.

Platoons for the holding of strong points will consist of not less than 30 men.

11. MACHINE GUNS.

The Brigade Machine Gun Company will support the attack on the right bank of the ANCRE with four Guns in the emplacements in

THIEPVAL WOOD in trenches Q 24, 4, 5 and 6.

They will support the attack on the left bank of the ANCRE with four Guns in the emplacements in the HAMEL Sub-sector, one in BULSON STREET, one in CONNANTRY AVENUE and two in old GERMAN TRENCH.

As soon as the 'B' line is taken the four Guns in THIEPVAL WOOD will advance to the attack behind the 8th R. Irish Rifles and will support the attack as opportunity occurs; on arrival at the 'D' line they will select the most suitable positions for the defence of the line.

As soon as the 'C' line is taken the four Guns in the HAMEL Sub-sector will proceed to Assembly Trenches in THIEPVAL WOOD vacated by the 15th R. Irish Rifles, nearest to Brigade H.Q. and will form part of the Brigade Reserve; the Officer in charge will report the arrival of these Guns to Brigade Headquarters.

The remaining eight Guns will be attached to Battalions, two to each Battalion of the Brigade and will accompany the Battalions in the attack.

12. (STOKES) TRENCH MORTARS.

The O.C., 107th Stokes Mortar Battery will detail two Mortars to accompany each of the following Battalions in the attack:- 8th, 9th and 10th Royal Irish Rifles.

The personnel of the other Six Mortars will be used as ammunition carriers for these Guns. Fifty rounds per Mortar will be carried in this manner.

13. BLOCKING PARTIES.

The O.C., 10th R. Irish Rifles will detail one party to block the trench running S.E., from D 8 and one party to block the trench running E. from D 8.

The 9th R. Irish Rifles will detail one party to block the trench running N.E. from D 9.

14. R.E., STORES.

The rear Platoon of each Company of the 10th R. Irish Rifles and the 9th R. Irish Rifles, and the two rear Platoons of the 8th R. Irish Rifles, will carry stores for the consolidation of the positions captured.

The stores will be picked up by the 10th R. Irish Rifles, on the ride 100 yards N. of ROSS CASTLE and by the 9th and 8th R. Irish Rifles North and South of GORDON CASTLE respectively.

15. MEDICAL.

Regimental Aid Posts will be established in WHITCHURCH STREET by the 8th, 9th and 10th R. Irish Rifles. Any change in the position of a Regimental Aid Post will be at once notified to the O.C., Collecting Post.

All casualties will be evacuated to the Collecting Posts at Q 30 c 9.4 and Q 36 c 7.6 under orders of the O.C., 110th Field Ambulance.

16. TRANSPORT.

All 1st Line Transport will move into Bivouac along the ENGLEBELMER - BOUZINCOURT Road on "Y" day.

All 1st Line Transport will be controlled by Divisional Headquarters in the first stage of the offensive.

The Brigade Transport Officer will keep in close touch with Divisional Headquarters.

Baggage Wagons will be loaded in accordance with Mobilization Store Tables and will remain on the first line bivouac ground when the 1st Line Transport marches off, and they will then be picked up by Divisional Train.

5.

17. BRIGADE HEADQUARTERS.

Brigade Headquarters will be established at Q 30 C 70.35 at 9 p.m. on "Y" day.

ACKNOWLEDGE.

M Day
MAJOR.
BRIGADE MAJOR.
107TH INF. BRIGADE.

Issued at ____

Copy No.1 to 8th R.Ir.R.
" No.2 to 9th R.Ir.R.
" No.3 to 10th R.Ir.R.
" No.4 to 15th R.Ir.R.
" No.5 to Bde M.G.Coy.
" No.6 to 107th T.M.Bty.
" No.7 to Bde. Transport Officer.
" No.8 to 36th Div. "G".
" No.9 to 36th Div. "G".
" No.10 to 36th Div. "Q".
" No.11 to 108th Inf. Bde.
" No.12 to 109th Inf. Bde.
" No.13 to C.R.E...36R
" No.14 to ....

INSTRUCTIONS ISSUED WITH OPERATION ORDER, No.1,
dated 21st June, 1916.

1. NOMENCLATURE OF DAYS.

The first and following days of the bombardment will be known as the U. V. W. X and Y days. Z day will be the day of the assault.

2. DRESS, ETC.

When moving up to AVELUY WOOD on the night Y/Z men will be equipped as follows:-

Packs and Great Coats will not be carried but Haversacks will be worn on the back in the place of the Pack.

A waterproof sheet with cardigan inside will be rolled and carried on the back of the belt.

Every man in the second and third Platoons of each Company will carry either a Pick or a Shovel.

Men will caryy in their Haversack their Rations for Z day and their Iron Rations.

Every man will carry two Sandbags tucked into his Belt.

The full establishment of Wire Breakers and Wire Cutters will be carried by the two leading Platoons of each Company; men carrying them will wear a white tape on their left shoulder straps.

One hundred and seventy rounds S.A.A. per man will be carried.

Every man will carry two Mills Grenades, one in each side Pocket.

Every man will cary two Smoke Helmets and Goggles.

Officers will wear Trousers and Puttees and the same Equipment as the men.

3. BOMBING SQUADS.

Bombing Squads referred to in O.O. No.1 will be composed as follows:-

Two Bayonet men each carrying 4 Bombs in Pockets.
Two Throwers each carrying 12 Bombs in Haversack.
Two Carriers each carrying 12 Bombs in Buckets.
One Leader carrying 6 Bombs in a bag.
Two spare men each carrying 12 Bombs in Buckets.

4. RUNNERS.

Runners will be detailed as follows and will wear a Black Band on each arm:-

Per Company .... 6.
Per Battalion Hqrs .. 8.
Per Brigade Hqrs .... 4 from each Battalion,
two from Brigade Machine Gun Company, 2 from Stokes Trench Mortar Battery.

5. AMMUNITION AND BOMB STORES.

Advanced Dumps have been established in front line in THIEPVAL WOOD at intervals along the trench.

Brigade Stores are at Q 30 B 2.7 and at Q 30 D 5.9.

6. FLAGS.

Five yellow flags with one blue strip in the middle will be carried by each Company; these Flags are only to be used to indicate the most advanced Infantry in any particular area. They are not to be stuck into the ground but should be carried and waved by hand.

7. COMMUNICATION TRENCHES.

ENNISKILLEN AVENUE and CROMARTY AVENUE will be up trenches. ELGIN AVENUE and SANDY AVENUE will be down trenches.

8. CONTACT AEROPLANES.

Every effort must be made to carry out the instructions already issued re Contact Aeroplanes; the red flares will be carried only by Officers and reliable N.C.Os.

9. WOUNDED MEN.

All ranks must be cautioned that they are not to fall out to take wounded men to the rear; the wounded men will be collected after the Battle.

10. PRISONERS.

All Prisoners will be evacuated to Brigade Headquarters; escorts need not exceed one to six Prisoners.

11. WHITE FLAG.

No attention is to be paid to any White Flag put up by the enemy.

12. BRIGADE O.P.

The Brigade O.P. is at Q 23 C 5.4.

13. VERY PISTOLS.

Very Pistols and ammunition for same will be carried in the attack.

14. MAPS.

All Officers will carry 1/20,000, 57D, S.E., and 57C, S.W. and the special Corps Map. These Maps will be referred to in reports and messages. Maps of our trenches are not to be carried.

15. INFORMATION TO THE ENEMY.

No papers or orders of any kind which might give information to the enemy will be carried by Officers or men. Compliance with this order will be verified by inspection prior to going into the Assembly Trenches.

All ranks are to be warned that if taken Prisoner they are only bound to give their name and rank and should refuse to answer any other questions.

16. BRIGADE CARRIERS FOR CONSOLIDATING MATERIAL AND AMMUNITION.

One N.C.O. and 20 men will be required from 8th, 9th, and 10th R. Irish Rifles, for carrying work, under Brigade orders.

They will be utilized in carrying up consolidating material, ammunition, etc, to Battalions as may be required.

Further orders as to their rendezvous, etc, will be issued later.

17. AMMUNITION CARRIERS FOR BDE. M. GUN COMPANY.

Twenty seven men will be detailed by 8th, 9th, 10th, and 15th Bns. R. Irish Rifles to be attached to the Brigade Machine Gun Company as carriers of Ammunition.

These together with the five men per Battalion attached to the Brigade Machine Gun Company will make up the required total of eight carriers per Gun. Further orders re this will be issued.

-+++++++++++++++++++++++++++++-

SECRET.

EXTRACTS FROM SIGNALLING INSTRUCTIONS AND DIVISIONAL ARTILLERY ORDERS FOR ATTACK.

18th June, 1916.

SIGNAL COMMUNICATION.

1. Cable Lines.   Every unit must go forward with its full establishment of cable.

Cables laid out during an advance must be run outside communication trenches.

When lateral communication cannot be managed by arrangement, the onus of providing the same lies with the Southern unit.

Places should be selected in the enemy's line where Signal offices are to be established, and at least three alternative lines should be run to each.

It is better to have a few points connected by alternative lines than more points connected by only a single line.

Enemy's lines found in the hostile trenches should not be cut by Infantry; they should be left to be dealt with by Signallers.

Sign Posts to signal offices in hostile trenches should be erected as soon as possible.

When a Headquarters moves forward linemen must be left to hand over the lines to the formation in rear taking over.

Should it be necessary to retire from a position that has been reached, any cables that have been run forward to it must be cut.

2. Visual (ground) Divisional reading stations have been selected as follows:-

        32-nd Division.   W.15.b.6/3. Landmark from front, two southern trees on MEULES ridge.

        36th Division.   Q.22.d.8/8. Landmark from front, single tree on MESNIL ridge.

        49th Division.   Q.29.c.2/4. Landmark MESNIL Chateau.

These stations are primarily intended for their own divisional front, but all must be prepared to take a message from any station in front which is endeavouring to send.

Messages will only be sent back by visual; Stations in rear will not answer or acknowledge.

Only messages equivalent to priority should be sent and they should be limited to six words.

Code as laid down for communication between ground and aeroplanes may be used.

It is hoped that one big French lamp per Battalion and 7 per Signalling Company will be available.

Practically all the ground between our trenches and "D" line is visible from the visual reading station

        x   x   x

5. Pigeons.   A loft will be established at Corps Headquarters. Each of the four leading Brigades will be furnished with 6 pigeons. A reserve of 8 birds will be with the Brigade in Divisional Reserve for 32nd and 36th Division.

The pigeons should be kept well forward and not at Brigade Headquarters.

Pigeons will only be used when all other means of communication have failed.

Messages must be properly addressed and show the unit from which despatched and time of despatch.

Pigeons cannot fly at night, and must therefore be released in time to reach Corps Headquarters before dark.

x   x   x

7. Rockets. 5 red rockets in quick succession, repeated at short intervals until acted on, will continue to represent the S.O.S. signal. Rockets will only be sent up at points where the enemy's infantry is attacking.

8. Code. The amended list of Code Calls issued under G.91/5/7 of June 12th, 1916, will be used for all messages by visual, aeroplane, balloon, wireless, or pigeon or by forward telephone lines.

The code calls will be used as a Station call and also as a code name to denote a unit in the "address to" "text" or "address from" of a message.

These code calls will not be used in messages transmitted from Divisional or Heavy Artillery Headquarters, but will be decoded at the Signal office.

The writer of any message emanating from or passing into the forward area and also of any message to be sent by visual, wireless or pigeon will be responsible for inserting the code name in his message.

------------------oOo------------------

PRISONERS OF WAR.

Escorts to Prisoners will take due precautions to ensure that prisoners do not destroy any papers, and no conversation will be permitted among the prisoners or between prisoners and escort.

Officers and Warrant Officers should be marched separately and under a different escort.

Regimental escorts will return to their units after furnishing full information of the place and circumstances under which the capture was effected.

------------------oOo------------------

EXTRACTS FROM 36TH Artillery DIVISIONAL ORDER, No. 1.

x   x   x

4.   There will be one F.O.O. with the Headquarters of each Battalion attacking. These F.O.O's. will be under the sole orders of the Artillery Liaison Officers at Infantry Brigade Headquarters, and will only advance when told by him to do so. They should be accompanied by 3 telephonists (one a linesman), 2 miles of wire, 2 Telephones, flags, discs and lamps.

x   x   x

6.   If any 'Re-Bombardment' is ordered during 'Z' day or afterwards, it will last 30 minutes, the last 5 minutes of which will be intensive.

x   x   x

7.   B/173 Brigade R.F.A., will be ready to advance to a position already chosen, by the fork roads at Q.23.d.6.0, on receiving orders from R.A.H.Q., This Battery will not be ordered to advance until the 'C' line has been reached and the Infantry have commenced consolidating it.

If the advance of the Infantry against 'D' line is held up and a fresh attack has to be made against this Line, the following Batteries will be advanced to positions E. of the to cut the wire:-

      A/153;   B/153;   A/172;   B/246;   C/246.

Officers from these Batteries should, if possible, be the F.O.Os. who are to be at Battalion Headquarters as laid down in para. 4.

-+++++++++++++++++++++++++++++++-

INTENSIVE BOMBARDMENT & TABLE OF LIFTS-
(THIEPVAL SUB-SECTOR).

Time.

-55 to 0.0.   18-pr. Batteries on all trenches (Fire and Communication) up to 'C' line inclusive.
Intensive Bombardment.   4.5" How. Certain Trenches and Strong Points in 'A' and 'B' lines.
2" T.M. Bombarding Front Line Trench in THIEPVAL Sub-sector.
9.45" T.M. CRUCIFIX System, M.G's in Q.24.b. ST. PIERRE DIVION RAILWAY SAP in Q.18.c.

0.0.
(0.0.-0.3)   All fire lifts off the Front Trench and Communication Trenches between Front and Support Trenches to Support Trench and Trenches in rear (exclusive of 'C' line).
2" T.M. Stop firing.
9.45" T.M. on ST. PIERRE DIVION and main CRUCIFIX REDOUBT.

0.3.
(0.3-0.18)   All fire lifts off the Support Trench and Communication Trenches between Support and Reserve Trenches to Reserve Line and Trenches in rear, including 'C' line.
9.45" T.M. on ST. PIERRE DIVION up to 0.10 (Stops).
The T.M. on CRUCIFIX REDOUBT stops firing.

0.18.
(0.18-0.28)   All fire lifts off reserve line to a parallel line about 400 yards E. of Reserve line and Trenches E. of this line.
Sections of 18-pdr. and 4.5" How. walk up Communication Trenches between 'B' and 'C' lines at 100 yards per minute and on reaching 'C' line commence bombardment of that Line.

0.28.
(0.28-1.18). All fire lifts to 'C' line and approaches to it from 'D' line.

1.18.   All fire lifts off 'C' line on to 'D' line and approaches to it from the E.

(1.18-2.38) Sections of 18-pdrs and 4.5" How. walk up approaches between 'C' and 'D' line at 100 yards per minute and on reaching 'D' line commence bombardment of that line.

2.38.   All Fire lifts to form a barrage 300 yards E. of 'D' line and approaches to it from the E.

    Note.   All 4.5" Howr. and Trench Mortars lift their fire in each case 3 minutes before the times laid down for 18-pdr.

MAJOR.
BRIGADE MAJOR.
107TH INF. BRIGADE.

36th DIVISION ORDER No. 39.

29. 6. 16.

1. Zero has been postponed for 48 hours.

> June 29th becomes Y.1 day.
> June 30th " Y.2 day.
> July 1st " Z day.

The programme for Z day will be as originally arranged.

2. Troops of this Division will remain in their present position until Y.2 day, when they will move to assembly positions under orders to be issued shortly.

During Y.1 and Y.2 days Battalion Commanders will take steps to see that Infantry billeted in villages conceal themselves on the approach of hostile aircraft.

3. The following measures will be carried out during the 48 hours postponement :-

(a) Concentrated bombardment and night raids will be carried out in order to deceive the enemy.
Concentrated bombardments will take place as follows:-

> Y.1 day   4 - 5.20 p.m.
> Y.2 day   8 - 9.20 a.m.

(b) Wire cutting will be completed.

(c) Advantage will be taken of favourable weather to destroy hostile batteries.
Subject to the above, heavy howitzer and heavy gun ammunition must be economised.

Work on communications, especially over the River ANCRE, and repair of trenches will be carried on as far as possible.

Issued at
7 a.m.

LT. COLONEL. G.S.

Distribution as for 36th Div. Orders 34 to 38.

Appendices :-
G. H. I. K. L. M. N.
O. P. R. S. T. U. &
Tracing.

"A" Form.
MESSAGES AND SIGNALS.
Army Form C. 2121.

SECRET

TO W.2 (122 Field By ??)

C.E. X Corps takes over
R. ANCRE at 8.0 a.m Y.2 day (30.6.16)
Z day is 1.7.16. Programme for Z
day as originally arranged.
Meanwhile pay special attention to crossing
of ANCRE, for which you have one detachment
of 135 A.T. Coy R.E.
Concentrated bombardments will take place
 Y.1 day 4 – 5.30 p.m
 Y.2 day 8 – 9.20 a.m.

From
Place Y P
Time 10.15 a.m

"A" Form
MESSAGES AND SIGNALS.
Army Form C. 2121.

PRIORITY

TO W Z

Sender's Number: E/2
Day of Month: 1/7
AAA

SEND A PARTY TO REPAIR
RAILWAY LINE ROAD GAUGE FROM LEVEL
CROSSING AT HULEY NORTHWARDS AND
CLOTHE ROAD NORTHWARDS FROM LEVEL TOWARDS
STATION IN Q.15.B.

From C.R.E. 26

"C" Form (Duplicate).
MESSAGES AND SIGNALS.

Army Form C. 2123.
(In books of 50's in duplicate)
No. of Message

Lieut FARGHER reports at 9.24 am rails badly damaged at R24A26 and Barrage on it aaa He is working beyond this and will return to it when it quietens aaa

Received 10.21 am

FROM PLACE & TIME   WZ   9.55am

"A" Form
MESSAGES AND SIGNALS

Army Form C. 2123.

No. of Message _____

Prefix _____ Code _____ m. | Words | Charge | This message is on a/s of. | Recd. at _____
Office of Origin and Service Instructions | | | | Date _____
| Sent | | H.2 Service. | From _____
| At _____ m. | | |
| To | | (Signature of "Franking Officer.") | By _____
| By | | |

TO W Z

Sender's Number.	Day of Month	In reply to Number	AAA
E/10	17	C H 9	

IS THERE ENOUGH MATERIAL ON

SPOT FOR REPAIR OF RAILWAY

From _____
Place X P
Time 12.50 p.m.

The above may be forwarded as now corrected. (Z)

Censor. | Signature of Addressor or person authorised to telegraph in his name.
* This line should be erased if not required.

"C" Form (Duplicate).
MESSAGES AND SIGNALS.

Army Form C. 2123.
(In books of 50's in duplicate.)

No. of Message ....

Service Instructions. NJ

Charges to Pay. £ s. d.

Office Stamp.

Handed in at .... Office 11.52 a.m. Received 12.5 p.m.

TO XP

Sender's Number	Day of Month	In reply to Number	AAA
	1		

QB inform me safe at
108
Q18 6 5520 still held by
enemy and our artillery on
it aaa Have withdrawn FARQHARS
section towards HAMEL and instructed
him to report VP for
information as to when he
can proceed aaa

FROM WZ
PLACE & TIME

"C" Form (Original).   Army Form C.2121
MESSAGES AND SIGNALS.   No. of Message

Prefix	Code	Words	Received	Sent, or sent out	Office Stamp
Charges to collect	£ s. d.		From 30 By	At To By	
Service Instructions					

Handed in at   Office   m.   Received   m.

TO   X P

*Sender's Number	Day of Month	In reply to Number.	AAA
EN9			

FARGHER and section detailed your
E2 are in HAMEL trenches
aaa please instruct whether you
wish them left there or
withdrawn here pending developments
aaa

FROM
PLACE & TIME   V2

* This line should be erased if not required.
W 12550/4108 75,000 Pads. A. J. W. & Co. 11/15 Forms/C.2123.

"A" Form.
MESSAGES AND SIGNALS.
Army Form C. 2121.

TO	W.Z.			
Sender's Number.	Day of Month	In reply to Number		
M	17	C.H.9		AAA

F FIRE PREVENTS SECTION WORKING

LET IT STOP ~~COMING~~ OUT OF FIRE

~~COMING~~ IN THE HAMEL DISTRICT.

"A" Form.   Army Form C. 2121.
MESSAGES AND SIGNALS.   No. of Message ....

[Form largely illegible — faint pencil handwriting. Partial readings:]

Sender's Number: A 10   Day of Month: 17   In reply to Number: E 4   A A A

[Message body too faint to transcribe reliably. Visible fragments include: "... have ... you ... any ... take ... aaa ... regarding this ..."]

From Place: W2
Time: ...

"A" Form. Army Form C. 2121.

MESSAGES AND SIGNALS. No. of Message

Prefix	Code	m.	Words	Charge	This message is on a/s of:	Recd. at m.
Office of Origin and Service Instructions.			Sent		Service.	Date
			At m.			From
			To			
			By		(Signature of "Franking Officer.")	By

TO W.Z. 17

Sender's Number.	Day of Month	In reply to Number	AAA
E 13.	17	CH 10	

NO FURTHER INFORMATION.

From X.P
Place
Time 4.8.P

The above may be forwarded as now corrected. (Z)

Censor. Signature of Addressor or person authorised to telegraph in his name.

* This line should be erased if not required.

(4198) Wt. W14042—M14. 300000 Pads. 12/15. Sir J. C. & S.

"C" Form (Original).
MESSAGES AND SIGNALS.

Army Form C. 2123.

Prefix	Code	Words	Received From	Sent, or sent out At	Office Stamp.
Charges to collect			By	To	
Service Instructions.				By	

Handed in at .... Office .... m. Received .... m.

TO

*Sender's Number	Day of Month	In reply to Number	A A A

Lieut YOUNGS section are now employed in evacuating wounded aaa Lieut FARGHERS section and remainder employed with under Colonel PLACKER aaa I have no news yet of Lieut BENBONS section aaa

Rec'd 4-20

FROM
PLACE & TIME

"A" Form.
MESSAGES AND SIGNALS.

Army Form C.
No. of Message ....

Prefix .... Code .... m.	Words	Charge	This message is on a/c of :	Recd. at .... m.
Office of Origin and Service Instructions.				Date ....
	Sent		.... Service.	From
	At .... m.			
	To			By ....
	By		(Signature of "Franking Officer.")	

TO — XP

Sender's Number.	Day of Month.	In reply to Number.		AAA
CH7	12			
What	instructions	have	you	for
Lieut	FARGHERS	section	aaa	they
are	awaiting	your	orders	in
HAMEL	trenches	aaa	can	they
return	here	as	there	is
apparently	no	immediate	prospect	of
the	railway	requiring	repair	aaa
they	will	be	easily	available
here	aaa			

From: W 2
Place:
Time:

The above may be forwarded as now corrected. (Z)

Censor. Signature of Addresser or person authorised to telegraph in his name.

* This line should be erased if not required.

"A" Form.
MESSAGES AND SIGNALS.

Army Form C. 2121.

SIGNALS.

TO	W Z		H11

Sender's Number.	Day of Month	In reply to Number	AAA
E/16	1.7	C.H.13	

WITHDRAW Lt. FARGHERS SECTION TO MOUND KEEP AND FEED AND REST THEM. AAA

Ref YOUR C H 13 NONE AT PRESENT

From X D
Time 6.55 hrs

"A" Form.   Army Form C. 2121.

AB 11:53 am

MESSAGES AND SIGNALS.   No. of Message 156

Prefix ___ Code ___ m.	Words	Charge	This message is on a/c of:	Recd. at ___ m.
Office of Origin and Service Instructions	Sent			Date
Priority MFP	At ___ m. To By		Service (Signature of "Franking Officer.")	From By

TO { WZ   XP

| Sender's Number | Day of Month | In reply to Number | |
| G.O. 66 | 2 | | AAA |

Send	all	available	men	forthwith
to	report	G.V.	~~For~~	ASSIS
Addressed	W Z			
Repeated	X P			

From ~~35~~ R U
Place
Time 11 53 a

The above may be forwarded as now corrected.   (Z)   MB Spender Capt

Censor.   Signature of Addressor or person authorised to telegraph in his name

*This line should be erased if not required.

"A" Form. Army Form C. 2121.
MESSAGES AND SIGNALS.   No. of Message_____

TO   W.Z.   A/2

Sender's Number: E.18.   Day of Month: 1.7   AAA

TRENCHES IN THIEPVAL WOOD REPORTED
CROWDED WITH PRISONERS aaa SEND
A SECTION TO ROUND THEM UP
AND MARCH THEM BACK TO
MC MAHONS POST aaa REPORT
FIRST TO T.B AND G.V. STATING
YOUR ORDERS aaa

From: X.P

"C" Form (Original).
MESSAGES AND SIGNALS.

Army Form C.2123

Prefix	Code	Words	Received From 23	Sent, or sent out At	Office Stamp
Charges to collect			By	To	
Service Instructions				By	

Handed in at   Office   m. Received   m.

TO   XD

*Sender's Number | Day of Month | In reply to Number. | A A A

No 1 Section has left for THIEPVAL WOOD and is reporting to TB and GV aaa

FROM
PLACE & TIME   W Z

"C" Form (Original).
MESSAGES AND SIGNALS.

Army Form C. 2123

Have sent no 1 Section under Capt MCILDOWIE to report to GU aaa No 4 Section under Lieut FARGHER joining OW aaa other two Sections assembling AVELUY WOOD on their return aaa when can we move to MARTINSART please aaa

AND SIGNALS. Army Form C. 2121.

TO	O W	
	W Z	

Sender's Number: 570 Day of Month: 2.7. In reply to Number: AAA

OW will be on leave from WZ
Clarice Kinross now born formerly
WZ will take ul London
of OW near Lancashire Dump

Addressed O W
Repeated W Z

From: KP
Time: 4.30 am

MESSAGES AND SIGNALS.

Prefix......Code......m.	Words	Charge	This message is on a/c of:	Recd. at......m.
Office of Origin and Service Instructions.	Sent		......................Service.	Date...............
....	At...............m.			From...............
....	To			
	By		(Signature of "Franking Officer.")	By...............

TO — X.P. — 15

Sender's Number.	Day of Month.	In reply to Number.	A A A
A121	2		

YOUNGS and BENSONS sections have returned and I are taking them to MARTINSART on your message 1.10 PM no reference aaa orderly will find me at 121st Old billet M'sart aaa Faughs section has joined 121st at MOUND KEEP aaa McILDOWIE and No 1 section are with 107th Brigade and are I understand engaged the consolidating captured German trenches aaa will you please instruct 107th Brig to send them back to M'sart when they have finished with them and I will try to phone

From
Place
Time

The above may be forwarded as now corrected.   (Z)

.... Censor. Signature of Addressee or person authorised to telegraph in his name.

* This line should be erased if not required.

No. of Message ....

Prefix .... Code .... m.	Words	Charge	This message is on a/c of :	Recd. at .... m.

Office of Origin and Service Instructions.

Sent

At .... m.
To ....
By ....

This message is on a/c of :

.... Service.

(Signature of " Franking Officer.")

Recd. at .... m.
Date ....
From ....
By ....

TO {

Sender's Number.	Day of Month.	In reply to Number.	A A A

*

the Jon but could not
quis Jon also at DRC
to Kidnualli so spoke to
GSO 3 who informed me that
the rest of my company
was at where back to
Kidnall aaa

From   OC   122   field amy

Place

Time

The above may be forwarded as now corrected.   **(Z)**

....

Censor.   Signature of Addressor or person authorised to telegraph in his name.

* This line should be erased if not required.

225,000. W 14042—M 44. H. W & V., Ld.   12/15.

MESSAGES AND SIGNALS.

PRIORITY

TO: W.Z. 416

				AAA
REF	ORDER	G O	66	YOU
WILL	NOT	SEND	THE	SECTION
JOINING	ON	to	report	G.U.
aaa	WHEN	YOUR	COMPANY	COMES
OUT	IT	WILL	GO	TO
MARTINSART				

From XP
Time 1.10 pm

"A" Form
MESSAGES AND SIGNALS.

Army Form C. 2121.

PRIORITY

TO: L.T.   I.

Sender's Number.	Day of Month	In reply to Number	AAA
E/3	1.7.		

PUT TRAMLINE INTO WORKING ORDER ALONG PAISLEY AVENUE AND THE SOUTH EAST SIDE OF THIEPVAL WOOD FROM END OF WOODEN TRAMLINE MAKE A ROAD FOR HANDCARTS &c GENERAL DIRECTION OF ROAD TO BE ACROSS OUR FRONT LINE TRENCHES TOWARDS THE CRUCIFIX. &c EMPLOY ONE SECTION FROM DIVISIONAL RESERVE ON ABOVE. REPORT COMPLETION.

From X.P.

Time 9.30 a.m.

Censor.   Lewis de Vitre

"A" Form.   Army Form C. 2123.
MESSAGES AND SIGNALS.   No. of Message_____

| Prefix | Code | m | Words | Charge | This message is on a/c of: | Recd. at_____ m. |
| Office of Origin and Service Instructions. | | | Sent At_____ m. To_____ By_____ | | _____Service. (Signature of "Franking Officer.") | Date_____ From_____ By_____ |

| TO | L.Y. | | | I₂ |

| Sender's Number. | Day of Month | In reply to Number | AAA |
| E.7. | 1/7 | | |

ACKNOWLEDGE MY E/3.

From X.P.
Place
Time 9.45 a.m.

The above may be forwarded as now corrected.   (Z) Cecil de Vere
                                               Censor.   Signature of Addressor or person authorised to telegraph in his name.
* This line should be erased if not required.

"C" Form (Original).
MESSAGES AND SIGNALS.

Army Form C. 2123.

Prefix	Code	Words	Received	Sent, or sent out	Office Stamp.
	£ s. d.		From	At .... m.	
Charges to collect			By	To	
Service Instructions.				By	

Handed in at .... Office .... m. Received .... m.

TO   XP   I 3

Sender's Number	Day of Month	In reply to Number	AAA
D7	1	63	

Iron tramway laid und in repair up to wimble trench which has been badly aaa further work impossible at present aaa

FROM PLACE & TIME   Ly 2.55 pm

"A" Form.
MESSAGES AND SIGNALS.

Army Form C. 2121.

TO X.P.   I 4

Sender's Number: D 10   Day of Month: 1.7.16   AAA

Tramway that we repaired has been broken up by recent bombardment. aaa Party repairing and ~~laying~~ proceeding with laying

From: L Y
Place: 6.40 h
Time:

J C Boyle

"C" Form (Original).
MESSAGES AND SIGNALS.

Army Form C. 2123.

Prefix	Code	Words	Received	Sent, or sent out	Office Stamp.
	£ s. d.		From	At m.	
Charges to collect			By	To	
Service Instructions.				By	

Handed in at .... Office .... m. Received .... m.

TO   XP   I 3

Sender's Number	Day of Month	In reply to Number	AAA
D7	1	63	

Iron tramway laid and in repair up to wimble trench which has been budged aaa further work impossible at present aaa

FROM PLACE & TIME   Ly 2.55 pm

"A" Form.
MESSAGES AND SIGNALS.
Army Form C. 2121.

TO: X.P.

I/4

Sender's Number: D 10
Day of Month: 1.7.16
AAA

Tramway that we repaired has been broken up by recent bombardment – a new Party repairing and ~~laying~~ proceeding with laying

From:
Place: LY
Time: 6.10 h

JCB?

"A" Form.
Army Form C. 2121.

MESSAGES AND SIGNALS.

No. of Message

Prefix	Code	m.	Words	Charge	This message is on a/s of:	Recd. at	m.
Office of Origin and Service Instructions.			Sent			Date	
MARITZ			At ___ m.		Service.	From	
			To				
			By		(Signature of "Franking Officer.")	By	

TO { L Y   I5

Sender's Number.	Day of Month	In reply to Number	AAA
E 15	17		

THE NAME OF YOUR ...
IS NOT ... T B ...
WORK ...
Addressed L Y
Repeated T B

From: A P
Place:
Time: 6.45 AM

The above may be forwarded as now corrected.   (Z)

Censor.   Signature of Addressor or person authorised to telegraph in his name.

* This line should be erased if not required.

"A" Form. Army Form C.2122.
MESSAGES AND SIGNALS.

TO: L.Y. I6

Sender's Number: E.17 Day of Month: 1.7. AAA

IS WATER SUPPLY PIPE LINE
IN THIEPVAL WOOD IN WORKING
ORDER

From: X.P.
Time: 7.30 hrs

"C" Form (Duplicate).
MESSAGES AND SIGNALS.

Army Form C. 2123.

Service Instructions.	Charges to Pay. £ s. d.	Office Stamp.

Handed in at............ Office............ m. Received............ m.

TO: XP

Sender's Number	Day of Month	In reply to Number	A A A
D12	1	E17	

No pipe water supply available
in THIEPVAL WOOD am
beyond immediate repair will wire
later if can repair

FROM PLACE & TIME:

"C" Form (Original).
MESSAGES AND SIGNALS.

Army Form C. 2123.

Prefix	Code	Words	Received From	Sent, or sent out At	Office Stamp
Charges to collect			By	To	
Service Instructions	TB			By	

Handed in at .... Office .... m. Received .... m.

TO XP   16

*Sender's Number	Day of Month	In reply to Number	A A A
C25	2	—	

Ref water supply at Elgin Avenue

FROM PLACE & TIME   LY   11.55 am

* This line should be erased if not required.

"A" Form.
MESSAGES AND SIGNALS.

Army Form C. 2121.

No. of Message _____

Prefix _____ Code _____ m.	Words.	Charge.	This message is on a/c of:	Recd. at _____ m
Office of Origin and Service Instructions.				Date _____
_____	Sent		_____ Service.	From _____
P468	At _____ m.			
_____	To _____			
_____	By _____		(Signature of "Franking Officer.")	By _____

TO { L.Y.

Sender's Number	Day of Month	In reply to Number	AAA
E/23	27	B.O.2	

When	T B	MOVE	BACK	90
TO	MARTINSART			

From X.P.
Place
Time 1.5 pm

The above may be forwarded as now corrected. (Z) _Cuervallit_
Censor. Signature of Addressor or person authorised to telegraph in his name

"C" Form (Duplicate).
MESSAGES AND SIGNALS.

Army Form C. 2123.
(In books of 50's in duplicate.)
No. of Message..........

41   TB

Service Instructions.

Handed in at......TB......Office....11-..a...m. Received..12-3.....m.

TO   XP   I 10

Sender's Number	Day of Month	In reply to Number	AAA
BO2	2		

TB whose orders I am under are moving back to MARTINSART aaa please instruct aaa the men are very much shaken and have no place to live as the colonade is full of wounded

FROM PLACE & TIME   Ly 11.40 am

"A" Form
MESSAGES AND SIGNALS.

Army Form C 2121.

PRIORITY
McPherson

TO: G.M.

SEND ONE COMPANY TO DIG
A COMMUNICATION TRENCH CONNECTING UP
No. 2 TUNNEL WITH HEAD OF INVERNESS
STREET WITH GERMAN SAP HEAD AT R.19.C
8-05 AAA IF FIRE PREVENTS WORK ON THIS
DIG A COMMUNICATION TRENCH CONNECTING UP
No. 5 TUNNEL WITH GERMAN SAP HEAD AT
R.19.C.2.4 AND REPORT COMPLETION AAA

SEND ANOTHER COMPANY TO CLEAR AND REPAIR
ROAD FROM LEVEL CROSSING IN Q.24.A VIA
MILL BRIDGE TO ST. PIERRE DIVION AND
REPORT COMPLETION.

From: GSO.1

"A" Form.
Army Form C. 2121.

MESSAGES AND SIGNALS.

No. of Message ....

TO: CRE 36th Div

Sender's Number: S/1
Day of Month: 1st
In reply to Number: E/1
AAA

These parties were sent off at 8.40 am on instructions from G.S.O. 1. aaa.

From: OC 16 R.I. Rif. P.

"A" Form
MESSAGES AND SIGNALS.

Army Form C. 2122.

TO: G.M.

K2

Sender's Number: E/9 Day of Month: 17 AAA

REF E/1 REPORT PROGRESS ESPECIALLY ON COMMUNICATION TRENCHES AND WHEN ONE YOU ARE DIGGING. ALSO PROGRESS ON ROAD AAA SEND OFFICER TO RECONNOITRE TRACK LEADING PAST HAMMERHEAD SAP R25 A 4 2 TO MOY A 13 AND REPORT WHETHER ITS VICINITY IS SUITABLE FOR A COMMUNICATION TRENCH. AAA IF IT IS SEND UP A COMPANY TO DIG IT.

From X.P.

Time: 12.45 pm

"C" Form (Duplicate).
MESSAGES AND SIGNALS.

Army Form C. 2123.

| TO | 6 R.B. 36 Div |

Sender's Number	Day of Month	In reply to Number	AAA
6/2	12	8/9	

Both parties road and communication trench are held up by Artillery fire and an officer has been sent to make reconnaissance per your 8/9 aaa

FROM PLACE & TIME   O.C. 1st R.B. L Rif

"C" Form (Original).
MESSAGES AND SIGNALS.

Army Form C.2123.
No. of Message... 384

TO ...... KP K4

Sender's Number	Day of Month	In reply to Number	A A A
0/10	1st	279	

Officer reports communication trench from HAMMERHEAD SAP quite impracticable AAA

FROM PLACE & TIME

"C" Form (Original).
MESSAGES AND SIGNALS.

Army Form C. 2123.

OC 9th Irish Fusiliers ordered up being engaged on the Road to support his Regiment aaa the support was urgently needed aaa shall I send another Coy to the road aaa

3/15 pm

"A" Form. Army Form C. 2121.
MESSAGES AND SIGNALS.

PRIORITY

TO G.M. K6

Sender's Number: E.12 Day of Month: 1/7 In reply to Number: S/5 AAA

DO NOT SEND ANOTHER COMPANY TO THE FRONT AAA THE COMPANY ORDERED IN E/1 TO DIG COMMUNICATION TRENCH SHOULD BE GETTING ON WITH IT

From: X.P
Time: 3.35 p.m.

"C" Form (Original).
MESSAGES AND SIGNALS.

Army Form C.2123.

TO: OHE No 4 Div

Sender's Number: A/6
Day of Month: 10th

Communication trench started from no 5 tunnel aaa The coy which was on the road has been sent by OC 9th R.F. to Fusiliers into trenches aaa Ends

FROM PLACE & TIME: OC 16 R.F. I Kef P
3 pm

"C" Form (Duplicate).
Army Form C. 2123.
(In books of 50's in duplicate.)

MESSAGES AND SIGNALS.

No. of Message

	Charges to Pay.	Office Stamp.
	£ s. d.	
Service Instructions.		

Handed in at .... Office .... m. Received .... m.

TO	XP	K8

Sender's Number	Day of Month	In reply to Number	A A A

Communication trench attempted several times but stopped by heavy shelling. O I/c suggested waiting until dark but is trying to carry on with it now aaa

4.20

FROM	GM
PLACE & TIME	3.40p

"C" Form (Original).
MESSAGES AND SIGNALS.

Army Form C. 2123.
(In books of 50's in duplicate)
No. of Message......36.7

Prefix....... Code....... Words.......	Received	Sent, or sent out	Office Stamp.
£ s. d.	From.......	At.......m.	
Charges to collect	By.......	To.......	
Service Instructions.		By.......	

Handed in at....... Office.......m. Received.......m.

TO   XP   K9

| *Sender's Number | Day of Month | In reply to Number | A A A |
| S/9 | 1st | | |

O I/c communication trench
reports progress impossible aaa
is trying to sap but
is very slow and
hampered by hostile MG fire
aaa would it be advisable
to wait until night aaa
Please wire instructions aaa

FROM: GM
PLACE & TIME: 6 pm

"A" Form
MESSAGES AND SIGNALS

Army Form C 2121

Prefix	Code	m.	Words	Charge	This message is on a/s of:	Recd. at ___ m.
Office of Origin and Service Instructions			Sent At ___ m. To By		Service. (Signature of "Franking Officer.")	Date From By

TO G.M.   K.C.

Sender's Number	Day of Month	In reply to Number	
E/4.	17.	S/9	AAA

COMPANY DETAILED TO DIG COMMUNICATION TRENCH IS TO CONTINUE SAPPING AND DIG IT AT NIGHT. AAA. THE REMAINDER OF YOUR BATTALION LESS THE COMPANY IN HAMEL TRENCHES IS TO REPORT FORTHWITH TO G.U. FOR WORK. AAA ACKNOWLEDGE.

ADDENDA

THIS EXCLUDES PARTIES UNDER ADJUTANT R.E.

From X.P
Place
Time 6.45 p.m.

The above may be forwarded as now corrected.   (Z)
Censor. Signature of Addressor or person authorised to telegraph in his name.
* This line should be erased if not required.

"C" Form (Original).
Army Form C. 2121

MESSAGES AND SIGNALS.

No. of Message

Prefix   Code   Words   Received   Sent, or sent out   Office Stamp.
                £   s.   d.   From   At   m.
Charges to collect   By   To
Service Instructions   By

Handed in at _____ Office _____ m. Received _____ m.

TO _____ XP

*Sender's Number | Day of Month | In reply to Number. | AAA

Communication trench abandoned owing to evacuation of A line AAA

FROM PLACE & TIME   GM 3.45am

"A" Form.
MESSAGES AND SIGNALS.

Army Form C. 2121.

TO: G.M

Sender's Number	Day of Month	In reply to Number	
E 224	2.7		AAA

DETAIL A PUSHING PARTY OF 60 MEN FORTHWITH TO ADJUTANT R.E. AAA THEY ARE NOT TO BE TAKEN FROM THE TWO COMPANIES ORDERED TO G.D. UNDER G.O.C.

Addressed G.M
Repeated Adjutant R.E
           LANCASHIRE DIV

From: X.P
Time: 10.53 p.m

"A" Form.
MESSAGES AND SIGNALS.

Army Form C.2...

Prefix	Code	m.	Words	Charge	This message is on a/c of:	Recd. at	m.
Office of Origin and Service Instructions.			Sent			Date	
			At	m.	Service.	From	
			To				
			By		(Signature of "Franking Officer.")	By	

TO C.E. 10th Corps

Sender's Number.	Day of Month	In reply to Number	AAA
* E/3	1/7		

Position of Field Coys NE. AAA 121st Coy in Divisional Reserve AT LANCASHIRE DUMP less 1 section attached to 107th Brigade in THIEPVAL Section aaa 122nd Coy in Divisional Reserve at MOUND KEEP less 2 sections attached to 108th Brigade one in HAMEL Sector one in THIEPVAL sector AAA 150th Coy in Divisional Reserve AT PAISLEY AVENUE THIEPVAL less two sections attached to 109th Brigade AAA 1st line transport at P.36.B AAA 16 R.I.R.(P) in Divisional Reserve at LANCASHIRE DUMP.

From C.R.E. 36 DIV
Place
Time 7.34. am

The above may be forwarded as now corrected.   (Z) [signature]

Censor. Signature of Addressor or person authorised to telegraph in his name.
* This line should be erased if not required.

"A" Form.
MESSAGES AND SIGNALS.

Army Form C. 2121

| Prefix | Code | m. | Words | Charge | This message is on a/c of: | Recd. at | m. |
| Office of Origin and Service Instructions. | | | Sent At ___ m. To ___ By ___ | | ___ Service. (Signature of "Franking Officer.") | Date ___ From ___ By ___ | |

TO G.O.C. 10th Corps.

| Sender's Number. | Day of Month | In reply to Number | |
| G.10 | 1/7 | | AAA |

Positions of Field Coys
R.E. AAA. 121 St. Coy R.E.
Divisional Reserve LANCASHIRE
DUMP less one section attached
to 107th Brigade also one
B 2nd Coy of other 2 Sections
in Divisional Reserve one went
forward to obtain Railway and
road from Hamel northwards
but prevented from doing
so by shell fire and enemy
holding Railway sap. the other
section gone to round up
prisoners in THIEPVAL Wood.
150 Coy one section with 108th
Brigade in HAMEL other section
with 108th Brigade in THIEPVAL

From C.R.E. 36th Div
Place
Time

The above may be forwarded as now corrected.   (Z)

"A" Form.
MESSAGES AND SIGNALS.

Army Form C.

Prefix	Code	m.	Words	Charge	This message is on a/c of:	Recd. at	m.
Office of Origin and Service Instructions.			Sent At m. To By		Service. (Signature of "Franking Officer.")	Date From By	

TO

Sender's Number.	Day of Month	In reply to Number	A A A
E/20	1/7		

No. 70 new ?? AAA 150th Coy one section in Divisional Reserve at PAISLEY repaired TRAMLINE and began track for hand carts on East side of THIEPVAL Wood but was stopped by fire AAA Lt Peacock killed AAA the whole of this Coy is now under the orders of 109th Brigade AAA 150 Coy again repairing railway broken by recent bombardment

From CRE 36 DIV
Place
Time 8.30 p.m.

The above may be forwarded as now corrected. (Z)

"C" Form (Duplicate).
MESSAGES AND SIGNALS.

Army Form C.2123
No. of Message

Charges to Pay. £ s. d.

M

Office Stamp.

Service Instructions

Handed in at .... Office .... m. Received .... m.

TO

Sender's Number	Day of Month	In reply to Number.	**AAA**

24 ... LANCASHIRE ...

PAISLEY ...

FROM

PLACE & TIME

"C" Form (Original).
MESSAGES AND SIGNALS.
Army Form C.2123

Office 1.57 m. Received ___ m.

TO (2)

To get up a fraction of this ammunition on tramway aaa It will have to go up gradually tomorrow aaa I am to make [?] start as soon as possible I must have fresh tracking party

FROM: Adjut R.E.
PLACE & TIME: LANCASHIRE DUMP 2am

"A" Form.
MESSAGES AND SIGNALS.

Army Form C. 2121.

TO: ADJUTANT R.F.
LANCASHIRE DUMP.

AAA

AS SOON AS POSSIBLE YOU WILL HAVE GOT IN TOUCH WITH BOMBARDIERS OR OC STATIONS AND HAVE TOLD THEM YOU ARE SENDING HIM SO MANY TRUCKLOADS OF S.A.A. AND THEN MUST PROVIDE PARTIES TO CARRY IT UP. AND I WILL TRY AN INCREASE YOUR PUSHING PARTY, MEANWHILE PUSH IT UP GRADUALLY AS BEST YOU CAN.

From: X.P
Time: 9.35 a.m.

"A" Form
MESSAGES AND SIGNALS.
Army Form C. 2121.

TO { Adjutant R.E.
Lancashire Dump } M1

Sender's Number: F 23
Day of Month: 27

GRENADE STORES THIEPVAL DEPLETED aaa SO CONTINUE SUPPLY OF S.A.A AND BOMBS.

From: X.B
Time: 10.30am

"A" Form.
Army Form C.2121.

MESSAGES AND SIGNALS.

No. of Message............

| Prefix | Code | m. | Words | Charge | This message is on a/s of: | Recd. at............ m. |
| Office of Origin and Service Instructions | | | Sent At......m. To...... By...... | | ....Service. (Signature of "Franking Officer.") | Date....... From....... By....... |

| TO | R U | Q | | M |

| Sender's Number. | Day of Month | In reply to Number | A A A |
| E.19 | 1.7. | | |

WILL YOU HAVE ANY LORRIES

AVAILABLE FOR ME ON

2.7.16 TO CONVEY R.E. STORES.

AAA IF SO KINDLY INSTRUCT CORPOR

MITCHELL. R.E TO SEND UP

BARBED WIRE. SCREW PICKETS -

SANDBAGS - EXPANDED METAL

TO C.R.E DUMP MARTINSART

From X P.
Place
Time 8.15am

The above may be forwarded as now corrected.   (Z)

Censor. Signature of Addressor or person authorised to telegraph in his name.
* This line should be erased if not required.

"A" Form.
MESSAGES AND SIGNALS.
Army Form C. 2121.

Prefix	Code	m.	Words	Charge	This message is on a/c of:		Recd. at	m.
Office of Origin and Service Instructions.			Sent				Date	
			At	m.		Service.	From	
			To					
			By		(Signature of "Franking Officer.")		By	

TO

M 3

Sender's Number.   Day of Month   In reply to Number   **A A A**

3 Coys of Pioneers + 2 Field Coys per G.D
(49) are placed at disposal of R.V.

They will all proceed to RISCO & on reporting
to G.O (107) the 2 Field Coys will pull
in way at LANCASHIRE DUMP + take
up R.E. stores, chiefly wire + stakes.

The remaining 2 Coys will dig C Trench
from RES 7 of THIEPVAL WOOD to about
A 12 reporting to G.O on the way

From
Place
Time

(Z)

Censor.   Signature of Addressor or person authorised to telegraph in his name.

"A" Form.   MESSAGES AND SIGNALS.   Army Form.
No. of Message_____

Prefix......Code......m.	Words	Charge	This message is on a/c of:	Reed. at............m.
Office of Origin and Service Instructions.	Sent		.................Service.	Date.......N......
....	At.........m.			From..............
....	To............			By................
....	By............		(Signature of "Franking Officer.")	

TO { 108   109 BDE   150 F CO RE
     122 F CO RE   16 RIR
     (CRE)   ADMS

Sender's Number	Day of Month	In reply to Number	A A A
9858	BDE		

THE FOLLOWING MOVES WILL TAKE
PLACE TODAY aaa 108 BDE
to FORCEVILLE aaa 109 BDE
to HEDAUVILLE aaa 122 and
150 F COS and 16
RIR P less 2 COS a letter
to 49 DIV and party
employed on tramway all to
FORCEVILLE aaa moves to be
undertaken as early as possible
aaa units to report how
soon they are clear aaa
Troops for FORCEVILLE by North
Route and then for HEDAUVILLE by
South route. aaa For information

From 36 DIV
Place
Time

The above may be forwarded as now corrected. (Z)
................................Censor.   Signature of Addressor or person authorised to telegraph in his name.
* This line should be erased if not required.
T. & W. & J. M., Ltd., London.   W 14042/M44. 75,000 12/15. Forms C 2121/10.

"C" Form (Original).
MESSAGES AND SIGNALS.

Army Form C. 2123.
(In books of 50's in duplicate.)

Prefix	Code	Words	Received	Sent, or sent out	Office Stamp.
	£ s. d.		From 3 JUL 1916	At	ARMY
Charges to collect			By 4218		YCF - 3. VII.16
Service Instructions.				By	TELEGRAPHS

Handed in at .... Office .... m. Received .... m.

TO

*Sender's Number	Day of Month	In reply to Number	**A A A**

[message body in pencil, partially legible:]
Position of ... ...
Trench water supply ...
... are thoroughly acquainted
with it and prepared to
...

CRE.
36 Div for information & action

S Lomp tod
AA oeg
36 Div

3/7/16

FROM
PLACE & TIME

This line should be erased if not required.

"A" Form.
MESSAGES AND SIGNALS.

Army Form C. 2121.
No. of Message _____

Prefix _____ Code _____ m.	Words	Charge	This message is on a/c of:	Recd. at _____ m.
Office of Origin and Service Instructions.				Date _____
_____	Sent At _____ m.		Service.	From _____
_____	To _____			By _____
_____	By _____		(Signature of "Franking Officer.")	

TO _____ R.E.

Sender's Number.	Day of Month	In reply to Number	AAA
E/7693	3/7		

No.

W. Smyth Lt
OC 180 Coy RE
Major RE
3.7.16

From
Place
Time

The above may be forwarded as now corrected. (Z)

Censor. Signature of Addressor or person authorised to telegraph in his name.
* This line should be erased if not required.

"A" Form.   Army Form C. 2121.
MESSAGES AND SIGNALS.

TO	O.C. 122 R.E.
	O.C 150 R.E.

Sender's Number.	Day of Month	In reply to Number	AAA
E/7693	3/7		

Have	you	any	men	left
on	WATER	SUPPLY	duties	in
Front	area.			

RE 36th Div

I have two sappers left in
employment on a water supply
here under the Town Major
I should like to get these back
if possible

Thorne
Major RE

From: CRE 36
Place:
Time: 6.30 p.m

"A" Form. Army Form C. 2121.

MESSAGES AND SIGNALS

No. of Message _____

Prefix _____ Code _____ m. | Words | Charge | This message is on a/c of: | Recd. at _____
Office of Origin and Service Instructions | Sent | | Service. | Date _____
 | At _____ m. | | | From _____
 | To _____ | | |
 | By _____ | | (Signature of "Franking Officer.") | By _____

TO CRC   Dvl Train
    Q
    Signals

Sender's Number.   Day of Month.   In reply to Number.
5893   5   AAA

Instruct 150 % Co R E to be
prepared to join 12 Division
for duty this afternoon as
Destination will follow
Somewhere near Abbey

addressed CRC
Repeated   Q
            Signals
            Dvl Train

From 86 Div
Place
Name

The above may be forwarded as now corrected.   (Z)

"A" Form.   Army Form C. 2121.
MESSAGES AND SIGNALS.   No. of Message

TO	107 Bde	Q	CRA
	108 Bde	Signals	CRE
	109 Bde	ADMS	Div Train

Sender's Number: G 911
Day of Month: 6
AAA

36 Div LESS troops attached to other Divisions will be prepared to move at 3½ hours notice after 7 a.m. tomorrow

From 36 Div

"A" Form. Army Form C. 2121.

MESSAGES AND SIGNALS

No. of Message............

Prefix............ Code............m. | Words | Charge

Office of Origin and Service Instructions.

Sent

At............m.

To............

By............

This message is on a/c of:

............*Service.*

(Signature of "Franking Officer.")

Recd. at............m.

Date............

From R1

By............

TO [illegible]

* Sender's Number	Day of Month	In reply to Number	AAA
	6		

[illegible]

From [illegible] 36

Place

Time 9 P[illegible]

The above may be forwarded as now corrected. (Z)

.... *Censor.* Signature of Addressor or person authorised to telegraph in his name. [illegible]

* This line should be erased if not required.

(A1) C. Ltd., London— W.14042/M.44. 150,000 Pads. 12/15. Form C.2121.

"C" Form (Original).
MESSAGES AND SIGNALS.

Army Form C. 2123.
(In books of 50's in duplicate.)
No. of Message ....

Prefix......... Code......... Words.........	Received From.........	Sent, or sent out At.........m.	Office Stamp.
£ s. d.			ARMY
Charges to collect	By.........	To.........	Y.C.F — 6. VII.16
Service Instructions.		By.........	

Handed in at......... Office.........m. Received.........m.

TO CRE 36 Div

Sender's Number	Day of Month	In reply to Number	**A A A**
42	5		

Relieve engine drivers on pumping engine at present supplied by 126 field Coy RE a.a.a. Report completion giving number of pumps taken over a.a.a. addsd oc 2/1.ca WR Fld Coy RE repld CRE 36 Divn Rflee this 6/7/14.

FROM
PLACE & TIME
CRE 49 Divn
7.55 pm

"C" Form (Duplicate).
MESSAGES AND SIGNALS.

Army Form C. 2123.
(In books of 50's in duplicate.)

No. of Message ....

Sm Eaf 55   KCO

Service Instructions.

Handed in at... YD3R .... Office. 5.5 p.m. Received 5.39 p.m.

TO   36 Divnl RE

Sender's Number	Day of Month	In reply to Number	AAA
TA40	8		

We have just received instructions from 49 Divn to report at HARPONVILLE at 8 pm aaa as our men are at present at work in THIEPVAL I fear this is impossible our men are about played out and require a rest

FROM   121 Field Co RE
PLACE & TIME   4.10 pm

Wt. 432—M437 500,000 Pads. H W V 5/16 Forms C.2123.

"A" Form
MESSAGES AND SIGNALS.

Army Form C. ???
No. of Message _____

Prefix	Code	m.	Words	Charge	This message is on a/c of:	Recd. at _____ m.
						Date _____
Office of Origin and Service Instructions		Sent At _____ m. To _____ By _____			_____ Service. (Signature of "Franking Officer.")	From _____ By _____

TO — OW 121 Coy RE

Sender's Number.	Day of Month	In reply to Number	
E 7724	8	T 440	AAA

GET TO HARPONVILLE AS SOON
AS YOU CAN TONIGHT. And
report arrival by wire. aaa
Lt FERRIER IS REJOINING.

From: RE 36 Divn
Place: RP
Time: 7 55 pm

The above may be forwarded as now corrected. (Z)

Censor. Signature of Addressor or person authorised to telegraph in his name.

* This line should be erased if not required.

"C" Form (Original).
MESSAGES AND SIGNALS.

Army Form C-2123.

Prefix	Code	Words	Received From By	Sent, or sent out At To By	Office Stamp.
Charges to collect					
Service Instructions.					

Handed in at .... Office .... m. Received .... m.

TO CRE 56th Divn

Sender's Number	Day of Month	In reply to Number	A A A
1632	9th		

You will rejoin 56th Divn forthwith and push march at 8 am tomorrow to HARPONVILLE aaa Authority GA 20 198 9th aaa You will leave an officer at 76th Bde HQ to hand over works to 25th Divl field Co among this morning aaa Acknowledge aaa Addsd OC. 150th Coy R.E. aaa Rptd CRE 26th Divn

FROM
PLACE & TIME

CRE 14th Divn
2.55 am

* This line should be erased if not required.

"A" Form Army Form C. ___.
MESSAGES AND SIGNALS.   No. of Message_____

| Code. | Words | Charge | This message is on a/c of: | Recd. at ___ m. |
| Office of Origin and Service Instructions | Sent At ___ m. To ___ By ___ | | _____ Service. (Signature of "Franking Officer.") | Date ___ From ___ By ___ |

TO { OC 122 RE

| Sender's Number. | Day of Month | In reply to Number | AAA |
| E/7729 | 9 | CH 821 | |

You have no orders from me. Coys march to HARPONVILLE at once.

From
Place CRE 36
Time 9-20 am

(Z) [signature]

"C" Form (Duplicate).
MESSAGES AND SIGNALS.

Handed in at 29 Divn

TO CRE 36 Divn

Sender's Number: CA 821
Day of Month: 7

Motor lorry has arrived here and driver states that his instructions are to take our forage and rations to HARPONVILLE tonight aaa As I have no instructions I am retaining the lorry here until the morning aaa Please wire what should be done with it then aaa

FROM PLACE & TIME: OC. 122 Field Coy

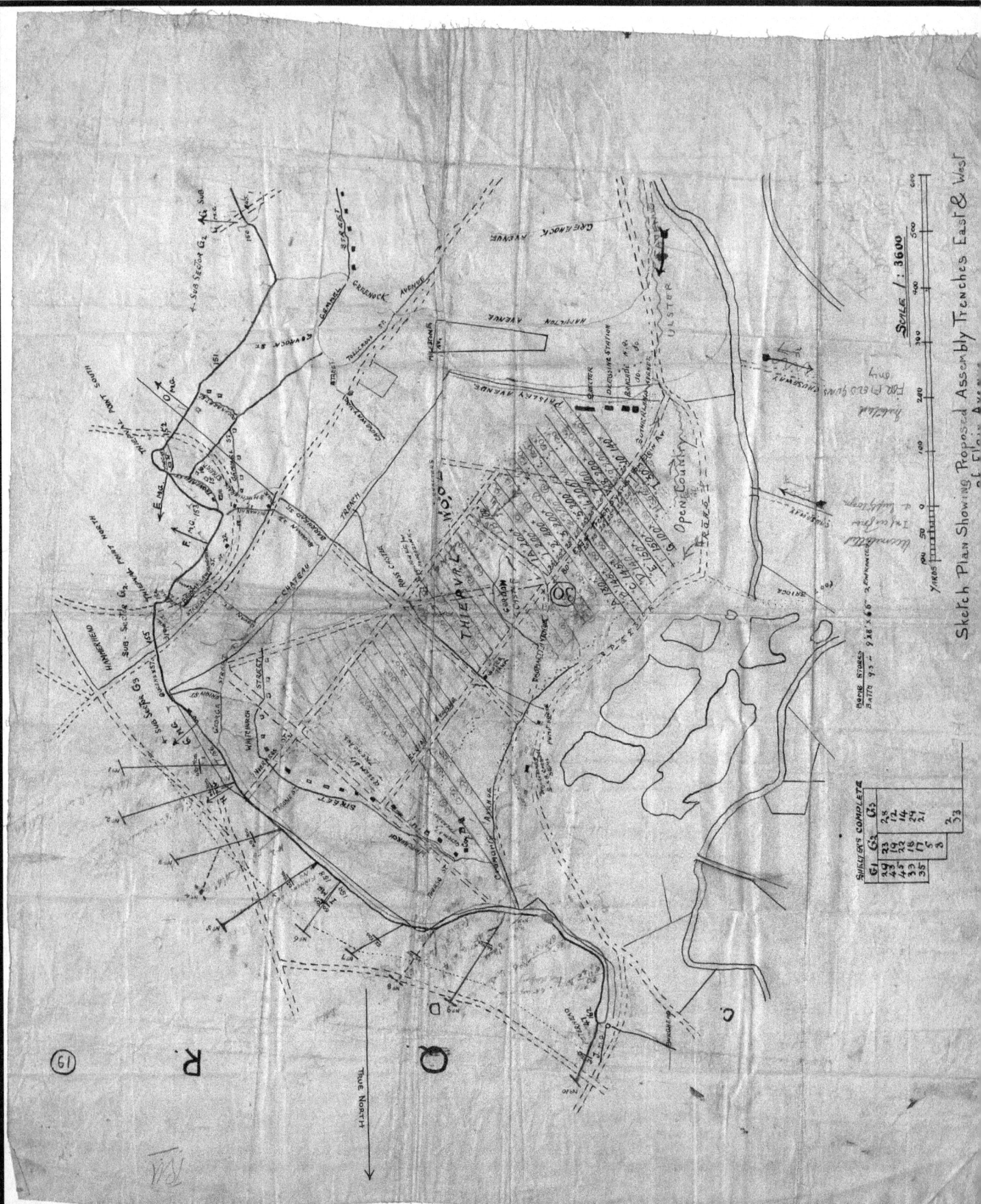

C.E., Fourth Army. E. 619
C.E., Xth Corps. R/264

Chief Engineer,

Xth Corps.

Please see that orders are given to all storemen, at dumps, to the efect that, after the commencement of fighting stores are not to be kept at the disposal of certain units, but issued to all that demand them.

This will enable Cavalry and Divisions which come up from Reserve to draw what they require from the nearest store.

Headquarters,   (Sd) R.U.H. BUCKLAND,
Fourth Army.

29th June, 1916.   Major General,

                                            Chief Engineer, Fourth Army.

Copies to:-

    Chief Engineer, Reserve Army.
    O.C., R.E., First Indian Cavalry Division.
    O.C., R.E., 3rd Indian Cavalry Division.
    O.C., R.E., 2nd Indian Cavalry Division.
    Chief Engineer, II Corps.

(2)

C.R.E., 25th Division.
C.R.E., 32nd Division.
C.R.E., 36th Division.
C.R.E., 49th Division.

For information and necessary action.

Headquarters,

    Xth Corps.   Captain, R.E.

30th June, 1916.   for Chief Engineer, Xth Corps.

COPY

M5

CRE 36th Divn

I desire to bring to your notice the work done by the late 2nd Lieut. D. Cole 16 RIR (P)

This officer was in charge of the tramway maintenance and traffic during the preliminary bombardment and during subsequent operations until he was killed on the tramway on morning of 3/7/16.

During this time 2nd Lieut Cole ran his job without a hitch in spite of considerable difficulties.

By his personality and example he got his repair gang to a high state of efficiency and pluck.

The numerous breaks in the line caused by shells were repaired rapidly and in consequence a great number of wounded were brought down the tramway and a large amount of ammunition and stores got up.

Whenever there was confusion or danger 2nd Lieut Cole was there putting things straight

He was a very fine officer and his death was a great loss.

The entire credit for what I consider to have been the successful working of the tramline belongs to him.

(sd) R.N. Burn
Capt RE.
Adjt RE.

4/7/16

P.T.O.

OC 16 R I R (P)

I cannot speak too highly of the cool, deliberate and clear headed manner in which the late 2⁴ Lieut D Cole 16 R I R (P) carried out his duties close behind the front line trenches.

Whenever and wherever any difficulty or confusion occurred in connection with his work, especially the trench tramway, whether it was sending up ammunition or evacuating wounded. 2⁴ Lieut Cole would go there and smooth it out, no matter what unit was concerned.

He was possessed of an unusual personality which impressed all who came in contact with him. He thought only of his duty regardless of danger which always surrounded him. He impressed his men with confidence, and fell gallantly carrying out his duties under heavy shell fire at AUTHUILLE on 3.7.16.

(Sd) P J Denys de Vitré
Lt Col CRE 36 Div

4.7.16

HQ 36 Div.

I forward above copies of two memos on the late 2⁴ Lieut Cole D. 16 R I R (P) which I have forwarded to OC 16 R I R (P).

(Sd) P J Denys de Vitré
Lt Col CRE 36 Div

4.7.16

SECRET.   Copy No. 18

                36th DIVISION ORDER No. 43.
                xxxxxxxxxxxxxxxx
                                                5. 7. 16.

1.   The Division, less Artillery, R.E., and Pioneers, will move to-day to area RUBEMPRE - HERISSART - TOUTENCOURT - PUCHEVILLERS.

2.   The moves will take place according to the attached March Table.

3.   The 16th R.Ir.Rif.(Pioneers) remain in their present position.

4.   The 150th Fld.Coy.R.E. will be attached to the 12th Division and will move to-day to the vicinity of AVELUY under orders issued by the 12th Division.

5   The 2 troops 6th Inniskilling Dragoons will return to the Corps Cavalry Regiment and the Cyclist Company to the Corps Cyclist Battalion, both moves taking place to-day.

6.   Railhead will be at ACHEUX.

7.   Divisional Headquarters will open at RUBEMPRE at 12 noon to-morrow.

Issued at
12.15 p.m.
                                                LT.COLONEL. G.S.

                        Copies to :-

No.1   G.O.C.   16   16th R.Ir.Rif.(P)
 2/3   Xth Corps   17   36th Div.Train.
  4   12th Div.   18   36th Div.Supply Col.
  5   25th Div.   19   A.D.M.S.
  6   29th Div.   20   A.P.M.
  7   32nd Div.   21   36th Signal Coy.
  8   49th Div.   22   File.
  9   C.R.A.   23   War Diary.
 10   C.R.E.   24   Q
 11   6th Innis.Dns.
 12   'B' Coy.Xth Corps Cyclists.
 13   107th Bde.
 14   108th Bde.
 15   109th Bde.

Administrative Orders
by
Lt. Col. P. T. Denis de Vitre, C.R.E. 36th Division.

5.7.'16

1. MOVES. The following is an extract of 36 Div. (Secret).
no.
The Division less R.A. + R.E + Pioneers will move to Rubempre Area on 6.7.'16.

The 150th Field Coy R.E. will be attached to the 12th Division, and will move on 5.7.'16. to the vicinity of AVELUY under orders issued by 12th Division.

The 122nd Field Coy R.E. will remain at FORCEVILLE until further orders.

H.Q. R.E. will open at RUBEMPRE at 12 noon on 6.7.'16

OC 150 Coy will leave surplus kits in village Dump at Forceville under Town Major + leave 1 man in charge of it.

Lieut. Colonel, R.E.
C.R.E. 36th (Ulster) Division

~~O.C.~~ C.R.E.
****

COMMUNICATIONS.

DURING BOMBARDMENT.

The three field Companies will keep up communication with Divisional Headquarters by Cyclists, for which purpose each Coy will attach a cyclist to H.Q.R.E. on "U" day.

The 16th R.I.R. (P) will do ditto.

In addition the 121st Coy will take over the Telephone in present 122nd Coy's Office.

The 122nd Coy in MOUND KEEP will use the Telephone on McMahons Post, and keep an orderly there for messages.

The 150th Coy in THIEPVAL WOOD can use the Telephone of 109th Brigade and keep an orderly there for messages.

The 16th R.I.R. (P) by runner to the exchange at MARTINSART in present 107th Brigade H.Q. where he should keep two orderlies for messages.

The Adjutant R.E. at Advanced Dump in AVELUY WOOD will use Telephone at McMahons Post, and keep an orderly there for messages.

DURING THE ASSAULT.

The same arrangements hold good.

N.B.

O.C. 36th Signals will try and get a Telephone fixed up with 16th R.I.R. (P) this will be extra to the above means of communication.

22/6/16.

Lt.Col.
C.R.E. 36th Division.

SECRET.

O.C. .... Field Coy, R.E.

Extract from ADMINISTRATIVE INSTRUCTIONS No. G/15/188.

RATIONS FOR CONSUMPTION ON 'U' DAY.

All rations for consumption on 'U' day by troops who will be in MARTINSART, MESNIL, AVELUY WOOD, HAMEL and TRENCHES must be sent up on 'T' day so as to reach the unit not later than 1 p.m. in order that the transport may get away at once and leave all roads and tracks clear for troops moving up and down that afternoon.

Brigades and units will make arrangements for getting in by day the rations of any units remaining in the trenches.

TRANSPORT IN MARTINSART, MESNIL & AVELUY WOOD.

All Regimental transport, Wagon lines of Artillery etc. and any other horses and vehicles of units including Cookers and Water Carts must clear Martinsart not later than 6p.m., and will move by the track (GRAHAM Road) leading to HEDAUVILLE, except the water carts and cookers in Hamel which may be retained until after the relief has taken place. They will follow the relieved Battalion when it marches out of HAMEL.

Infantry Transport and R.E. Transport coming out from the Forward Area will proceed direct to the Divisional Transport Camp along the ENGLEBELMER - BOUZINCOURT Road, except the 107th Infantry Brigade Transport which will go to VARENNES & LEALVILLERS

TRANSPORT IN HEDAUVILLE, VARENNES, FORCEVILLE & LEALVILLERS.

The Transport and details of all R.E. and Infantry Units in the above Villages (excepting 107th Infantry Brigade) will move out of those Villages after midnight on T/U. They must concentrate at the Divisional Transport Camp on the ENGLEBELMER - BOUZINCOURT Road by 5 a.m. on 'U' day.

Transport of the 107th Infantry Brigade will remain with the Units until the latter move up on X/Y and Y/Z nights. Instructions will be issued later with regard to it.

DIVISIONAL TRANSPORT CAMP ON ENGLEBELMER - BOUZINCOURT ROAD.

No tents except those required for the Divisional Ordnance Dump will be erected on the Camp.

The Senior Brigade Transport Officer will act as Divisional Transport Officer and he will allot times for watering and route for water carts, horses etc.

While the 121st, 122nd and 150th Field Companies Transport remains in the Divisional Transport Camp, the Transport Officer 16th R.I.R. (P) will be in charge of them in addition to his other duties.

Brigade Transport Officer and Transport Officer 16th R.I.R.(P) will report a Divisional Headquarters "Q" at 2.30p.m. daily from 'U' to 'Z' days inclusive.

23/6/16

Lt.Col.

SECRET.

O.C., 17th N.F. (Pioneers).
General Staff.
O.C. 206th Field Coy.R.E.
    218th Field Coy.R.E.
    219th Field Coy.R.E.
A.A. & Q.M.G.

   The 36th Division will run 30 trucks during operations on their tram line, and place them at disposal of the R.A.M.C., for evacuating wounded from PAISLEY AVENUE. These trucks will, therefore, return empty to railhead THIEPVAL WOOD, and opportunity may occur to put on R.E. stores, provided parties go with them to off-load promptly, and not interfere with 36th Division down trucks carrying wounded.

   The Traffic Officer 36th Division will be at R.E. Dump, N.E. corner of AVELUY WOOD, and Lieut. Dallin should get in touch with this officer, to see if any time table is arranged.

   If there is none, the 36th Division Dressing Station Officer, Dug-outs North, may be able to say when wounded are coming down. In any case, our parties taking up a truck of stores must have a signaller ahead to warn the approach of a "wounded" down truck, so that our up truck can be cleared off the rail, which may necessitate some prompt off-loading. 32nd Division has only accommodation rights on this line, and can only use it so long as we do not interfere with 36th Division service.

   It must be clearly understood by our parties that they must give way to the requirements of the 36th Division when they clash with our own.

          Sgd. E.P. Brooker. Lieut.Col.R.E.
            C.R.E., 32nd Division.

24-6-16.

C.R.E.,
 36th Division.

      For information.

24-6-16.
            Lieut. Col. R.E.
            C.R.E., 32nd Division.

H.Q. 36th Division.

"G".
****

I do not propose to replenish the Brigade Dumps in THIEPVAL WOOD as they were originally sited near the troops for the initial advance; but I do not think these the best places for sending additional stores to, because being off the Tramway stores require man handling to get there and man handling to get out of the WOOD.

It took 300 men about a week to get the stores there and I cannot expect to get that labour to replenish them.

There is still a good supply of stores in the Dumps, which can be taken.

Meanwhile I shall be forming advanced Dumps near Railway level crossing in Q.24.A., by trollies and pontoons or road, but as this will not be convenient for the 109th Brigade I shall endeavour to send up by limbered wagons, via. AUTHUILLE to R.25.A.4.1. failing which up the SUNKEN and THIEPVAL ROAD.

28. 6. 16.

Lt.Col.
C.R.E. 36th Division.

SECRET.   Copy No. 9

36th DIVISION ORDER No. 40.

29. 6. 16.

1. The moves shown on the attached March Table will take place on the 30th instant in order to bring troops into their positions for the assault on the 1st July.

2. A map showing the routes referred to was issued with 36th Division Order No.36.

3. C.R.A. will arrange that the following batteries do not fire during the moves :-

    D/246 & D/172, and any other battery the fire of which would interfere with these movements.

4. The G.O.C. 107th Brigade will move his Brigade from AVELUY WOOD at such an hour as to ensure the whole Brigade being across the ANCRE by zero on 1st July.

5. Except where special instructions are given, battalions will march by platoons at 100 yards distance, when moving to their positions of assembly.

6. The Field Companies R.E., less the Sections allotted to Brigades, will assemble in Divisional Reserve by zero at the following places ready to move at once.

    121st Field Coy.R.E., .. LANCASHIRE DUMP.
    122nd   "   "   " .. MOUND KEEP.
    150th   "   "   " .. PAISLEY AVENUE.

    The 16th R.Ir.Rif.(Pioneers) will assemble 200 yards South of LANCASHIRE DUMP at zero.
    Each of the above units will send 2 runners to McMAHON'S POST.

7. Advanced Divisional Headquarters will open at 9 p.m. on 30th at Q.25.d.9.0.

    PLEASE ACKNOWLEDGE BY WIRE.

Issued at
9.50 p.m.
                                            LT.COLONEL. G.S.

Distribution as for 36th Div. Orders 34-39

OPERATION ORDER BY C.R.E. 36th Division.

The Field Companies R.E., less the sections alloted to Brigades will assemble in Divisional Reserve by zero at the following places ready to move off at once.

† 121st Field Coy, R.E.   LANCASHIRE DUMP.
    122nd   "   "   "   MOUND KEEP.
    150th   "   "   "   PAISLEY AVENUE.

Each of the above Units will send 2 runners to McMahon's Post, Telephone Office.

✻ Adjutant R.E. will allot 121st Coy, R.E. 2 handcarts and the half of 122 Coy and 150th Coy, R.E. in Divisional Reserve 1 handcart each for carrying tools *extra to those carried by the Sappers.*

Coys' should take tools sufficient for rough bridging, making Machine Gun emplacements, defensive houses; saws will be useful.

30. 6. 16.

[signature]
Lt.Col.
C.R.E. 36th Division.

✻ *If O.C. 121 has any handcarts of his own he will use them instead of applying to Adj: for some.*

† *O.C. 121 will keep his men clear of the road.*

Firing against any Airship is absolutely prohibited, unless the Airship has revealed its hostile character unmistakeably by dropping bombs.

CONFIDENTIAL — ORIGINAL

Vol 11

WAR DIARY

OF

C.R.E. 36th (ULSTER) DIVISION

FOR MONTH OF

AUGUST 1916

CONFIDENTIAL

C.R.E.
36th (ULSTER) DIVISION

Army Form C. 2118.

WAR DIARY
or
INTELLIGENCE SUMMARY.
(Erase heading not required.)

Instructions regarding War Diaries and Intelligence Summaries are contained in F. S. Regs., Part II. and the Staff Manual respectively. Title pages will be prepared in manuscript.

Place	Date	Hour	Summary of Events and Information	Remarks and references to Appendices
MONT NOIR	1.8.16	—	Met + rode round hqr half / left sector with C.O.'s. Lunch at Batt H.Q. — conference H.Q. Group of Infantry and Machine Guns Conferences for C.E. Corps.	
		Noon	Received orders to supply 682 men / 8th Inniskilling Battalion on subsidiary line. Notify C.E. R.Sussex, O. 2.8.16 under further orders. Allotted 11th R.I.R. & R.F.C. 121	
	2.8.16	10 a.m.	Office work. Rode to see barbed wire defences of C.E. Y. Corps. Conferences with various C.E.'s Y. Corps. Visited demonstration of Trench Mortar school — one of garrison H.Q.s ready days onto Germans pallices completed timer. Workshop — visit Zest. R.	
	3/8/16	8 a.m.	Office work.	
		pm	Walked to see medical and wire defences div. Group, and various field works C.E. I Corps. N	
	4/8/16		Visited roads and R.E. dump being carried out by his Corps N	
	5.8.16		Office work.	
	6.8.16		Asked Col. Stewart & Lieut Smyth R.E. as Field Engineers inform unit 91 B R.I.R.(P) Base No 6 Infantry Battalion on subsidiary line. — Lieut. Wilson (121 B) & Lieut Thorne (15 D) Winter hut. Dated 3rd C.L. 5 Copies of Detail / Section / Field by 8 Inniskilling issued on 9/8/26 detached 107 Bgde. 36 Div Instructions 6/8/16 to detail 1 Section / Field by 8 Inniskilling issued on 9/8/26 detached Lieut Forsyth section on 9/8/16 moved to De Kennebar OAB to send unit 107 Brigade.	

Army Form C. 2118.

WAR DIARY
or
INTELLIGENCE SUMMARY.
(Erase heading not required.)

Place	Date	Hour	Summary of Events and Information	Remarks and references to Appendices
MONT NOIR	7/8/16	—	LIEUT HARLING. R.E. reported that 7 days of division's Hutting scheme for approx 5000 all ranks received latest Hutting panel at DETROIT at back of tunnel on Kemmel Hill. R.	
	8/8/16	—	G.O.C. conference as work on expansion units, + Hutting. 450 Labourers. O.C. No 2 Ruter of Repair regiment no SUBSIDIARY LINE. Sr Govt's Section 9/24 not attached for interment. Work tentatively handed over by C.E.V Corps to C.R.E. 36 Div.	
	9/8/16		No 8 Entrenching Battalion not available. 1 and two teams 1+6.6 per coy R. Inspected road 9 16 (R.1.R(?) = 9 Crowley or Wulverdinghe Hill R.	
	10/8/16		Hutting scheme. N	
	11/8/16		Hutting scheme as proposed near Ypres. N	
	12/8/16	—	Sunday. Hutting scheme as before 100 men 9 Lubwirenberg Battalion letters army by C.E. 5 Corps N	
	14/8/16		Passed Hartecourt Hutting hut. for men. R. Received report on amount of new two kitchen proposed for ovendo Hutting scheme. R.	

WAR DIARY
or
INTELLIGENCE SUMMARY.

(Erase heading not required.)

Army Form C. 2118.

Instructions regarding War Diaries and Intelligence Summaries are contained in F. S. Regs., Part II. and the Staff Manual respectively. Title pages will be prepared in manuscript.

Place	Date	Hour	Summary of Events and Information	Remarks and references to Appendices
MONT NOIR	15.8.16	—	Instructions to DETEVIS DUMP to allow 9 men making huts – moved Hqrs. & Fances.t	
	16.8.16		"	
	17.8.16		Organization of Hutting by wheel now lines out 6 huts a day	
	18.8.16		Selecting site for Hutson Church Recovery fork from A.D.O.N. 1 P.M. – Ink'd dr General Hartigan. Informal Visit of Inspection.	
	19.8.16		To C.E. IX Corps re Hutt grants & Huts to be prepared for (4) Divisions (4) divisional units.	
		4.30	Visited GOC 107 Bry re site for huts & arrangement of Huts.	
	20/8/16		Recvy. Received intimation UCT past four area with Intern cavalry – & Hutting party on division depot. Changed Reserve Hutt from LE ROMARIN to T.27.C.7.2.	
	21/8/16		Justified Hutt offered LETROMARIN at Double latter out your area – Transferred all machines were carted to a new site.	
	22/8/16		Inspection of Ruths and Dugouts. M.G. Stewart Brigade Westerly support line Hill 63 & F.W. last day of Hutt send for us. B. In effect of huts 6 per day.	
	23/8/16		Progress Rept. Dispatch received. D. Inventory detailed for un-hutting Huts & a small number on	
	24/8/16		Inspection of Hutting in progress by CRE O & CE IX Corps. Y	
	25/8/16		Arg. went to ha f a Bricks for municipality purpose at ProPolls. If 13 trollies sent daily ogreand for General Brigade. Receipt of uncompleting and intervening huts Annexes. K by Several Brigade Ceased Employ making huts. B	

Army Form C. 2118.

WAR DIARY
or
INTELLIGENCE SUMMARY.
(Erase heading not required.)

Place	Date	Hour	Summary of Events and Information	Remarks and references to Appendices
MONT NOIR	26/8/16	—	All night-working parties. Regt. working parties repaired trench stores near "RODGERS". Reg't working parties as before to getting up "RODGERS". Informed that on 28/8/16 m.g. Indershey of supply 7 G.O. Ranks. front.	
	27/8/16	—	Sunday. Intended relief of S/2 J.M.S support & and House Saturday 7 most of Div Relief ordered to take place not 7 earlier to be hulled down.	
	28/8/16	—	Packet 2nd Army School Ammunition at WISQUES.	
	29/8	—	Packet Horse Lines. Return and LA PLUS DOUVE FARM WORKS.	
	30/8	—	Says I have been allowed by Corps & left-wing furniture relieve in 2 mes a 3 pl man between lines — Proceeded GOC instructed. Regt-working parties supplied under Division.	
	31/8/16	—	Suddenly ordered to supply a by 16 R 1 R 19 for making a supercedes house of KING EDWARD II & NUGENT SUPPORT and Suffer 40/15 R 1 R 19 front with Australian Mining Cy. Bungos front to late there if HIGGINSON & CALGARY AVENUES & slightly advanced all other working parties. Re working parties after Div orgs	

Henry (signature)
Lt. Col. U.C. 36 Div

2/1/8/16

CONFIDENTIAL — ORIGINAL

Vol 2

WAR DIARY

OF

C.R.E 36th (ULSTER) DIVISION

FOR MONTH OF

SEPTEMBER 1916

CONFIDENTIAL

Army Form C. 2118.

CRE 36th (ULSTER) DIVISION

WAR DIARY
or
INTELLIGENCE SUMMARY.
(Erase heading not required.)

Instructions regarding War Diaries and Intelligence Summaries are contained in F.S. Regs. Part II and the Staff Manual respectively. Title pages will be prepared in manuscript.

Place	Date	Hour	Summary of Events and Information	Remarks and references to Appendices
ST JANS CAPPEL	1.9.16		On H.Q. move from MONTNOIR to ST JANS CAPPEL. N.	
"	2.9.16		present or	
	3.9.16		" "	
	4.9.16		" "	
	5.9.16		Preliminary trials in NEUVE EGLISE and Huts at PRAETZIGNIS — Hurry on to 4 to 6th Kings ?OME — 150 Field ½ life moves to DRANOUTRE N	
	6.9.16		Lt Col DE VITRE left. Visited DE SEUL DUMP. HQs of 121, 122 & 150 Field Coys. Arranged for move of Northern Section 122 from ALDERSHOT to ROMARIN and HQ & Section of 121 from ROMARIN to ALDERSHOT. Remainder of 121 to go into Artillery Shelters at DE KENEEBAR; moves to take place of on 8th.	
	7.9.16		Visited Dump, HQ 121, 122 & 150.Coys. Inspected huts in course of erection T.15.B. Three completed & one nearly completed. Visited Power and Arrangements for 2 Coys to work in KINGSWAY area. PICCADILLY on 9th under 150 Field Coy.	
	8.9.16		Visited KINGSWAY, BULLRING & PICCADILLY with Major ROYLES OC 15 Coy	[signature]

2353 Wt. W2544/1454 700,000 5/15 D.D.&L. A.D.S.S./Forms/C. 2118.

WAR DIARY
or
INTELLIGENCE SUMMARY

Army Form C. 2118.

Place	Date	Hour	Summary of Events and Information	Remarks and references to Appendices
ST JANS CAPPEL	9/9/16		Visited work in trenches by O.C. 122 Bn, m/RATION FARM, PLUS DOUCE, BENSON alleys, ONE SHELL Farm, STINKING FARM, GOBION FARM, S. MIDLAND FARM, also CALGARY AV; NUGENT SUPPORT, KING between Trenches & portions of TRAM Line.	
	10.9.16		Visited Horse lines & Mobile Vet. — 108 Field Ambulance, DAC HQ, DAC B Echelon, No 3 Coy A.S.C., 173. A. Battery. Visited 121st Coy Camps & saw Camp CASTLE hutting officer.	
	11.9.16		Visited 150 Coy Camp & inspected hutments. Inspected hutting & grounds between 150 & BUS Farm also of 3 lorries. ¼/121 at DERSNINE BAK. Visited huts in course of erection near NEUVE EGLISE, representing organisation. Arranged with OC Pioneers & OC No 3 Coy Pioneers for men & lorries from Tunnelling to work in CALGARY AV. Inspected Pioneer hire lines, A 153 battery, 13" R.I.R., 14 R.I.R., 108 MG Coy, 12 R.I.R., 9 R Irish F, 10 R Innis F, 8 R.I.R., 107 MG Coy, 15 R.I.R., 9 R.I.R., B 172 battery. & Visited C.E. IX Corps	

Army Form C. 2118.

WAR DIARY
or
INTELLIGENCE SUMMARY.
(Erase heading not required.)

Place	Date	Hour	Summary of Events and Information	Remarks and references to Appendices
ST JANS CAPPEL	12.9.16		C.E. 2nd Army orders C.R.E.	
	13.9.16		Conference of Field Coy Commanders at 121 Coy Aircraft. Visited site proposed for huts for 2 Coys Infy & 2 Coys of Pioneers in DRANOUTRE — DAYLIGHT CORNER. Visited G.O.C. Divn.	
	14.9.16		Visited C.E. 1x Corps. Inspected work in huts near NEUVE EGLISE. Inspected site for huts along the DRANOUTRE DAYLIGHT CORNER Road, and by means of a lorran reconnaissance when digging of cover from MESSINES was found in progress. The site proposed for 2 Coys of Pioneers is not adequate, as anything above the knees is in full view.	
	15.9.16		Inspected work LT STEWART acting O.C. of 121 Coy. Re work in underground KETSEK. Inspected work in No 3 Heavy T.M. Class site with O/C Heavy 1x Corps for work through stereoscope. 107 Bde Transport lines. AT Coy will erect a Langhine.	
	16.9.16		Visited 150th Tony HQ 108 & 109 Infry Bdes. Inspected work in huts for 2 Coys of Infry near AIRCRAFT Farm in DRANOUTRE — DAYLIGHT Corner Road	Initials

Army Form C. 2118.

WAR DIARY
or
INTELLIGENCE SUMMARY.
(Erase heading not required.)

Place	Date	Hour	Summary of Events and Information	Remarks and references to Appendices
STUDNS COPPEL	17.9.16		Sunday. Attended conference of 2nd A.D.C.R.A., Artillery, Bde Commanders and T.M. officers, discussed Artillery. Visited LOCREHOF Farm with OC Tram. No 10 be prepared for sleeping there as soon as ready for troops. Visited R.E. dump at LOCRE.	
	18.9.16		Visited T.M. Battery lines in 108 Brigade area with Artillery Bde Commander T.M. officer & R.E./22 Coy. Very heavy rain.	
	19.9.16		Visited work on Huts at AIRCRAFT Farm also O.C. Pioneers. Inspected fuel overhead shields at IX Corps Park.	
	20.9.16		Inspection work in KINGSWAY and PICCADILLY CTs & supports in 109 Bde and with O.C. Pioneers and O.C. 150 T. Coy. Several points were brought in during inspection. Very wet rain.	
	21.9.16		Visited with "Q" Transport lines of B153, B172, A172, 107 M.G. Coy, 107 Bde Mortars, 108 Bde Mortars, & 108 M.G. Coy, and decisions as to accommodation.	
	22.9.16		Visited work in front line 107 Bde & supports in New Brigade's trench. Menin Eglise & R.E./22 Coy, O.C. 121 Coy. Also visited Artillery men.	

Army Form C. 2118.

WAR DIARY
or
INTELLIGENCE SUMMARY.
(Erase heading not required.)

Instructions regarding War Diaries and Intelligence Summaries are contained in F.S. Regs., Part II. and the Staff Manual respectively. Title pages will be prepared in manuscript.

Place	Date	Hour	Summary of Events and Information	Remarks and references to Appendices
ST JANS CAPPEL	23.9.16		Presentation of medal ribbons by Corps Commander.	
	24.9.16		Sunday. Visited NEUVE EGLISE Rest Billets in C.E. IX Corps to discuss Railway question re NEUVE EGLISE – LINDEN HOEK line. Fine day, near BRONCOUTRE.	
	25.9.16		Visited R.A. Hdrs. Line with O. and S.C.R.A. and discussed upon the question of accommodation. Visited OC's 122 and 121 Corps. Very fine day.	
	26.9.16		Visited CE IX Corps & inspected concrete cupolas for OP's at IX Corps Park. Lecture to School at ST MARIE CAPPEL. Fine day.	
	27.9.16		Inspected motor park line from NEUVE EGLISE to LINDENHOEK with Capt. HIGGINSON OC 109 Rly. Coy, & arranged for tramway from whatever. Inspected work at SHANKILL HUTS (NEUVE EGLISE HUTS). Visited CRE 16 Div. Some rainfall.	
	28.		Inspected tramline & accommodation & remounting of RA Workshop Corps RA. Attended to inauguration of motor pump from tramway from rear at NEUVE EGLISE to DANYLGOT (Corrie, carried 20 tons of stores).	
	29.		Lecture to officers & NCO's. Visited O.C.150 Coy & Northern O'Brien. Bomb at WAKEFIELD HUTS.	

Army Form C. 2118.

WAR DIARY
or
INTELLIGENCE SUMMARY.
(Erase heading not required.)

Place	Date	Hour	Summary of Events and Information	Remarks and references to Appendices
STUART CASTLE	30.9.16		Kindly No 1, 2, 14 Cop Sent Train and division upon resumption Inspection works. 122nd Divis by RE with O/C O/C Huttn Capt CASTLE on leave during W Lieut HARLING is in charge of Construction of Huts in workmen hampoine to IX Corps of Park	Major Kent Lieut Col RE 36 Div CRE 8 1/10/16

SECRET ORIGINAL (Pages 7 to 11) Vol 13

WAR DIARY

OF

C.R.E. 36th (ULSTER) DIVISION

FOR MONTH OF

OCTOBER 1916

SECRET

CRE 36th (ULSTER) DIVISION 7

Army Form C. 2118.

WAR DIARY
or
INTELLIGENCE SUMMARY.
(Erase heading not required.)

Instructions regarding War Diaries and Intelligence Summaries are contained in F. S. Regs., Part II. and the Staff Manual respectively. Title pages will be prepared in manuscript.

Place	Date	Hour	Summary of Events and Information	Remarks and references to Appendices
ST JANS CAPPEL	1.10.16		Lieut KNOX took over charge of Hutting Coy and important work in huts with CRE Nr NEUVE EGLISE (SHANKILL HUTS), ~~Districts~~ AIRCRAFT FARM (DERRY HUTS) + 107th M.G. Coy.	
	2.10.16		Visited work carried on by 122nd & 2nd Army in 108th Bde work CE IX Corps. Very wet day.	
	3.10.16			
	4.10.16		Various work in 107 Brigade area with Jr STEWART.	
	5.10.16		Visited KORTEPYP, ALDERSHOT + BULFORD Camps with Q and discussed upon alterations to be formed. Visited work in 107 Brigade area with Major BOYLE.	
	6.10.16		Reconnoitred area for Ammo Dumps to Battery positions with a view on: Also CE IX Corps men ride & discussed questions with him.	
	7.10.16		Various work in 108 Bde area by 122 Field Coy R.E. with a Colonel of Russian General Staff.	

W.M. Lieut. Colonel
CRE 36 (Ulster) Div
C.R.E. 3644

SECRET

Army Form C. 2118.

WAR DIARY
or
INTELLIGENCE SUMMARY.
(Erase heading not required.)

Instructions regarding War Diaries and Intelligence Summaries are contained in F.S. Regs., Part II. and the Staff Manual respectively. Title pages will be prepared in manuscript.

Place	Date	Hour	Summary of Events and Information	Remarks and references to Appendices
	8.10.16		Visited huts at 108 M.G. Coy, 107 M.G. Coy & B.M. Transport. 107 T.M.B. this day.	
	9.10.16		Visited Specialist School, 108 F.A. Mobile Vet Section, huts B173, C173, N°3 S.A.C., N°2 S.A.C., B153, D173 & D153. 10 & 11th Innis. Killing F.Zs. Inspected water supply arrangements for WAKEFIELD HUTS. Fine day.	
	10.10.16		Office work all day. Fine weather.	
	11.10.16		Visited huts in Transport Lines of 107 & 108 Bdes. Visited position of No 9 107 Bde with O.C. 121 Bty. Term line from D.G. KENNEBAR hut in Terry Hallow, which was very difficult for trucks with ballast.	
	12.10.16		Visited 108th Transport Lines. C, 153. HQ 122 I. Bdy Bde. HQ 108 Sec. SHANKILL HUT & BERRY HUTS.	
	13.10.16		Visited 2nd Army Workshops morning. Went over area of 109 Bde as far as REGENT DUG OUTS.	

SECRET.

Army Form C. 2118.

WAR DIARY
or
INTELLIGENCE SUMMARY.

(Erase heading not required.)

Place	Date	Hour	Summary of Events and Information	Remarks and references to Appendices
	14.10.16		Visited Hubert horse line Asylum. 108 F.Amb. N°3 Cav A.S.C. D.163, 121 D.Coy, N°1 SPS, N°1875, A.172, 107 Brigade Transport lines, 105 M.G. Coy, 9 R.I.R, 12 R.I.R, KORTE PYP. Visited Brigadier commanding 107 & 109 Brigades. Spoke to Sunday. Visited 109 Bde and was with O.C. 15th (Northumb) Reconnaissance train for Tramway.	
	15.10.16			
	16.10.16		Visited erection of Officer hut at KORTE PYP Northern. Scheme to 10th R.I.R. at KORTE PYP. Visited hut at N.G. Coy 107th Bde. Visited T.M. School at BERTHEN.	
	17.10.16		Visited line with O.C. School Army) (itinerary) SOUVENIR Farm R.E. Farm KINGSWAY, ULSTER ROAD, horse lines to ST QUENTIN CABT. LA PLUS DOUCE, + NORTH MIDLAND Farm.	
	18.10.16		Visited H.Q. BAC & Ammunition dumps, 121 Coy & 152 Coy.	
	19.10.16		Heavy rain. Visited DE SEULE and STEENWERCK PARKS. Was 2nd Army workshops BAILLEUL. Wing Benzine in operation. Visited "109 Brigade and was into an Officers ([?]) 17. Cav C4 to front and a line for lorry Sandbags (Report). Visited O.V. O.B.E.	

2353 Wt. W3544/454 700,000 5/15 D.D.&L. A.D.S.S/Forms/C. 2118.

SECRET

WAR DIARY
or
INTELLIGENCE SUMMARY.

Army Form C. 2118.

Place	Date	Hour	Summary of Events and Information	Remarks and references to Appendices
	21.10.16		IX Corps & Ammunition Dumps. Visited road & 2nd & 6th Spitfire Mortars at Trench Mortar School BERTHEN.	
	22.10.16		Visited filling camps with O.C. 8th Sentinelany Battalion, BULFORD, KORTE PYP. 167 A.T. Coy. Inspected dumps 1. DEBROCKEN Road. Inspected site for T. Mortars. G.O.C. R.A. Visited KORTE PYP & 107th AU Transport Camps, 122 Ing C8 Camp & 56 KENNEDBAR. Trench tramway & inspected scheme in use from NEUVE EGLISE to DAYLIGHT Corner.	
	23.10.16		Visited RED LODGE & NEUVE EGLISE, lookor place to arrange for scheme.	
	24.10.16		Visited Trench Mortar School BERTHEN to see 2" TM just off a tramway trolley. Very useful.	
	25.10.16		All day in office.	

Army Form C. 2118.

WAR DIARY
or
INTELLIGENCE SUMMARY.

(Erase heading not required.)

Instructions regarding War Diaries and Intelligence Summaries are contained in F. S. Regs., Part II. and the Staff Manual respectively. Title pages will be prepared in manuscript.

Place	Date	Hour	Summary of Events and Information	Remarks and references to Appendices
	26.10.16		Visited RATION FARM, wall protecting M.G. Emp'. hit by shell. To improve concrete wires protecting M.G. damaged. Inspected tramway between RATION FARM & SOUVENIR Dump, O.P. in PLUM ST. WIND SAFE.	
	27.10.16		WIND DANGEROUS. Visited work in 109 Rd. Are work OC 150 Rdrs. a/a 28 November. Communication Trenches have fallen in very badly, chiefly Nr 1 & front where camouflets. Water has been hammering up & camo more damage. Rain fell in afternoon.	
	28.10.16		WIND SAFE. Visited STEENWERCK, BULFORD & KORTEPYP.	
	29.10.16		Visited R.E. dumps nr b'tns BROEKEN. Very wet day	
	30.10		Notice from Second Army that 2/Lt JACKSON OR 25 a/c's Shirely to proceed to command a field Coy. 2/Lieut WEDGEWOOD of 136 A T Coy attached to learn duties of a/c'r.	
	31.10		CRE proceeded on leave	

2353 Wt. W2544/1454 700,000 5/15 D. D. & L. A.D.S.S./Forms/C. 2118.

ORIGINAL
Page 12-15
Vol 14

SECRET

War Diary

of

C.R.E 36th (Ulster) Division

For Month of

November 1916

WAR DIARY
or
INTELLIGENCE SUMMARY.
(Erase heading not required.)

CRE
36ᵗʰ (ULSTER) DIVISION

Army Form C. 2118.

12

Instructions regarding War Diaries and Intelligence Summaries are contained in F. S. Regs., Part II. and the Staff Manual respectively. Title pages will be prepared in manuscript.

Place	Date	Hour	Summary of Events and Information	Remarks and references to Appendices
ST. JANS CAPPEL	1.11.16		CRE on leave.	
	2.11.16		Very wet	
	3.11.16		Wet morning	
	4.11.16		Bombardment of enemy trenches	
	6.11.16		Very wet morning	
	7.11.16			
	8.11.16		Great floods. R. Douve rose 8-10 feet & flooded all right sector	

T 6 & 7.

Army Form C. 2118.

WAR DIARY
or
INTELLIGENCE SUMMARY.
(Erase heading not required.)

Place	Date	Hour	Summary of Events and Information	Remarks and references to Appendices
	11.11.16		Lt Col KING arrived at BOULOGNE from leave about 1.30 p.m. & proceeded to HAZEBROUCK by train arriving at ST JANS CAPPEL about midnight.	
	12.11.16		Visited HQ of all Field Coys. Corps.	
	13.11.16		Visited BULFORD & KORTEPYP camps, H.Q. 107 + 108 Brigade & 121 Field Coy. Capt JACKSON handed over duties of Adjutant to 2Lt WEDGWOOD, and him self to take over Commander 121st Field Coy R.E.	
	14.11.16		Visited 109th Brigade H.Q. with O.C. 150 Field Coy R.E. Spent evening in HQ.	
	15.11.16		Visited Brick works at MERVILLE where army written was drawn up. Visited 108th Field Coy area with O.C. 122nd Field Coy R.E. and Major GILES R.E.	
	16.11.16		Attended conference of Trench Tramway Drivers at 11 a.m. Visited 107th Brigade area with O.C. 121 Coy R.E. and end of day spent evening clear.	

Army Form C. 2118.

WAR DIARY
or
INTELLIGENCE SUMMARY.

(Erase heading not required.)

Place	Date	Hour	Summary of Events and Information	Remarks and references to Appendices
	7.11.16		Headquarters. Visited Camp with Hutting Officer.	
	16.11.16		Thorn & Anysley Camps.	
	19.11.16		Sunday. Visited WAKEFIELD HUTS & Transportation with Staff Captain 109 Bde & OC 150 Field Coy RE.	
	20.11.16		Visited front line trenches of 107 Bde with OC 121 Coy.	
	21.11.16		Visited KORTEPYP Camp with Q. Conference & demonstration on wire management to General Catour & officers in charge of 107 & 109 Bde wiring parties by 30 - 109 Bde at WAKEFIELD Huts.	
	22.11.16		Visited Trench Tramway system in 107 & 109 Bde sectors with CE IX Corps.	
	23.11.16		Attended Conference at IX Corps Hqrs. of Trench Tramway Comrs. Visited A.S.C Camps with OC 3 & 6 Div Trains.	
	24.11.16		Visited BULFORD Camp with Brigadier 108 Bde to advise upon plan for improvement of Camp generally.	
	25.11.16		CRE remained in camp.	
	26.11.16		Visited 150 & 128 & 1/6 RIRR re proposed move of Hqr Brigade.	

Army Form C. 2118.

WAR DIARY
or
INTELLIGENCE SUMMARY.
(Erase heading not required.)

Instructions regarding War Diaries and Intelligence Summaries are contained in F. S. Regs., Part II and the Staff Manual respectively. Title pages will be prepared in manuscript.

Secret

Place	Date	Hour	Summary of Events and Information	Remarks and references to Appendices
	26.11.16		Visited SHANKILL Huts to close shop. Handed over shelter Eng.	
	27.11.16		Visited STEENWERCK. O.C. 150 Coy R.E. Reconnoitre. Visited MIDLAND Farm into O.C. 171 Coy R.E. & discussed plans for dugouts.	
	28.11.16		Visited 122 Field Coy R.E. BAILLEUL Workshop. Discussed work in September 25 But men into O.C. 106 Field Coy R.E.	
	29.11.16		Inspected accommodation in Hill 63 with O. Went to SMYTH. Visited G.O.C. Trench & SUBSIDIARY LINE BOYOISA Farm & 25 But area & Returned via DOUVE & KANADA Farm. Farm.	
	30.11.16		Afternoon Conference J Trench Tramway Board	

W.A.M [signature]
Lieut Col R.E.
CRE 36 Div

Confidential.

Vol 15

WAR DIARY
of
C.R.E. 36th DIVISION

December 1916.

Army Form C. 2118.

16

WAR DIARY
or
INTELLIGENCE SUMMARY.
(Erase heading not required.)

Instructions regarding War Diaries and Intelligence Summaries are contained in F. S. Regs., Part II. and the Staff Manual respectively. Title pages will be prepared in manuscript.

Place	Date	Hour	Summary of Events and Information	Remarks and references to Appendices
ST JANS CAP	1.12.16		Thick fog. Visited site of tramway for ammunition supply to Batterie near ALOUETTES Farm. Visited work in 108 Bde area with OC 122 F Coy, many to say it was possible to walk everywhere in daytime. Visited Stone quarries MONT NOIR. Newports.	
	2.12.16			
	3.12.16		Visited back area of 108th Bde area with GSO 2. Visited CRE 25 Divn.	
	4.12.16		Capt McILDOWIE arrived from 122 Coy to take over appointment under Visited Subsidiary Line now approaching Hill 63 with OC 15 PIR(P) OC 150 F Coy, RE & two Coy Commanders of 16 PIR(P)	
	5.12.16		Three officers Kingsway. 109 RE area move to right of Neuve Eglise. 150 Coy to return to Hill 63. HQ to ALDERSHOT. 121 Coy trimmers + HQ to MONMOUTH Camp SPANDOEK Visited KINGSWAY and 107 & 108 Bde BAER areas with CE	
	6.12.16		I Corps. Raw + hail. Nmer bangours. Visited Support line with CISO by near 109 RE area between DOUVE and ANTONS Farm	
	7.12.16		Visited Sites near BAILLEUL Stadium for Rear Camps for Reinforcements &c.	

WAR DIARY
or
INTELLIGENCE SUMMARY

Army Form C. 2118.

Place	Date	Hour	Summary of Events and Information	Remarks and references to Appendices
ST JANS	8.12.16		Office work. Wet day.	
	9.12.16		CRE inspected work in the billeting area to 6 chief	
	10.12.16		ditto	
	11.12.16			
	12.12.16		Snow	
	13.12.16		CRE runner to work in office	
	"		CRE & TTO attended meeting of Trench Tramway Board.	
			Visited POLLUX & IX Hy (B. gun positions now being	
			demonstrated at BULFORD.	
			Return in late afternoon & evening.	
			Visited follies in HD. corner & microchigan to Poederhoek x	
			Aurora forts.	
			Visited Trench Tramway at ALOUETTE Farm.	
			Inspected works in ILC at KORTEPYP/BULFORD.	
			Visited KORTEPYP and BULFORD Camp. Inspection lines with	
			... from HD BKE	
			Visited Schurty Inchaclen St MARY CAPPEL SIX KEMMEL DAK	
			... SPUR DEICKE ... ALDERTS ...	
			... WHITE GATES WIND OXENROLL	

Army Form C. 2118.

18

WAR DIARY
or
INTELLIGENCE SUMMARY.
(Erase heading not required.)

Place	Date	Hour	Summary of Events and Information	Remarks and references to Appendices
	19.12.16		Got orders to move to BEAUVOIR to a Battery of 108 wagons. Went to BEAUVOIR ready. Proceeded on consolidation of open scrap during afternoon.	
	20.12.16		Afternoon lecture and demonstration by O.C. R. Eng. Special Mynah R.E. Visited PETIT-MUNQUE Farm, proposed billet for 150 TC, R.E. Visited HYDE PARK gallery, and tramway from ST QUENTIN to DEKENNEBEAK.	
	21.12		Visited DE SEVLE Dump.	
	23.12.16		Visited 108 forward area into OC 172 TC, RE. Saw MAJOR BOYLE R.E. who was i/c the CRS when CRS proceeded on leave. Known horses came R DOUVE to floor. Slung gate to dugout. Into floor cairn.	
	24.12.16		Visited HEAD. MAJOR BOYLE and Hunting Officer BULFORD CAMP, R.S. Park De SEULE, STEENWERCK PARK, Surgn. Consolidation BAILLEUL Hosp. Dental school ST-MARIE CAPPEL	

WAR DIARY
or
INTELLIGENCE SUMMARY.
(Erase heading not required.)

Army Form C. 2118.

Place	Date	Hour	Summary of Events and Information	Remarks and references to Appendices
ST JAN 25.12.16 CAPEL	25/12/16		XMAS DAY. Office work. Visited T.M. practice in 108 & 109 Bde areas with G.O.C. R.A. Major BOYLE.	
	27/12/16		Visited 107 Bde area with O.C. 131 Fd Co R.E. but have received C & E horses in 30 days leave.	
	28/12/16		Rode to 8 Bde area. Talk to Koenake Bn. have been talking with G.O.C. R.A. and O.C. 131 Fd. Co. R.E.	
	29/12/16		Visited T.H. practice in 107 Bde area with G.O.C. R.A. and O.C. 131 Fd. Co. R.E.	
	30/12/16		Visited with G.O.C. 109 Bde & new trenches for Whittley front line held by S.W. Borde Av. & Johannas Spruce AV. Saw G.O.C. [explained absent?] from Batt. lets his [a/ect?] with Capt GREEN and settled some details.	
	31/12/16		A HAPPY NEW YEAR L.B.Boyle	

Vol 16

Confidential

War Diary

of

C.R.E. 36th Division

From 1/1/19 to 31/1/19.

Army Form C. 2118.

20

WAR DIARY
or
INTELLIGENCE SUMMARY.   SECRET

(Erase heading not required.)

Instructions regarding War Diaries and Intelligence
Summaries are contained in F. S. Regs., Part II.
and the Staff Manual respectively. Title pages
will be prepared in manuscript.

Place	Date	Hour	Summary of Events and Information	Remarks and references to Appendices
ST JAN CAPEL	1-1-17 P.M		Visited 121 H.L. at Dranoutre & then saw Bg T.E.T.O. & visited 107 Bde re costs.	
	2-1-17		Visited 109 Bde with Capt Smyth re special work & recce'd new Hill 63.	
	3-1-17		Visited MIDLAND FARM defences with O.C. 171 Tunnels Co.	
	4-1-17		Saw NXVI & XXXVII, held O.C. Wks Batts had conference with Brunton re redu Corps to arrangement Plonka Bynes undermines thouse 1914. Recce'd front line & Plutz Mill road with Architect. Busy at office.	
	5-1-17		Met C.E. TRAINING OFFICER.	
			Staff Officer YESTEENU WORKS & de Cecle chamber.	
	6-1-17		Visited MIDLAND FARM defences & Subsidiary lines & Kent Posh with & went P.M.S. to Saw Sugar Mills trench in Kirklands & Lonely Farm & [illegible]	

2353 Wt. W2511/4454 700,000 5/15 D.D.&L.   A.D.S.S./Forms/C. 2118.

Army Form C. 2118.

21.

WAR DIARY
or
INTELLIGENCE SUMMARY.   SECRET
(Erase heading not required.)

Place	Date	Hour	Summary of Events and Information	Remarks and references to Appendices
	8-1-17		His Grenier. He poured down 5 or 6 ons per while in Mann area. Inspected new Observation Farm perfectly formed. He was a Gillant have fallen. Inspected sites for huts with A.A. & Q.M.G. Shutting Officer also called in O.C. T. Tramways.	
	9-1-17		Inspected works with O.C. No. 1st area tramways work progressed. Met Railway Officer who informed me of this proposal. Called on C. R. E. 1st Corps.	
	10-1-17		Called in Tramway Office. Shewed him suggestions to R.E. for tramway work. Connecting up to future 2 section 121st D.C. never had to moment Camil way, Gullet being shelled.	
	11-1-17		Called in 105 Bde & 107 Bde re labour to repair of damaged trenches. Met Electric Light Officer H.Q. Estree Gulleine.	

Army Form C. 2118.

22

WAR DIARY
or
INTELLIGENCE SUMMARY.
(Erase heading not required.)

Place	Date	Hour	Summary of Events and Information	Remarks and references to Appendices
	12-1-17		Office – Visited H.P. Cornie & collieries – Saw Major Gordon. Fieldman H.Q. Organisation office & Electric lighting. Register.	
	13-1-17		Visited 108 Bn available at 150 per will stands –	
	14-1-17		Visited 107 Ama works with O.C. 121 Fd. Co. Saw O.C. Works Battn. re new men arriving.	
	15-1-17		Office –	
	16-1-17		Visited works of 171 Co. also front line by Boyles Farm.	
	17-1-16		Snow Storm – Visited front line works 108.109. Bde areas.	
	18-1-16		Office – Snow storm all day.	
	19-1-16		Visited 184 Fd Co. re armoured pillboxes for Coast Defence – Visited Div. Specialist School –	
	20-1-16		Met O.C. 3rd Tunnellers Co. Canadian Engs. re sites for M.G. posts in line 63 –	
	21-1-16		Visited 2nd Army workshops HAZEBROUCK. Stamping machines with hulling of coy.	

WAR DIARY
INTELLIGENCE SUMMARY

Army Form C. 2118.
SECRET
23

Place	Date	Hour	Summary of Events and Information	Remarks and references to Appendices
ST JANS CAPEL	22/23-1-17		Visited Sector Line. Curri A.P. Front line & Survey from Mal. FARM. BOCHE RAID on or Rig. H.T.	
	23-1-17		Inspected damage done by enemy bombardment on 2-2-1-17	
	24-1-17		Kestul work done by Wks Battn with O.C. Wks Battn & Capt McSheery	
	25-1-17		Office –	
	26-1-17		Lieut. CUTTING arrives back from leave at 10.30pm 121 Field Coy R.E. took over billets at PETIT PONT, & 122 moved to DRANOUTRE. CRE arranged for their being left. MAJOR BOYLE hands over the men mules waggons to 150 Coy	
	27-1-17		122 Field Coy R.E. at DRANOUTRE. Visited HEUVRE EGUSE Baths, manurepipes front army to front. Wired 121 Coy & 150 Coy	
	29-1-17		Visited ANNEROFT Avance SUBSIDIARY Lne into OT. 150 Coy & arranged for wiring.	
	30-1-17		Visited Keystedge mk Bryan Commence to OT.122 & Keener in line of wire behind AGNES ST.2 wires dug nets in MIDLAND FARM. Capt LEWIN assumes command of 121 Coy	

WAR DIARY
or
INTELLIGENCE SUMMARY.

Army Form C. 2118.

SECRET

Place	Date	Hour	Summary of Events and Information	Remarks and references to Appendices
	31/1/17		Vadas Rd 121 Cmy Rd. Inspected RA Tramway to ALOUETTE Farm. LT STEWART left 121 Coy to take over duties as TOWN LT FARGHER left to take up duties with No 2 Field Survey Coy. LT WALSH took over charge of tramway coy.	Mmf Frost Lieut Col RE CO 3rd Bn

Vol 17

War Diary
of
C.R.E. 36th Division
February 1917.

Army Form C. 2118.

25.

SECRET

WAR DIARY
or
INTELLIGENCE SUMMARY.
(Erase heading not required.)

Instructions regarding War Diaries and Intelligence Summaries are contained in F.S. Regs., Part II. and the Staff Manual respectively. Title pages will be prepared in manuscript.

Place	Date	Hour	Summary of Events and Information	Remarks and references to Appendices
ST JANS CAPPEL	1/2/17		Attended Trench Tramway Board with Trench Tramway officers. Bnig for Cork previous. Visited RATION FARM and SUBSIDIARY line work OC 121 F Coy made arrangements requirements for wire entanglements. Run held pm.	Appx K
	2/2/17		Visited new site for Army Butting with others & VCRA and decision in build of ammunition trench tramway. Visited tottering positions on Kemp sector. Run hour pm.	Appx K
	3/2/17		Wrote GE IX Corps re shortage of wire entanglement materials. Visited Cork Park BAILLEUL times & contracting workshops. Their own work in joining with a School of Instruction in Horkmanning. MIDLAND FARM FORT OSBORNE ONE SHELL FARM RATION FARM in. LA PLUS DOUVE. Very heavy frost.	Appx K
	4/2/17		Office work. Very hard frost. Lieut CRISWELL joined presently 132 Coy.	Appx K
	5/2/17		Office work. Some snow, temperature up to zero.	Appx K

WAR DIARY
or
INTELLIGENCE SUMMARY.

Army Form C. 2118.
SECRET

(Erase heading not required.)

Instructions regarding War Diaries and Intelligence
Summaries are contained in F. S. Regs., Part II.
and the Staff Manual respectively. Title Pages
will be prepared in manuscript.

Place	Date	Hour	Summary of Events and Information	Remarks and references to Appendices
	6.2.17		Visited OPs, Scheme work OC 122 and Reconn. with OC CTs + TM Emplacements, also reconnnr. a line for tramway through WULVERGHEM to BEKENZIGAK. Hard frost.	manu X
	7.2.17		Office work. Returning reinforcements for new work. Hard frost. Ps.	manu X
	8.2.17		Visited Trench Tramway Supt. Improvements works in progress. Tree as B. Scheme Sh 28 E S.22.a. Hard frost.	manu X
	9.2.17		Returned at Burnwood School at ST MARIE CAPPEL. Remarks for field work opposite the G.	manu X
	10.2.17		Office work.	manu X
	11.2.17		Daylight thaw. Visited NEUVE EGLISE Bns, BULFORD, ALDERSHOT and KORTE PYP Camps.	manu X
	12.2.17		Slight frost during night.	manu X
	13.2.17		Pushed entries of 7 Batts Hosp to OC 121 Coy. R cumming extr. for Reon aln MERIDIAN ROAD from MISSOURI Farm to SURREY Land and Old CT from end of MEDICINE HAT Trench to BOYLES FARM CT with TC 122 DC Md Reproduction Scheme being satisfactory.	manu X

Army Form C. 2118.

WAR DIARY
or
INTELLIGENCE SUMMARY.

(Erase heading not required.)

Place	Date	Hour	Summary of Events and Information	Remarks and references to Appendices
	14.2.17		Office work. Snow during night - Snow during day.	
	15.2.17		Visited work on new Trench line for R.A. near PIGGERIES. Also HEATH new GAS Trench mk - 121 Cry. Snow during day.	
	16.2.17		Thaw. Nothuum importnt.	
	17.2.17		Stayed indoors.	
	18.2.17		Office work. Thawing hard. Capt. SMYTH 180 T Coy accompanied Runners when demonstrating demolition of wire Supp. with ammonal into. Visited MIDLAND Farm Mac BRIDGE Minimum site with OC 122. 9th Fy. day.	
	19.2.17			
	20.2.17		Visited HILL 63 defences with - OC 121 8th Fy CO. Very wet.	
	21.		Indoors.	
	22.		Indoors.	
	23.		Visited CE. IX Corps. Conference with OCs 121 + 180 Cry.	
	24.		Visited work in entrance from 24 W. Ry towards ORCHARDS Strong Winner Sanguine.	

WAR DIARY or **INTELLIGENCE SUMMARY**

Army Form C. 2118.
SECRET
28

Place	Date	Hour	Summary of Events and Information	Remarks and references to Appendices
	25.2.17		Sunday. Visited Buit School ST MARIE CAPPEL and School Army workshops, HAZEBROUCK. The 20 H.P. Browne Fan Engine which was lent by 121 Tunl Coy is running efficient in these workshops.	MM/R
	26.2.17		Visited Tunnel dug outs with OC 171 Coy. Visited Front line on top of Dep Section.	MM/R
	27.2.17		Visited MIDLAND FARM, MEDICINGHAT TSAD, NUGENTS SUPPORT, ONE SHELL proof BENSON CUTTAGES with OC Lemon huns.	MM/R
	28.2.17		Visited the farm bin tracks + the tops of the Right Section and enlarging the Left section also CURRIE Avenue, R communications line for OP3 in MIDLAND Fm.	MM/R

M.G. al C. Knot
Lieut Co RE

CRE 36 Div
CRE.36.16.82.

War Diary

of

C.R.E. 36th Division

for month of March 1917.

SECRET

Army Form C. 2118.

29.

WAR DIARY
or
INTELLIGENCE SUMMARY.
(Erase heading not required.)

Place	Date	Hour	Summary of Events and Information	Remarks and references to Appendices
ST JANS CAPEL	1.3.17		Very fine mo clear day. Visited Subsidiary Emd gun Emery 3, & reconnoitred target MG Emplacements into OE.12.14	
	2.3.17		Visited work on T.M's in Eppleterre, also Bn HQ & Bug HQ dug outs with OC Repair into & view to taking in Cable.	
	3.3.17		Visited Rifle Range who OEO 2, also to harm army Innermp. BAILLEUL. Muddy day. Depart from sunny fine night.	
	4.3.17.		Sunday. Visited L' KENNEBAR and MONMOUTH Camp	
	5.3.17		Visited BUS Farm & DE KENNEBAR with Q. Snowshowing reps— many Interrupted matters during afternoon. Stay for dinner night. Visited Whitchurch Searchlight Corner on DE KENNEBAR with — a view to putting in a Section of 1500 Hy Rs. Lecture to 107 Bde at RED LODGE. Lecture to 108 Bde at KORTEPYP.	
	8.3.17		Visited work on Bn HQ in JPS & markes sites for new mg. own int. to DURHAM Posts	

2353 Wt. W25441/1454 700,000 5/15 B. D. & L. A.D.S.S./Forms/C. 2118

SECRET

Army Form C. 2118.

WAR DIARY
or
INTELLIGENCE SUMMARY.
(Erase heading not required.)

Instructions regarding War Diaries and Intelligence Summaries are contained in F.S. Regs., Part II. and the Staff Manual respectively. Title pages will be prepared in manuscript.

30

Place	Date	Hour	Summary of Events and Information	Remarks and references to Appendices
	9.3.17		Orders received that 11th ANZAC Corps will take over 36th Div area.	
	10.3.17		Visited G.N.Y.2 between DAYLIGHT Corner and LINDENHOEK also KEMMEL before new trenches. Arrange for 2 sections 150 long & 109 bypasses to carry out repair the starting on 11th inst. Orders received from G. that New Zealanders Div. will take over the front held by 36th Div. on the present between 11th & 15th inst. Th 36th Div. to take over the sector of the front between Pt. WULVERGHEM - WYTSCHAETE Road to KETCHEN Av. inclusive. Th 107 Fd. to take over the line & Cummings Bypass at 12 noon 14th inst.	
	11.3.17		Arranges with CRE New Zealanders for liaison Officers & men to proceed to state new Div. work. CRE 36 Cunipers to the bill of work referring following arrangements. Relieving never took place.	
			150 Field Coy R.E. Nidigfrom PETIT MUNQUE to MON MOUTH Camp	
			" 1 " " ALDERSHOT "	
	12.3.17		CRE 16th Divn Comes to take CRE 36th	

2353 Wt. W2544/1454 700,000 5/15 D.D.&L. A.D.S.S./Forms/C. 2118.

SECRET   Army Form C. 2118.

WAR DIARY
or
INTELLIGENCE SUMMARY.
(Erase heading not required.)

31

Place	Date	Hour	Summary of Events and Information	Remarks and references to Appendices
	13.3.17		Following amm dumps places.	
			121 Field Cy. HQr & 2 sections from PETIT PONT to LURGAN Camp.	
			2 " " " to BOIS Fm.	
	14.3.17		Following amm dump places.	
			122 Field Cy. 2 sections NEUVE EGLISE Hutments BULFORD LINDENHOEK	
			2 " " " NEWMARKET Camp.	
			150 Field Cy. 1 section from DEIRENMBEAK to MONMOUTH Camp.	
			1 " " PONT de ST QUENTIN " "	
	15.3.17		Following amm dump places.	
			121 Field Cy. 1 Section from LURGAN Camp to BUS Fm.	
			CRE discusses Defence work with OsC 121 & 122.	
			Hutton Cy on formation moved to NEWMARKET Camp.	

SECRET Army Form C. 2118.

WAR DIARY
or
INTELLIGENCE SUMMARY.
(Erase heading not required.)

32

Place	Date	Hour	Summary of Events and Information	Remarks and references to Appendices
	16.3.17		CRE returned to his office.	
	17.3.17		Visited site for M.G. Emplts on Lock Lm & B Lm.	
	18.3.17		Visited PALL MALL SP 8 & 9 & Vag. b with Brig. over 107.	
			Visited Camp but HQ with Q. Major BOYCE, 110 Coy, returning from leave.	
	19.3.17		Visited MONMOUTH Camp, freeing trench LINDENHOEK/Borders.	
			N.G.HQ 2. M.	
	20.3.17		Visited tunnel dug outs in KEMMEL Hill. Snow storm for time during early morning.	
	21.3.17		Visited with OC Pioneers this by Major, RESERVE Trench, KERR ST and KELLY Trench, & communication trenches for trench relay Posts running South from LACACHE Farm.	
	22.3.17		Visited Regtl area with OC 121 & 122 concerning Siting of M.G. Empts etc. Snow fell heavily at intervals with bright thirsty sunshine.	
	23.3.17		Visited with OC Engr Section with OC 122. Visited whips for B 2. HQ.	

WAR DIARY
or
INTELLIGENCE SUMMARY

Army Form C. 2118.
SECRET
33

Place	Date	Hour	Summary of Events and Information	Remarks and references to Appendices
	24.3		Office work	month/R
	25.3		Visited Sector between LINDEN HOEK and HANEBEETS Farm.	month/R
	26.3		Raining. Office work	month/R
	27.3		Snow fell during morning, cleared in the afternoon. Office work	month/R
	28.3		Visited work on ~~G.H.Q~~ trenches 108. Fort Victoria & M.G. emps. SPY Farm. Inspected wire between ROMMEL and LINDENHOEK with an Officer of the Division into a view to securing same.	month/R
	29.3.17		Visited work in rear of front line with G.O.C.'s Reserve Arm.	month/R
	30.3.17		Reconnoitred Coln Gp 2 bayonets HQ RSK OL 175 Tunnelling Coy who have fitted a tramway. The following Infantry working parties have been supplied to the Cheese Cop Tunnels: 121 Middlesex 115 122 " " 135 152 " " 215 men. · 45 Foot-Intermediate Sec.	month/R

Army Form C. 2118.

SECRET 34

WAR DIARY
or
INTELLIGENCE SUMMARY.

(Erase heading not required.)

Instructions regarding War Diaries and Intelligence Summaries are contained in F. S. Regs., Part II. and the Staff Manual respectively. Title pages will be prepared in manuscript.

Place	Date	Hour	Summary of Events and Information	Remarks and references to Appendices
	31.3.19		Various work in A/B lines also GOWER ST.	Run Home Lont
				Maint Arms Erectonics CRE 36th Div

Vol 19

War Diary

of

C.R.E. 36th Division

1st April 1917 to 30th April 1917

Army Form C. 2118.

WAR DIARY
or
INTELLIGENCE SUMMARY.
(Erase heading not required.)

35

Place	Date	Hour	Summary of Events and Information	Remarks and references to Appendices
ST JANS CAPPEL	1.4.17		Held conference with OC 121 & 122 & 2 Lt LINDEN HOEK and discussed proposals for work. Visited CE IX Corps. Rain & heavy snow worked.	
	2.3.17		Visited sites for 3 batteries with Staff Officer RA & discussed arrangements for screening. Snowfall during afternoon. Rain during morning.	
	3.4.17		Heavy snowfall during forenoon, heavy lines & snow during morning. Night work stopped owing to weather. Visited RE Park STEELE. Fine afternoon.	
	7.4.17		Visited KEMMEL with G & OC 171. Visited work in hyper section up to Regents dugouts. OC 175 started 2 tunnel dug outs, J 12.18.9	
	5.5.17 10.20pm		Near aerodrome near cafe. Recruits a hair for a French Tunneller from KINGSWAY to Dy section	

Army Form C. 2118.

36

WAR DIARY
or
INTELLIGENCE SUMMARY.
(Erase heading not required.)

Place	Date	Hour	Summary of Events and Information	Remarks and references to Appendices
	5.4.17		with OC 121 Coy.	
	6.4.17		Mng to relief of troops in the line, all infantry parties cancelled till anyng of 8th when 1 Battalion will be available, am morng of 10th when two battalions will be available, natives arrival of 36 porahun. Visited Supp. Section into CE IX Corps.	
	7.4.17		Visited Special Works Park RE at AIRE. have reported for young officer attending as scheme on Hygiene. Visited bivouacs in vicinity of REMMEL with officer from Belgian Mission with a view to taking tracings from the ruins of same. Visited Commander of Pioneers 180 12 & 122 Divs. Very fine day.	
	8.4.17			
	9.4.17		Inspection lines of QUEENS GATE to Pte Gravenstafel. The in over CT. practically a stream. Clear hot day. V.S. 107th at STANLY PARK MESS. Inspected work on tunnel dug outs for Bdy HQ Hasher Mews Dunes H.Q. Camps.	

2353 Wt. W2544/1454 700,000 5/15 D. D. & L. A.D.S.S./Forms/C. 2118.

WAR DIARY
or
INTELLIGENCE SUMMARY.

Army Form C. 2118.

37

Place	Date	Hour	Summary of Events and Information	Remarks and references to Appendices
	10.4.17		Visited Sec & Div'l H.q. with OC 16 Cay & OC 175 Tunnellers Coy. Visited work in tunnel by 150 Coy with O.p.	man/R
	11.4.17		Visited work with Brigadier 109 Brigade. Snow.	man/R
	12.4.17		Visited CE IX Corps. All superving parties crew work on 2pm 14th and no more available. Visited 20½ mm/g the mes'y servicing infantry with work. Brigadier 109th to assisting 4 platoon present	man/R
	13.4.17		Visited work by Brunen with OC 16 RIRP.	man/R
	14.4.17		Office work	man/R
	15.4.17		Visited work in OP's in KEMMIS with OC 150. Rain.	man/R man/R
	16.4.17		Visited work in ayfter Luton with OC 121 Coy. worked in tunnels improving with work.	
	17.4.17		Infantry worked supplies with Q.	
	18.4.17		Snow fell during night. Visited LINDENHOEK 13, some disorders. Scenery of work from ment to KEMMEL with Scenery Officer 16th Corp.	man/R

Army Form C. 2118.

38

WAR DIARY
or
INTELLIGENCE SUMMARY.
(Erase heading not required.)

Place	Date	Hour	Summary of Events and Information	Remarks and references to Appendices
	19.4.17		Visited Second Army Workshops Hazebrouck & CROIX Rouge where information for training is being collected.	mm/A
	20.4.17		Heavy artillery firing all day, wrote informing men we stopped in an active situation we expected, whenever his not moving. Visited OE121 Pbg & 16 R.I.R.R. Inspected new HQ Camp Kemmel new	mm/A
	21.4.17		Visited work on HQ tumble-wagons & C.T.s Div area.	
	22.4.17		Visited the advance group Commanders Augmts into 6 V& RA	mm/A
	23.4.17		Visited QUEENS GATE CT now battling near Regent Street into. Kemmel day. Inspected 130 the lorry for BOULOGNE.	mm/A
	24.4.17		Visited Second Army Workshops BAILLEUL, Capes River STEENWERCK and LA CLYTTE in men to obtain French transp. Visited LINDENHOEK	mm/A
	25.4.17		Visited site for Camps near BRANDHOEK with Q. Infantry working platoons had a day off for improving own	mm/A
	26.4.17		Visited work on REDAN AV, GEORGE ST VIGO ST, auth- Corps GOOCH acting OE121 Div area	mm/R

WAR DIARY
or
INTELLIGENCE SUMMARY.
(Erase heading not required.)

Army Form C. 2118.

39

Place	Date	Hour	Summary of Events and Information	Remarks and references to Appendices
	27.4.17		Visited BOARDMAN TRENCH, QUEENS GATE, SHEPPERDS LANE and RESERVE LINE.	map/X
	28.4.17		Visited work in own sector. Kemmel Hill, Queens Gate, & Buttalean Hy Regiments - Engnrs. This day.	map/X
	29.4.17		Sunday. Attended demonstration with District Hydraulic Jack forcing pipes, below a change of command. 50ft 2in or 3 h.p. pump, moved a trench 20ft wide & 8 feet deep. Inspected trenches of 150 & 164 Regt.	map/X
	30.4.17		Inspected work in tramway between LINDENHOEK and KEMMEL. Also work in QUEENSGATE area. Battalion HQ at VROULANDHOEK. Attended inspection of 122 D.Inf. Transport. Very fine day.	map/X

N. C. Ayrton Kaw ?/??
Capt 354 Siege

Confidential

Vol 20

War Diary

of

C.R.E. 36 Division

for month of May 1917.

WAR DIARY or INTELLIGENCE SUMMARY

Army Form C. 2118.

40.

Place	Date	Hour	Summary of Events and Information	Remarks and references to Appendices
ST JANS CAPEL	1.5.17		Very fine day. Visited being ammy workshops HAZEBROUCK and others. 2 Tm Cons pr Orders Pommery, and Spare pumps. M.G. mornings. Visited LINDENHOEK Dumps. Inspected Transport and animals of 121 Siege Bty. R.A. LT WEDGWOOD proceeded on Kindness leave to Inspection. Capt. McILDOWIE 122 Bty acting Adjt.	Apps/K
	2.5.17		Visited work on C.T.s GEORGE ST. VIGO ST with Capt GOUGH 121? Bty. Major LEWIN OC 121 Bty. returned from leave.	Apps/K
	3.5.17		Visited work on QUEENS GATE C.T. with OC 122 + arranged for carrying up Trenches - REGENT ST Dugouts. Leicester Sq. with Sapps for R.A.P. very hot day.	Apps/K
	4.5.17		Visited HQ Camp near BRANOUTRE and later Made Supply points. Gave a wiring demonstration to 10 Sappers at METEREN.	Apps/K
	5.5.17		Inspected site for Reserves in STUIVERBERK, with OC 121 Bty RA. Very hot day.	App/K
	6.5.17.		Sunday. Inspected site for Inftry Camp with Q. Visited HQ Camp. Visited 10,11,12 Shafts Boileau with OC 122 & hope agreement as to sites for new H Construction. On implementing with an infantry Regiments.	Mods/K

Army Form C. 2118.

41

WAR DIARY
or
INTELLIGENCE SUMMARY.
(Erase heading not required.)

Place	Date	Hour	Summary of Events and Information	Remarks and references to Appendices
	7.5.17		Visited work on CTS & Trench Tramway wrk 0 & 121 Tloy in Right Sector Hampshire	man/R
	8.5.17		Visited work on GEORGE ST & KINGS WAY wrk O, C, 16. R.I.R.R. Attended Conference at IX Corps HQ at 3.30pm. Some rain fell last night.	man X
	9.6.17		Visited work in Right Sector wrk OC, 12 OC, 13 & arrangements for stores & reserves	man/R
	10.5.17		Inspected water supplies in area near BRANDHOEK very hot day	man/R
	11.5.17		Visited LINDENHOEK, work on new track thoroughly started in the evening. Very hot day	man/R
	12.5.17		Visited LINDENHOEK where received orders. Arrangements for up of ammunition for front. T.M. Bombs & Grenades with shortly to tear up by rail to LINDENHOEK. 122 Tloy accurately started labour carrying these Tramway on Motor Maps from LINDENHOEK to DAYLIGHT Corner, & move from proper, the work	man/R

WAR DIARY
INTELLIGENCE SUMMARY

Army Form C. 2118.
42

Place	Date	Hour	Summary of Events and Information	Remarks and references to Appendices
ST JANS CAPPEL	12.5.17		Gangs put eventually the amended work — 60 Cm trucks by shifting on rail.	Man/R
	13.5.17		Visited work on tramway between SUICIDE CORNER (KEMMEL) and DAYLIGHT CORNER. Reconnoitred for a line of Comm up into Eyp.-Railway in KEMMEL. Front-Shown from new camp.	Man/R
	14.5.17		Visited work on SHEPPERD'S LANE & QUEENSGATE. Went into P.A.L & 16 R1 RP and arranged new work to be started.	Man/R
	15.5.17		H.Q. of 36th Division moved from ST JANS CAPPEL to new camp at M.3.5.C. just West of DRANOUTRE. (ULSTER CAMP) Visited work in Rgr. Sector whn. acting O.E. 121 Coy. Major LEWIN O.C. 121 Coy damaged his knee & proceeded on leave for 10 days. Ram Fille	Man/R
DRANOUTRE	16.6.17		Conference of Divisional C Rs at Div H.Q. Visited C.E. 1 x Corps, prinned a/or & Harrison for back Seaside craters. Rain fell during day. Scotia.	Man/R
ULSTER CAMP.				

WAR DIARY
or
INTELLIGENCE SUMMARY.
(Erase heading not required.)

Army Form C. 2118.

43.

Instructions regarding War Diaries and Intelligence Summaries are contained in F. S. Regs., Part II. and the Staff Manual respectively. Title pages will be prepared in manuscript.

Place	Date	Hour	Summary of Events and Information	Remarks and references to Appendices
	17.5.17		Heavy rain fell during morning. Various water supply arrangements in back area.	front.
	18.5.17		Various work on Tramways in Sept & Reg sections. Arranged tentative work on to Dyptouk supplemen - accommodation Reps - forges etc as tramulu augments in view of construction and pulling in of into rail points to formed supplies.	front.
	19.5.17		Finished m-sim for a "paper" from KEMMEL supply near VROILAND KRUISIK to be found on M WULVERGHEM WYTCHAETE Road near R.E. Dump. Rd -- OC 167 A.T.Coy. Inspected work on dugouts at REGENTST sy mtr. Various [illegible] of WYTCHAETE between nth-OC Free Coy & explained plan of attack.	front
	20.5.17		Had a conference wir Coy Officers to discuss consolidation. Attended a conference of CRES w - CRS P.W. at Sevren tramwarys. I am desirous to relay our main tramway 9b track in each case drivers, G.Penn & Cony. are only 96 track to post portal traction come him in it. concern of Pioneers from 11th Bn to work on it.	front

Army Form C. 2118.

44

WAR DIARY
or
INTELLIGENCE SUMMARY.

(Erase heading not required.)

Instructions regarding War Diaries and Intelligence Summaries are contained in F. S. Regs., Part II. and the Staff Manual respectively. Title pages will be prepared in manuscript.

Place	Date	Hour	Summary of Events and Information	Remarks and references to Appendices
	21.		Inspected work in forward area with OC 150 Flu RE. Area letup for Coy of 114 Fw Pioneers.	Appx/R
	22.		Inspected work on tramline between DAYLIGHT CORNER and LINDENHOEK. Purchased 4500 sft run of 3"x 3" run at AIRE. Rainfall during night. 11th Sw Pioneer Started work on tramway.	Appx/R
	23.		Inspected site of Assembly Trenches in Ry. nr Sector. Visited KEMMEL Chateau Grounds to see proposed route by Lyn Railways for Connection which sent team to can line at LINDENHOEK.	
	24.		Visited LINDENHOEK area arranged for 1 Coy of Pioneers to work on bridging trenches for guns. Visited O. C. SPANBROEK Group R.A.	
	25.		As Tunnelled dug outs for Bgd-Hqs have always been completed, arranged work on 2 September with Pioneer Companies by 2 Batteries of 16 R.I.R. Improved dug outs which Pioneers of 16 R.I.R. to Started work immediately.	

Army Form C. 2118.

WAR DIARY
or
INTELLIGENCE SUMMARY.
(Erase heading not required.)

45.

Instructions regarding War Diaries and Intelligence Summaries are contained in F. S. Regs., Part II. and the Staff Manual respectively. Title pages will be prepared in manuscript.

Place	Date	Hour	Summary of Events and Information	Remarks and references to Appendices
	26.5.17		Visited work on KINGSWAY LINE. Inspected completed trenches in pillars. KINGSWAY, STRAND, VIGO ST, GEORGE ST.	mult.
	27/5/17		Lt Colonel King killed by shell fire during night of 27/28.	VB
	28/5/17		Major A CAMPBELL posted to duty as CRE vice 9.30 p.m. Lt Colonel King. Visited at team H.Q.	VB
	29.5.17		Rtn to advanced H.Q. 121 + 122 Tn Cos. Pioneer Bn were engaged in digging Reo subways pioneer dump.	VB
	30/5/17		Visited work with OC 122 Tn Co. Visited 121 + 150 Tolls Pioneer Bn. Rearranged details of work of RE. etc.	VB
	31/5/17		Visited work with 121 Tn Co. decided site of work and what is started. Visited 121 Tn C. H.Q. Tr 16 DLI HQ.	

Alan Shellmere
CRE 36 Divn.

Vol 21

Confidential

War Diary

of

C.R.E., 36th Division

June 1917.

WAR DIARY
or
INTELLIGENCE SUMMARY.
(Erase heading not required.)

Army Form C. 2118.

Place	Date	Hour	Summary of Events and Information	Remarks and references to Appendices
	1/6/17		Verified that the Huns left in MKindi Nov at 12n & returned from their raid whilst our Albinos received me marching. New 121 & 150 meaning that raid whilst	
	2/6/17		Touring Albinos in the C.C. Conference with O.C. Pioneers & W.O.C.V. in who Pioneers are sending this all Op up	
	3/6/17		Inspected line trouble much took to lift Hyde road creek he ordered to three harbours up	
	4/6/17		debited keep right Hyde. New Pioneers and OCs up	
	5/6/17		To OCs office & interviewed. Renwick & seer CB	
	6/6/17		To investigate about it LAGMORE FARM new OCs of Cabango & 129 BN didn't Barnes, Cain & Thorne inner till me 23 BNs evacuated Cain & Thorne at duty CB	
	7/6/17		Albinos attacked at 9.10 A.M. Two conferences in C.C. BN's started Nil at 9 A.M. to be carried out successfully and not always accept to final attempts there not with to be started till much more engineering work be. After at night very successful night ink. Wiring & road, all ranks IC worth tack 20 attempt on OPs huts most violent. tr left job returned OP. to be attacked at night doing much effective & damage. OC of road. Pioneers on rail	
	8/6/17			

WAR DIARY
or
INTELLIGENCE SUMMARY.
(Erase heading not required.)

Army Form C. 2118.

Place	Date	Hour	Summary of Events and Information	Remarks and references to Appendices
VLAMERTINGHE	9/6/17		Circulated A Co. at Dranoutre re when by H.Q. Pioneers at the with (2 O.C.) Attack Pioneers. Who noted over to G.A. the a/vehs. Saw O.C. Pioneers & arranged detail with G.A. Co. Pros. by phone.	
ST JANS CAPPEL	10/6/17		Removed H.Q. to ST JANS CAPPEL. Co. training.	
	11/6/17		Saw B.S.M. & O.R.S. at drill, inspected horses & S.A.A. & S.Q.	
	12/6/17		Saw O.C. IX Corps inspected horses of B.L.	
	13/6/17		that found BLACK LINE and O.C. of B.L. was confining section & decided edge of King Point.	
	14/6/17		Saw O.R.S. 16th re huneter on BLACK LINE revision of BLACK LINE a left flank. & agreed re strms of	
	15/6/17		Inspected BLACK LINE Pioneers saw trench & noticed by adv. and ted state of ground.	
	16/6/17		Inlie.	
	17/6/17		that to BLACK LINE. Trench men with Chief of Saw O.R.s 11 & 19 C.O.	
	18/6/17		that in A Trench LINE with Chief of Saw O.R.s 11 & 19 C.O.	

Army Form C. 2118.

WAR DIARY
or
INTELLIGENCE SUMMARY.
(Erase heading not required.)

Instructions regarding War Diaries and Intelligence Summaries are contained in F. S. Regs., Part II. and the Staff Manual respectively. Title pages will be prepared in manuscript.

Place	Date	Hour	Summary of Events and Information	Remarks and references to Appendices
ST JANS CAPEL	19/6/17		New CRS. 11th & 19th Div. Saw OC Fields & Bearers re details of relief into the line.	
ULSTER CAMP	20/6/17		To Thanvey Corners Cuts MD 10mm. Arrived ULSTER CAMP Noon.	
	21/6/17		Went round bank of MAUVE LINE XCTS a 0.20 21 26 & 27 Sheet 28.B. started at 2.50mm. Rdz Met OC/161FAB. Sheet 28.S.E. 9mm. Saw OC/161FAB	
	22/6/17		Visited Bn MAD Posts. Underground Tunnels.	
	23/6/17		Visited MAUVE LINE N & OC 160. Left cars 3.30am. Scattered shelling of forward area interfered with work. Saw rested B 15 & 25 Sept 28.	
	24/6/17		Visited 120 & 40 es KNOLL. Wimfgoo and CRS Posts at MESSINES — WYTSCHAETE RIDGE.	
	25/6/17		Inspected Reserve line (late MAUVE) out at Dr. Grd at 5mm. Very Inspected Lock. Ruffy/Baer arranged attack of relief out.	
	26/6/17		To Corps HQ at Noon. OC Corps 37=D=	
	27/6/17		Inst & inst. Relieve line with CRS 97th Dr. Went to Corps HQ. Onedunkit Ridge of Battens. Started 5mm. Very Quiet	

Army Form C. 2118.

WAR DIARY
or
INTELLIGENCE SUMMARY.

(Erase heading not required.)

Place	Date	Hour	Summary of Events and Information	Remarks and references to Appendices
ULSTER CAMP	28/6/17		New BQ F.Co. Co solved damaged horses for a night 275- 20th and several other hit card not reverse them	
	29/6/17		To VII Corps HQ to arrange unit of this & horses vans & arranged rects sorted supply horses. CRS FWATOU	
KATOU	30/6/17		Co. F.Mereo handed to MCLENNING H.S.	

Densfell
Lt Cols
CRS 36th D
3/8/17

— Secret —   Copy No. 74

C.R.E. 36th Division Operation Order No. 21.   28/6/17.

Reference 1/100,000 Sheet H A Z E B R O U C K, 5a.

1. 121st, 122nd, and 150th Field Companies, R.E., and 16th R.I.R. (Pioneers) will move by road from IX Corps area to XIX Corps area, in accordance with attached march table.

2. Starting Point — LA CLYTTE Cross Roads.

3. Head of column will pass starting point at 5 a.m., 30/6/17.

4. Order of march:-

    16th R.I.R. (Pioneers) less 2 Companies
    121st Field Company, R.E.
    122nd Field Company, R.E.
    150th Field Company, R.E.
    2 Companies 16th R.I.R. (Pioneers).

5. Marches on 1st and 2nd July, 1917 will be under orders of senior officer present. Conditions as laid down in paras. 6, 7, 8, and 9 to be complied with.

6. All moves must be completed by 10 a.m. each day.

7. Distances of 500 yards to be maintained between units.

8. A mounted officer will precede the column to warn control posts of its approach.

9. Second Line transport will accompany units.

10. Usual halts of 10 minutes before clock hour to clock hour to be given.

11. Reports to head of column which will be under command of Lt. Colonel C.F. Meares, Commanding 16th R.I.R. (Pioneers).

12. O.C. 16th R.I.R. will detail a representative to report to O.C. XIX Corps Troops Supply Column, 29 GRAND PLACE, POPERINGHE on arrival. The duties of this representative will be to accompany a lorry delivering rations at WINNEZEELE and WATOU.

13. ACKNOWLEDGE.

A. Campbell

Lt. Colonel, R.E.
C.R.E. 36th Division.

Copy No 1. to 121st Fd. Co. R.E.
      2. to 122nd "
      3. to 150th "
      4. to 16th R.I.R. (P).
      5. 36th Division "G"
      6. 36th Division "Q"
      7. XIX Corps "G"
      8. C.E. XIX Corps.
      9. C.E. IX Corps.
    10. Town Major POPERINGHE
    11. O.C. 36th Div. Train
    12. A.D.M.S. 36th Divn.
    13. A.D.V.S. 36th Div.

Copy No 14 D.A.D.O.S. 36th Div.
      15 A.P.M. 36th Divn.
      16 A.P.M. 19th Corps.
      17 Claims Officer 36th Div.
      18 Area Commdt. WATOU.
      19 XIX Corps Reinforc. Camp.
      20 Sub. Area Cmdt. No. 1.
      21.   "   No. 3.
      22.   "   No. 5.
      23.   "   No. 9.
      24. WAR DIARY.
      25. FILE.

MARCH TABLE.   To accompany C.R.E. 36th Division Operation Order No 21.

Serial No.	Date	Unit	From	To	Route	Remarks
1.	June 30th	16th R.I.R. (P) (less 2 Coys.) 121st Field Co.R.E.	KEMMEL Area	WATOU	RENINGHELST - POPERINGHE - ST.JAN-TER-BIEZEN.	(a) Not to enter RENINGHELST before 5 a.m. (b) Site of Camp and Tents will be obtained from Area Comdt. WATOU. (c) H.Qrs. to be located at Camp
2.	June 30th	122nd Field Co.R.E. 150th Field Co.R.E. 2 Cos. 16th R.I.R. (Pioneers)	KEMMEL Area	POPERINGHE	Via RENINGHELST	Billets from Town Major POPERINGHE.
3.	July 1st	122nd Field Co.R.E. 1 Co. 16th R.I.R. (Pioneers)	POPERINGHE	WINNEZEELE	ST.JAN-TER-BIEZEN - WATOU.	Tents will be delivered to unit at WINNEZEELE.
4.	July 1st.	150th Field Co.R.E. 1 Co. 16th R.I.R. (Pioneers)	POPERINGHE	WORMHOUDT	ST.JAN-TER-BIEZEN - HOUTKERQUE.	Billets from Area Commandant.
5.	July 2nd.	150th Field Co.R.E. 1 Co. 16th R.I.R. (Pioneers)	WORMHOUDT	LEDERCKEGHEM	ZEGGERS CAPPEL - BOLLEZEELE.	Billets from XIX Corps Reinforcement Camp.

Vol 22

Confidential

War Diary
of
C.R.E. 36 Division

For month of July 1917

Army Form C. 2118.

WAR DIARY
or
INTELLIGENCE SUMMARY.
(Erase heading not required.)

Place	Date	Hour	Summary of Events and Information	Remarks and references to Appendices
WATOU	17/7/17		*[handwritten entries illegible]*	

Instructions regarding War Diaries and Intelligence Summaries are contained in F. S. Regs., Part II. and the Staff Manual respectively. Title pages will be prepared in manuscript.

WAR DIARY
or
INTELLIGENCE SUMMARY.
(Erase heading not required.)

Army Form C. 2118.

Place	Date	Hour	Summary of Events and Information	Remarks and references to Appendices
WATOU		6/7/17	Abandoned [illegible] well at WATOU. Temporarily abandoned [illegible] wells at WINNEZEELE. [illegible] successful well at WINNEZEELE down 17 feet. AS	
	7/7/17		Inspected wells at WATOU & WINNEZEELE. [illegible] better at [illegible] block. AS	
	8/7/17		Inspected well at MEKKEGHEM. [illegible] [illegible] SAND and [illegible] [illegible] [illegible] at 8 feet. Saw CE XIX Corps [illegible] [illegible] of [illegible] [illegible]. AS	
	9/7/17		[illegible] well at MEKKEGHEM. [illegible] well [illegible] [illegible] at 9–10 feet [illegible] flowing well. [illegible] Inspected wells at WATOU [illegible] afternoon. AS	
	10/7/17		Inspected wells WINNEZEELE.	
	11/7/17		To MEKKEGHEM. [illegible] [illegible] [illegible] H.Q. at WIZERNES. AS	
	12/7/17		Inspected wells WATOU & WINNEZEELE. AS	
	13/7/17		Inspected well at MEKKEGHEM. [illegible] details of [illegible] of 150th [illegible] [illegible] [illegible] [illegible]. AS	

Army Form C. 2118.

WAR DIARY
or
INTELLIGENCE SUMMARY.
(Erase heading not required.)

Place	Date	Hour	Summary of Events and Information	Remarks and references to Appendices

WA 203

Confidential

War Diary

of

6 R.E. 36th Division

for month of August 1917.

Army Form C. 2118.

WAR DIARY
or
INTELLIGENCE SUMMARY.
(Erase heading not required.)

Instructions regarding War Diaries and Intelligence Summaries are contained in F.S. Regs. Part II. and the Staff Manual respectively. Title pages will be prepared in manuscript.

Place	Date	Hour	Summary of Events and Information	Remarks and references to Appendices
POPERINGHE	1/8/17		Companies concentrated at L16A. Pioneers working to Cab. front of grand EAST of YPRES with OC's 121 & 122. Got up as far as high grand between ST JEAN & POTIJZE but no sign of rain open up the miles. Enfilised topography from t OC's of Companies. Heavy rain in night of 31/7st & all took very heavy.	
	2/8/17		Shore and companies took to see line and dumps. Very wet seemed light had still further deteriorated. Ground frozen all day then of interest. New CCS 55th on dumps and road indent. River no 24 in charge of Co.	
	3/8/17		Adjt to la CCS 55th & divisional RE dump in morning. Low cy Dir Col in afternoon to inspect. Probably 2nd rain Field. Rain at night & all returned to lay.	
MERCY CAMP	4/8/17		Companies marched in afternoon relieving Co of 55th Divisional RE and to MERCY CAMP. Engineers to YPRES POTIJZE Road. Engineers rees dear end of road. Coming in Rue DIXMUDE YPRES. Weather slightly better but heavy showers afternoon all	
	5/8/17		through Col at 5 am. Much rig toorchbed during days Co all Mrs MS-TMS. Miserable day.	

Army Form C. 2118

WAR DIARY
or
INTELLIGENCE SUMMARY
(Erase heading not required.)

Instructions regarding War Diaries and Intelligence Summaries are contained in F. S. Regs., Part II. and the Staff Manual respectively. Title Pages will be prepared in manuscript.

Place	Date	Hour	Summary of Events and Information	Remarks and references to Appendices
Morslede Camp.	6/8/17		Inspected front RS Stys & Eff. Three lorries of 121 x 150. Letter over Bgos and accommodation of Eff. and Lorries of hi. Light lorries arrived also to institute of wounded horses.	
	7/8/17		To MIKETTE. Lao QQ 121 x150. 100 killed & 1000 wounded Visited Lorries in afternoon.	
	8/8/17		Sec. O & XX Cops SC. Inspection dank evacuated train at Ypres (new)	
	9.8.17		Hosted Oct 121 x150. Went & made an enoccial anglt of 9, 10.	
	10/8/17		Inspected horse line & motors	
	11/8/17		Conference of Sub Commders at Q. Horses. QO 121 x150 to and QC 121 x150	
	12/8/17		Visited Field Co. Went away night of 11/12 and all inspected horses evening & evening Qand RSA 17 around in Pop.	

WAR DIARY
or
INTELLIGENCE SUMMARY

Army Form C. 2118

Place	Date	Hour	Summary of Events and Information	Remarks and references to Appendices
MORLEY CAMP	13/8/17		Inspected H.Q. Hicks &c. CANAL & Coteaux N WIELTJE. Relieved O.C. 150th S.C. & inspected work nr H.Q. Instructed.	
	14/8/17		Inspected part of Nos 4, 5, 6 Sucks. Progress well but much hampered by enemy & so soft that very little can be held under than in trenches.	
	15/8/17		14th Cas. Det. H.Q. to CROTON & CAPTAIN TRENCHES. M.O. H.Q.s WIELTJE DUGOUTS.	
	16/8/17		Attack made on LANGEMARCK – GHELUVELT LINE. Field H.Q. short put. 2 Lt THORNE & Cdr Killed. Lieut BROMYATE wounded.	
	17/8/17		Visited Companies working after 16/8.	
WINNEZEELE	18/8/17		Companies relieved in morning and marched thro' Brigade Trenches to WINNEZEELE area. March Rep to WINNEZEELE.	
	19/8/17		Visited 101. F.Co. Companies resting.	
	20/8/17		Visited 122 & 150. Companies drilling, reloading equipment etc.	

WAR DIARY
or
INTELLIGENCE SUMMARY

(Erase heading not required.)

Army Form C. 2118

Instructions regarding War Diaries and Intelligence Summaries are contained in F. S. Regs., Part II. and the Staff Manual respectively. Title Pages will be prepared in manuscript.

Place	Date	Hour	Summary of Events and Information	Remarks and references to Appendices
WIMEREUX	21/8/17		Visited 101 F.A.D. Also dismounted men in close rest billet. Relieving & clearing wagons. JB	
	22/8/17		Conference setting. Visited 150th F.A. & inspected lines. Received information that horses would not be seen down at present. JB	
	23/8/17		Army HQ to BARASTRE. Conference interrupted by rail during in town early in 24/8. Self & ADVS. JB	
BARASTRE	24/8/17		Sr. CRE gun. Arranged to lend him 25th & ph. officer of 2/Co & to attend to Force there. Send him 2 chargers. JB	
	25/8/17		Inspected right sector with CRE. Gave new truck sheets y all gate. JB	
	26/8/17		Inspected centre sector with OC 64th FAB. JB	
	27/8/17		Inspected left sector with officer of 70th FAmb. Ways Rain. Run to Arras. JB	
	28/8/17		Visited HQZ, EQUANCOURT, NEUVILLE and RUYAULCOURT in connection with vetted sample. Rain all round complete. JB	

WAR DIARY
or
INTELLIGENCE SUMMARY.

Army Form C. 2118.

Place	Date	Hour	Summary of Events and Information	Remarks and references to Appendices
BRIEFTES	1/8/17		To Capt H.Q. then R BECKINGHAM. Saw OC 150th Infantry Bde	
	2/8/17		Left AD. + Only party to RECONNOITRE the site for further Devonport Bde site for screen ships works etc reserves in platoons	
YPRES	3/8/17		moved HQ to YPRES. There 101 stabs at MDS. Selected site on right of right Inf Bde tent will tent with G.O.C. of relief site for them.	

M. Marshall Devos
Col 3rd SA
3/8/17

SECRET.   Copy No...16

C.R.E. 36th DIVISION OPERATION ORDER NO 24.

2/8/17.

Reference BELGIUM Sheet 28 N.W. 1/20,000

1. Field Companies R.E. of 36th Division will relieve Field Companies R.E. of 55th Division on 4th inst. Moves as on attached march table.

2. "Orders for Movement of Troops in XIX Corps Area", which have been issued to all concerned, will be strictly adhered to.

3. Accommodation for attached Infantry (who will accompany dismounted portion of Company) exists at forward billets allotted.

4. Rear Headquarters of all Companies will be established at Divisional R.E. Dump (H.8.a.5.9), 10 % of dismounted personnel of each Field Company will be left at this point on march forward to form personnel of yard. The extra R.E. Officer of 121st and 150th Field Companies will also be left at this point. Accommodation for officers and men is available.

5. Each Company will send forward an advanced party of 1 Officer and 4 O.R. to take over billets. 1 Officer and 2 O.R. to go to Forward billets, 2 O.R. to horse lines. In addition, 121st and 150th Field Companies will send forward personnel to take over dumps as follows:-

    121st Field Company, R.E.
         1 N.C.O. and 2 Sappers for POTIJZE DUMP.

    150th Field Company, R.E.
         1 N.C.O. and 6 Sappers for ST. JEAN DUMPS.

    These parties to leave camp at 8 a.m.

6. Tools for work are available at forward billets, and will be taken over from Companies relieved. Tool carts will be left at horse lines. Only carts limbered G.S. to be taken to forward billets. These will be offloaded and returned to horse lines.

7. Guides from 55th Division will meet Companies at GOLDFISH CHATEAU (H.11.a.85.05) at 4 p.m. on 4th inst.

8/

(2)

8. M.O. i/c R.E. will remain at Divisional R.E. Dump (H.8.a.5.9).

9. Completion of move to be reported by wire.

10. ACKNOWLEDGE.

                                    Lt. Colonel, R.E.
                                    C.R.E. 36th Division.

Copy No 1. 121st Field Company, R.E.
       2. 122nd   "
       3. 150th   "
       4. M.O. i/c R.E.
       5. 36th Division "G"
       6. 36th Division "Q"
       7. 36th Divisional Signal Co.
       8. C.R.E. 55th Division.
       9. C.E. XIX Corps.
     10. A.P.M. 36th Division.
     11. D.A.D.O.S. 36th Divn.
     12. A.D.M.S. 36th Divn.
     13. D.A.D.V.S. 36th Divn.
     14. O.C. 36th Divl. Train.
     15. Claims Officer 36th Divn.
     16. WAR DIARY.
     17. FILE.

MARCH TABLE TO ACCOMPANY O.O. NO 24.
(Reference BELGIUM Sheet 28) 727

Date	Unit	From	To	Remarks.
4/8/17.	121st Field Coy. R.E.			
	Dismounted	L.16.a.	RUE DIXMUDE, YPRES (I.8.a.4.7) H.2.c.0.8	To march at 12 noon.; Relieves 422nd Fd.Co. R.E.
	Mounted	L.16.a.		
-do-	122nd Field Coy. R.E.			
	Dismounted	L.16.a.	I.3.c.4.3.	To march at 12.30. p.m. Relieves 423 Fd. Co. R.E.
	Mounted	L.16.a.	H.2.c.0.8.	
-do-	150th Field Coy. R.E.			
	Dismounted	L.16.a.	I.1.b.8.1.	To march at 1 p.m. Relieves 419th Fd. Co. R.E.
	Mounted	L.16.a.	H.1.c.4.3.	

S E C R E T.   Copy No... 11

C.R.E. 36th DIVISION OPERATION ORDER NO 25.

Reference BELGIUM Sheet 28 N.W. 1/20,000.

16/8/17.

1. The 61st Division will relieve the 36th Division in the line between the 17th and 19th instant.

2. The Field Companies R.E. of the 36th Division will be relieved by the Field Companies of the 61st Division on the 18th instant, as follows:-

    121st Field Co. R.E. by 479th Field Co. R.E.
    122nd Field Co. R.E. by 476th Field Co. R.E.
    150th Field Co. R.E. by 478th Field Co. R.E.

3. Advance parties from each Field Company of 61st Division are reporting to the forward billets at 2 p.m. on 17th inst. O.Cs. Field Companies will hand over to the O. i/c each party all work now in hands, trench maps, and all maps dealing with work in this area.

4. The incoming Field Companies will take over all billets, wagon lines, Trench and Area stores (including motor bicycles) as laid down in Fifth Army General Circular Memorandum No 1 page 21 (A.R.O. 328) dated 1/1/17. A receipt will be obtained for the bicycles and forwarded to this Office.

5. Field Companies will hand over all dumps in their charge.
    Stock sheets showing stocks in ST. JEAN Dump, Divisional Emergency Dump, and POTIJZE Dump, will be handed over to the Field Companies concerned. Copies of these stock sheets will be sent to this Office.

6. Companies will also inform their reliefs of any advanced dumps of tools, wire, pickets, etc., their location, and the approximate quantities of these materials in each. A note of the quantities so handed over, and their location will be sent to this Office.

7. C.R.E. 61st Division is detailing one man from each relieving Company to take over wagon lines and back billets. These men will arrive at back billets about 1 p.m. on the 17th inst.

8. C.R.E. 36th Division will hand over to C.R.E. 61st Division all plant, machinery, materials, and stores, in Divisional Dump at H.8.a.5.9., on evening of 17th inst. A stock list showing all above mentioned stores will be prepared by W.O. i/c 36th Div. R.E. Dump, in duplicate.
    On completion of handing over, all personnel at the dump will rejoin their units.
    Full particulars as to civilian labour employed at Dump will also be handed over.

9/

(2)

9. The incoming companies will not take possession of back billets and horse lines before 11 a.m., or forward billets before 12 noon on the 18th instant.

10. Movements of companies after relief will be communicated later.

11. Field Companies ACKNOWLEDGE.

Captain, R.E.
for C.R.E. 36th Division.

===========================

Detail of distribution.
===========================

Copy No 1 to 121st Field Co.R.E.   7 to 107th Inf. Brigade.
        2 to 122nd Field Co.R.E.   8 to 108th Inf. Brigade.
        3 to 150th Field Co.R.E.   9 to 109th Inf. Brigade.
        4 to 36th Division "G"   10 to C.E. XIX Corps.
        5 to 36th Division "Q"   11. to WAR DIARY.
        6 to C.R.E. 61st Div.   12 to FILE.

S E C R E T.   Copy No. 23.

C.R.E. 36th DIVISION OPERATION ORDER NO 26.
✼✼✼

Reference BELGIUM & FRANCE - Sheet 27
1/40,000.
                                                    17/8/17.

1. The 36th Division will move to the WINNEZEELE Area on the 17th, 18th, and 19th instant.

2. The Field Companies R.E. (Dismounted portion) will move by bus on the 18th inst., in accordance with attached March Table.

3. Mounted branch, transport, and cyclists will move by march route, starting from wagon lines at 8.30 a.m.

4. Companies will be accommodated in their Brigade Groups.
    An advance party should be sent as early as possible on 18th inst., to report to Area Commandant of area in which their Company will be located, and find out what accommodation has been allotted to them by their Brigade.
    A rendezvous in the area should be arranged at which these advance parties will meet the company on arrival.

5. The WINNEZEELE areas are approximately as follows:-
                                            Map reference
    121 - WINNEZEELE Area No 3 - D.25 (part of), J.1,2,3,
                                            7,8,9, and 14 (part of)

    122 -   "   "   No 2 - J.4,9,10,15 (part of) and
                                            16 (part of).

    150 -   "   "   No 1 - J.5,6,11,12,17,18, and
                                            K.1 (part of).

6. Transport bringing kits etc., from Forward Billets can follow after the company transport.

7. Attention is directed to 36th (Ulster) Division Administrative Instructions supplementary to 36th Div. Order No 135, copy of which is attached.

8. C.R.E's Office will move on the 18th inst, opening at WINNEZEELE at 3 p.m.

9. Completion of moves to be reported by orderly.

10. ACKNOWLEDGE.

                                            Captain, R.E.
                                            for C.R.E. 36th Divn.

Issued at 7.30 p.m.

P.T.O

COPIES ISSUED.

```
Copy No 1. to 121st Field Co.R.E.      13 to. C.E. XIX Corps.
        2. to 122nd      "             14 to. Area Comdt. WINNEZEELE No 1.
        3. to 150th      "             15 to.   "       "       "      No 2.
        4. to 121st Coy. Wagon Lines   16 to.   "       "       "      No 3.
        5. to 122nd Coy. Wagon Lines   17 to. 36th Div. Signal Coy, R.E.
        6. to 150th Coy. Wagon Lines   18 to. A.P.M. 36th Division.
        7. to C.R.E. 61st Division.    19 to. D.A.D.O.S. 36th Division.
        8. to 36th Division "G"        20 to. A.D.M.S. 36th Divn.
        9. to 36th Division "Q"        21 to. D.A.D.V.S. 36th Divn.
       10. to 107th Brigade.           22 to. O.C. 36th Divl. Train.
       11. to 108th Brigade.           23 to. WAR DIARY.
       12. to 109th Brigade.           24 to. FILE.
```

FOR
18th August 1917

MARCH TABLE to accompany C.R.E's Order No 25.

Reference BELGIUM & FRANCE Sheet 27, 1/40,000 and BELGIUM, Sheet 28 N.E., 1/20,000.

No	Unit	From	Time	To	Remarks.
1.	121st Field Co. R.E. Dismounted	Forward Billet	—	WINNEZEELE No 3 Area	Debus on road at H.9.a.5.4. to H.8.d.7.4. (Sheet 28 N.E.) at 11 a.m. Debus at DROGLANDT J.12.b. (Sheet 27)
	Mounted	H.2.c.0.8.	8.30 a.m	—do—	By march route.
2.	122nd Field Co. R.E. Dismounted	Forward Billets H.2.c.0.8.	—	WINNEZEELE No 2 Area —do—	Debus as No 1.
	Mounted	H.2.c.0.8.	8.45 a.m		By march route.
3.	150th Field Co. R.E. Dismounted, and attached infantry	Forward Billet	—	WINNEZEELE No 1 Area	Debus as No 1.
	Mounted	H.1.c.4.3.	8.30 a.m.	—do—	By March route.

N.B. 109th Bde. is in WINNEZEELE No 1. — 108th Bde. is in WINNEZEELE No 2. — 107th Bde is WINNEZEELE No3.

SECRET.   Copy No. 15

C.R.E. 36th DIVISION OPERATION ORDER NO 27.

22/8/17.

1. The 36th Division (less Artillery), accompanied by a Divisional Supply Column, will be transferred from the XIX Corps 5th Army, to the IV Corps, 3rd Army.

2. The Division will move by rail, commencing on 23rd inst.

3. The 36th Division (less Artillery) on arrival in IV Corps Area will be accommodated in the area about BARASTRE at present occupied by the 59th Division.

4. The 36th Division (less Artillery) will then relieve the 9th Division (less Artillery) in the line, under orders to be issued later. Relief will be completed by 10 a.m. 31st inst.

5. The Field Companies, R.E. will move as laid down in Q.C.55/8/206 dated 20th inst., and accompanying entraining programme as corrected, which have been circulated to units.

6. Further instructions as to supplies and transport are contained in Q.C.55/8/206 dated 21st inst., which has also been circulated.

7. Attention is directed to O.C./137/1 dated 21st inst., addendum to 36th Div. Order No 137 which is in possession of units. O.C. 121st Coy. will render return called for therein direct to H.Q. VIII Corps.

8. Extracts from "STRATEGICAL MOVE OF 36th DIVISION (less Artillery)" issued by A.D.R.T., HAZEBROUCK Area, as far as they concern the Field Companies, are given below:-

From Fifth Army   Via ST. POL   To Third Army.

        A.   CASSEL
        B.   ESQUELBECQ.
        C.   CAESTRE.

All trains will be consigned to ACHIET-LE-GRAND.

Train Number From Stations.			Serial Numbers	Date	March	Time of dept.
A.	B.	C.				
1.	2.	3.	4.	5.	6.	7.
	8.		3681 (121 Coy.)	23/8	H.T.68	17.30
7.			3682 (122 Coy.)	"	H.T.67	16.51
		9.	3683 (150 Coy.)	"	H.T.69	18.05

2.

9. During the move Field Ambulances will be with their Brigade Groups, and will collect the sick of their respective Brigades.

10. Instructions regarding leave will be issued later.

11. Field Companies ACKNOWLEDGE.

[signature]

Captain, R.E.
for C.R.E. 36th Division.

COPIES ISSUED:-

No 1 to 121st Field Co.R.E.
   2 to 122nd Field Co.R.E.
   3 to 150th Field Co.R.E.
   4 to 36th Division "G"
   5 to 36th Division "Q"
   6 to 107th Brigade.
   7 to 108th Brigade.
   8 to 109th Brigade.

No 9 to A.D.M.S. 36th Division.
10 to C.E. XIX Corps.
11 to VIII Corps.
12 to C.E. IV Corps.
13 to 36th Div. Signal Co.R.E.
14 to 36th Divisional Train.
15 to WAR DIARY.
16 to FILE.

****

SECRET.   Copy No. 18

C.R.E. 36th DIVISION OPERATION ORDER NO 29.

26/8/17.

1. Field Companies R.E. of 36th Division will relieve Field Companies R.E. of 9th Division on 28th, 29th, and 30th inst., as detailed below.

2. 121st Field Company, R.E. relieves 63rd Field Company, R.E. on 28th instant.

Advanced billet	- METZ EN COUTURE	- 4 sections.
Horse lines	- NEUVILLE	

    Advance party has already been sent to METZ. Advance party of one N.C.O. and three sappers to be sent to NEUVILLE on evening of 27th.

    Company to march at 8 a.m. on 28th, taking only essential transport to METZ by day. Any other transport to move forward on night of 28th - 29th.

3. 150th Field Company, R.E. relieves 90th Field Company, R.E. on 29th inst.

Advanced billet	- HERMIES	- 2 sections.
Horse lines, and) back billet)	- BERTINCOURT	- 2 sections.

    Advance party has already been sent to HERMIES.

    Advance party of one N.C.O. and three sappers to be sent to BERTINCOURT on evening of 28th instant.

    Company to march at 8 a.m. on 29th inst. No transport to be taken into forward billet till after dark. Section moving into HERMIES to move in small bodies.

4. 122nd Field Company, R.E. will relieve 64th Field Company, R.E. on 30th instant.

Advanced billet	- BARINCOURT WOOD (Q.7.d.central)	- 3 sections.
Rear billet and) Horse lines)	- RUYALCOURT.	

    Advance party has already been sent to advanced billet.

    Advance party of one N.C.O. and three sappers to be sent to rear billet on evening of 29th.

    Company to march at 8 a.m. 30th inst. No transport to go beyond rear billet till after dark.

    Route via YTRES.

5/

(2)

5. On completion of reliefs, the Field Companies of 36th Division will be under C.R.E. 9th Division until the command of the Divisional front passes to G.O.C. 36th Division. Date and time of this will be communicated later.

6. Completion of reliefs to be reported to this Office by orderly.

7. Field Companies ACKNOWLEDGE.

[signature]

Lt. Colonel, R.E.
C.R.E. 36th Division.

COPIES ISSUED:

No 1 to 121st Field Company, R.E.
   2 to 122nd Field Company, R.E.
   3 to 150th Field Company, R.E.
   4-7 to C.R.E. 9th Division.
   8 to 36th Division "G"
   9 to 36th Division "O"
  10 to C.E. IV Corps.

No 11 to 107th Inf. Bde.
  12 to 108th Inf. Bde.
  13 to 109th Inf. Bde.
  14 to 36th Signal Co.R.E.
  15 to A.D.M.S. 36th Divn.
  16 to D.A.D.V.S. 36th Div.
  17 to 36th Divl. Train.

No 18 to WAR DIARY
   19 to FILE.

SECRET.   No E/S.C/9.   Copy No. 15

INSTRUCTIONS FOR THE OFFENSIVE.

Reference :-
BELGIUM, Sheet
28 N.W. 1/20,000.

EMPLOYMENT OF PACK TRANSPORT ON "Z" AND SUBSEQUENT DAYS

1. The Divisional Pack Transport Column (as laid down in Administrative Instruction No 1 dated 15th July) will assemble at "PACK CAMP", H.12.b.70.95 by 9 p.m. Y/Z night at which hour the four sections of the column will come under the orders of the Divisional Pack Transport Column Commander.

2. The 21 mules from 16th R.I.R. (P) will report to their respective Field Companies at H.8.a.5.9. at 4 p.m. on "Y" day. They will bring with them in addition to their ordinary pack saddles and crates one 20 ft. length of light rope lashing for tying loads.

3. All animals will be loaded with barbed wire and screw pickets at the Divisional Dump and will rendezvous as in para. 1, completely loaded.

4. The Divisional Pack Transport Column will bivouac on Y/Z night in "PACK CAMP".
   107th and 109th Brigade Sections and R.E. and Pioneers Sub-Sections will move forward under the orders of the Column Commander on "Z" morning in sufficient time to enable the head of the column to cross the Canal at zero hour. The remainder of the Column will await further orders in "PACK CAMP".

5. At zero hour the Column Commander will establish his Headquarters beside the Divisional Telephone Exchange (C.B) on the CANAL BANK so that he will be in touch with the two Brigade Headquarters at WIELTJE and with Divisional Headquarters.
   He will arrange for runners from each unit to be available to take messages to the Pack Transport Sections.

6. At zero hour the R.E. and Pioneers Sub-sections will move forward from the Canal under their respective commanders, via No 5 track to I.3.a.35.35 and forward from there via Nos. 4, 5, and 6 tracks

7. How far the pack transport will work forward will depend on the tactical situation, the state of the ground and the requirements of the respective units. Information on the latter point will be obtained from Brigade Headquarters of 108th and 109th Infantry Brigades at WIELTJE.
   The pack transport will not advance further East than the original "NO MAN'S LAND" until permission is received from Brigade Headquarters.

8. Each Sub-section will carry a white board with a letter "D" painted on it and mounted on a pole 4' long, which will be stuck in the ground to mark the position of the most forward dump.

(2)

9. On arrival at the line OXFORD ROAD, the sub-sections will halt, and the Officer i/c Pack Transport 122nd Field Co. R.E. will report at Brigade H.Q. in WIELTJE for further instructions.

10. On completion of the first trip, the material for the second trip can be drawn from any of the Forward Dumps.

11. As soon as the pack transport has completed its allotted task on "Z" day it will return to bivouac in "PACK CAMP", to which place also the water carts and cookers of the units will move on "Z" day under Brigade arrangements.

Rations for the transport personnel and forage for animals will be delivered at "PACK CAMP" by the Divisional Train on "Z" day for consumption on "Z" + 1 day. Rations for the fighting troops for that day will have already been dumped in forward area.

12. ACKNOWLEDGE.

McDowell Capt. RE

for Lt. Colonel, R.E.
C.R.E. 36th Division.

14/8/17.

COPIES ISSUED :-

Copy No. 1. to 121st Field Company, R.E.   9. to 36th Division "G"
2. to 122nd Field Company, R.E. 10. to 36th Division "Q"
3. to 150th Field Company, R.E. 11. to 107th Brigade.
4. to O.i/c Wagon Line 121st Coy. 12. to 108th Brigade.
5. to O.i/c Wagon Line 122nd Coy. 13. to 109th Brigade.
6. to O.i/c Wagon Line 150th Coy. 14. to A.P.M. 36th Divn.
7. to 16th Royal Ir. Rifles (P). 15. to WAR DIARY.
8. to Div. Pack Transport Officer. 16. to FILE.

Confidential

WAR DIARY Vol 24

of

C.R.E. 36th Division

for month of September 1917.

Army Form C. 2118.

WAR DIARY
or
INTELLIGENCE SUMMARY.
(Erase heading not required.)

Instructions regarding War Diaries and Intelligence Summaries are contained in F. S. Regs., Part II. and the Staff Manual respectively. Title pages will be prepared in manuscript.

Place	Date	Hour	Summary of Events and Information	Remarks and references to Appendices
YPRES.	1/9/17		*[illegible handwritten entry]*	
	2/9/17		*[illegible handwritten entry]*	
	3/9/17		*[illegible handwritten entry]*	
	4/9/17		*[illegible handwritten entry]*	
	5/9/17		*[illegible handwritten entry]*	
	6/9/17		*[illegible handwritten entry]*	

Army Form C. 2118.

WAR DIARY
or
INTELLIGENCE SUMMARY.

(Erase heading not required.)

Place	Date	Hour	Summary of Events and Information	Remarks and references to Appendices
VITZ.P.	7/9/17		Round Cliff dutn with G.O.C. 109. 93. Propos tour for Doctor BEAUVOIR & ROSHROUCOURT.	
	8/9/17		Round night sector. Good arrangements had been made for O.C. 107. 93 & 108. 131. in afternoon.	
	9/9/17		To A90 in morning, rabble of to be delivered in 107 & 108 & 107. 108 in afternoon.	
			VACCINATION TYPE Re: Septimis.	
			To AMIENS to see VICTOR VICTOR MALETZ that our angle MERCER	
			got 107 108 but	
			L.L.H. dicty took 107 109 L.50	
	10/9/17		To C.Off. dicty with O.C. 101. Propos in af. fair. To VIEW in afternoon.	
	11/9/17			

WAR DIARY
or
INTELLIGENCE SUMMARY.

(Erase heading not required.)

Army Form C. 2118.

Place	Date	Hour	Summary of Events and Information	Remarks and references to Appendices
YPRES	15/9/17		[illegible handwritten entries] To ROCQIGNY in afternoon. Sent Reinforcement Camp.	
	16/9/17		[illegible]	
	17/9/17			
	18/9/17			
	19/9/17			
	20/9/17		To ROCQUIGNY	
	21/9/17			

Army Form C. 2118.

WAR DIARY
or
INTELLIGENCE SUMMARY.
(Erase heading not required.)

Place	Date	Hour	Summary of Events and Information	Remarks and references to Appendices
METZ.	28/9/17		And left Debr with OC B/RIR. Saw site for hut of 122 RIR n/ Lus. OC Hoq & R1C2. NB	
	29/9/17		And Cade ashes in OC 16/RIR + 19 RIR	
	1/9/17		In O left Site with OC 14 RIR B	
	2/9/17		Self left Debr with OC 22 A G.S.04 and site of proposed Dental line. To run damp N facing	
			To night with OC 122 Sus CE re houseing of Horses. NB	
	27/9/17		Visit Debr with OC 122. NB	
28.9.17	—		C.R.E went on leave. O.C 122 (Major Hawdi) acting CRE	
			Started 16th R.I.R.(D) on clearing Velu Château.	
			Saw Brigadier 108 and. A.C.S 122 and 121.	
29.9.17	—		To reinforcement camp Rocquigny. % Berlin canal and turned with O.C./D	
30.9.17	—		Rouse right centre with G.S.O.3	

Frans Epinoti, R.E.
C.R.E. 36th (Ulster) Division

Vol 25

Confidential

WAR DIARY

of

C.R.E. 36th Division

for month of October 1917

Place	Date	Hour	Summary of Events and Information	Remarks and references to Appendices
YTRES	1/10/17	-	Went round INTERMEDIATE line in right sector with CE. and GSO2 IV corps. CE requires main parallel fence fixed without diagonals, as this portion of line is in full view. Fence from to be in entirety with traverses 24' wide instead of 12' as at present. MG positions sited. Dugouts for these to be started with tunnelling company and working parties from Burgain.	Q
	2/10/17	-	Round new switch line with OC 150⁰. Trench dug to depth of 3'-6". All line this tun been viewed up to R.43 and trench dug to depth of 3'-0".	Q
	3/10/17	-	Round INTERMEDIATE line in right sector with CE & GO2 IV corps. Sited new MG positions. ROGUIGNY reinforcement camp in afternoon.	Q
	4/10/17	-	Went round with OC 121. Thence line in immediate line. Went to BAPAUME & see OC 248th Tunnelling Coy.	Q
	5/10/17	-	122nd Coy in morning. 150th Coy in afternoon.	Q
	6/10/17	-	Bought bitts of & arrival turks in Quens. Went to VAREIMES in dark line.	Q
	7/10/17	-	150th Coy. Saw GOC 109th Brigade in dark line.	Q
	8/10/17	-	Saw GOC's 107 and 108 and went to right sector with 2/21st Field Coy.	Q
	9/10/17	-	To 122nd Coy. ROGUIGNY reinforcement camp in afternoon.	Q

Army Form C. 2118.

WAR DIARY
or
INTELLIGENCE SUMMARY.
(Erase heading not required.)

Instructions regarding War Diaries and Intelligence Summaries are contained in F. S. Regs., Part II. and the Staff Manual respectively. Title pages will be prepared in manuscript.

Place	Date	Hour	Summary of Events and Information	Remarks and references to Appendices
TO 19 YPRES.	10/10/17	—	Saw O.C. 107, 108" and 109" M.G. Companies in their billets and obtained particulars of M.G. positions and their outposts.	B
	11/10/17	—	To 108" Brigade and then to 21st Div Hqrs. S to O.C. Comp. to talk returns from leave.	B
	12/10/17	—	Est. complete return Div. Hq. Change over to new Camp.	C
	13/10/17	—	To Right Sector of Stonehenge Line with O.C. 91 and O.C. W. Sheeter 28th D Coy. Excellent of MG outposts. Talked wiring to Pioneer MG	
	14/10/17	—	To Left Sector with O.C. 150. Sur [illegible] the mechanism of S.A. French set of change stopping and quite feasible wiring quite satisfactory. MG	
	15/10/17	—	To Centre Sector with O.C. 122. MG	
	16/10/17	—	To Right Sector with O.C. 121. to ROCQUIGNY & Obs. M.P. neptusine	
	17/10/17	—	To Left Sector with O.C. 150 & G O.C. 109 & 3. MG	
	18/10/17	—	To Centre Sector with O.C. 122. MG	
	19/10/17	—	To Right Sector with O.C. 121. Went to EQUANCOURT. MG	
	20/10/17	—	To Left Sector with O.C. 150. Saw Lot of left of R.R. line. MG	

Army Form C. 2118.

WAR DIARY
or
INTELLIGENCE SUMMARY.
(Erase heading not required.)

Instructions regarding War Diaries and Intelligence Summaries are contained in F. S. Regs., Part II. and the Staff Manual respectively. Title pages will be prepared in manuscript.

Place	Date	Hour	Summary of Events and Information	Remarks and references to Appendices
YPRES.	21/10/17		Vars DUYNKERK — HEEMING road with O.C. 122. Lens Bhef highest moving. MB	
	22/10/17		To METZ. Dead line of repairs of road METZ — PLACE MONT MARE. Sheets of BERTINCOURT Inspected line of sintex between R4, R4A, R3. MB	
	23/10/17		G Return unto the with CE. MB	
	24/10/17		G Left sects of Coke Brigade with O.C. 122 Inspected RB 1. between G sintex of R4, R5, R6. MB	
	25/10/17		G Right Brigade with O.C. 21. MB	
	26/10/17		G Left Brigade with O.C. 150. MB	
	27/10/17		Conference of Cos RO. Moving standing at YPRES in afternoon. RO.	
	28/10/17		Reconnaissance of road. OXFORD VALLEY — PIONEER VALLEY. RO.	
	29/10/17		To TRESCAULT Re repairs of road. G Cos RO. moving MB	

WAR DIARY
or
INTELLIGENCE SUMMARY.

Army Form C. 2118.

Place	Date	Hour	Summary of Events and Information	Remarks and references to Appendices
YPRES.	30/10/17		To CRS RO. Kockoigny in mng. Saw C.E. of Intermediate line W of with D.M.G.O. afternoon	
	31/10/17		METZ - PLACE - MORTE MARE ROAD with O.C. Senior Co. who was to RUYAUL COURT, METZ & BRIDGE IN COURT. connect line.	

Alan Bell White
CRS 38 Jnr Sx
31/10/17

Confidential

War Diary

of

CRE 36' Division

for month of November 1917

Vol 26

Army Form C. 2118.

WAR DIARY
or
INTELLIGENCE SUMMARY.

(Erase heading not required.)

Instructions regarding War Diaries and Intelligence Summaries are contained in F. S. Regs., Part II. and the Staff Manual respectively. Title pages will be prepared in manuscript.

Place	Date	Hour	Summary of Events and Information	Remarks and references to Appendices
YPRES.	1/11/17		To YPRES with OC 150 to see site for Dump B. Took OC 151/CN/P to see tank needed & YPRES road. Packed view from BRIEKER [illegible] look in meanwhile.	
YPRES.	2/11/17		To METZ. Explained work unit to OC 121. Shew CoE 109 SB also conferences with OC Eng to RE of OC RE & to take. Shewls not altogether satisfactory.	
	3/11/17		To ROYAUCOURT & BRETINCOURT found roads OK	
	4/11/17		To METZ. Found roads unit O.C. 121. Shew to Col. Influence nothing.	
	5/11/17		To YPRES. Shew to LURGAN SWITCH with Col GRAVES & NEUVILLE & ROYAUCOURT.	
	6/11/17		To TRESCAULT & PLACE MORTEMARE Roads. Shew to OC 150 & G.O.C 109 S.B. with CofE. Saw OC 150 & G.O.C 109 S.B.	
	7/11/17		To METZ. Shew Roads.	
	8/11/17		To METZ. Shew to ROYAUCOURT, BERTINCOURT & Rd to H.Q.	
	9/11/17		To YPRES etc. to TRESCAULT, PLACE MORTEMARE & METZ. Shew CRE ST.	

Army Form C. 2118.

WAR DIARY
or
INTELLIGENCE SUMMARY.
(Erase heading not required.)

Instructions regarding War Diaries and Intelligence Summaries are contained in F. S. Regs., Part II. and the Staff Manual respectively. Title pages will be prepared in manuscript.

Place	Date	Hour	Summary of Events and Information	Remarks and references to Appendices
	10/11/17		TO MR52 - TRESCAULT YMSTZ PLACE MORSTMORES MRSO JB	
	11/11/17		YMSTZ, RUYAULCOURT Caus OC 121 4722 JB	
	12/11/17		To HERMIES RUYAULCOURT. JB	
	13/11/17		To MSTZ - TRESCAULT road in morning to ALBERT Ruffuran JB afternoon to OC 16 RIC (?) in morning. To Cars in afternoon. JB	
	14/11/17		Capture of OC 121 122 & OC 16 RIC (?) in morning. JB	
	15/11/17		To TRESCAULT, PLACE MORTEMARE + PLACE ST HUBERT. Hew to HERMIES. Caus OC 121, 122 750 Yds. C.E. noted morning. JB	
	16/11/17		+ TRESCAULT + PLACE MORTEMARE. To A.D.M.S. Caus O.C. 122. JB	
	17/11/17		To HERMIES with OO 122. New offices of 56th Rations B missing. JB	
	18/11/17		To TRESCAULT Wood Sir Huge Margement + panuelus to Cookers cantonment. To new site of BARRELS to Cars revival. JB	
	19/11/17		To HAVRINCOURT WOOD SUNKEN WOOD C /2 15? 26.05 R.M. /2 268 (?) Cars evacuated by sunken TRESCAULT RIBECOURT Road. JB	

2353 Wt. W2544/1454 700,000 5/15 D.D.&L. A.D.S.S./Forms/C. 2118.

WAR DIARY
or
INTELLIGENCE SUMMARY

Army Form C. 2118.

(Erase heading not required.)

Place	Date	Hour	Summary of Events and Information	Remarks and references to Appendices
	20/11/17		Troops moved off at intervals after zero and covered enemy back from TEESCOURT & R13K-COURT. Quiet afternoon and night. Some enemy seen approaching R13K-COURT. Held O.R. Killed O.R. wounded. 1 O.R. enemy evacuated came up. Two dead enemies & a wounded load 122 shells & 1/2 15" shells under reg. shell. All known enemy dead. Were huge and covered or none. Repaired in former battle ridge ind. no evidence. AG	
	21/11/17		Entered fire a TUECOURT - R13COURT and under CK WCB. Saw enemy in the Magazine at WTHRO several and craters joined by surge trye. Enemy attempt remember of R13 under reg. rifle informed ammunition NORTH OF CA'17 K 30 road. Two HCC11K8 toward GRANCOURT. AG	
	22/11/17		Stopped work at TUECOURT - R13COURT road after anything made under cover overhead and to the rear. Repaired ground in afternoon. AG	
	23/11/17		Repaired AKEM 160 - GRANCOURT, INCEN160 - DEMICOURT ROADS. Reduced roads in section to work 16 C.I.R. ? 21 PRB & 12 15" PRB PG near firm METZ & HAVEINCOURT WOOD & recent of MRRN160. AG	

WAR DIARY
or
INTELLIGENCE SUMMARY.
(Erase heading not required.)

Army Form C. 2118.

Instructions regarding War Diaries and Intelligence Summaries are contained in F. S. Regs., Part II. and the Staff Manual respectively. Title pages will be prepared in manuscript.

Place	Date	Hour	Summary of Events and Information	Remarks and references to Appendices
	24/11/17		Taken over ACHEIT - GRANCOURT KAREMER-BEMICOURT Road preparing well. Rain during night. OB	
	25/11/17		Rain during night. Men todo shale red act int tithe kept open. Seitin RE or aspect 10/25 n energadatin.	
	26/11/17		Recorded relieving try from Capt. D. Noet to in front of GRANCOURT and refl in infantry 2D 16RIR P 21 n 150 Road proposed OB	
	27/11/17		10 it + 15th Feb & 16 RIR P/2CD made last from we relief near still in ACEMIER. The n roads relayed from ens train. may it of 20/21 during day of 21 Kans FC 258 17 CO-25 n rite 4/1 tps C 2 n 29t	
	29/11/17		Unt n rode entered. Changed into st Covain. OB Railway from to Railway at about it tops in Egypt and asphalt. second new to cucuaie rivals.	
	30/11/17		Today rain from hose sel sent n Rearr line. New OB Guide n afternoon & traged into OB	
	31/11/17		Rec. CRE Guide n ent entailed factors of to c= r pawn. but of the stated frictent. OB	

W. B. M. Ellis Cap. 30 th tot

SECRET.

AMENDMENT TO C.R.E. 36th DIVISION
OPERATION ORDER NO 30.

Reference para 11 of Operation Order No 30 dated 17/11/17.

Arrangements have been made under which a cavalry patrol will precede the main body of the cavalry by about 15 minutes, and give warning so that the road can be cleared.

Sentries should be warned that until the arrival of this patrol road is not to be cleared on account of the arrival of isolated mounted men.

(Sd) A Campbell

Lt. Colonel, R.E.
C.R.E. 36th Division.

18/11/17.

To all recipients of O.O.30.

SECRET.   Copy No. 10

C.R.E. 36th DIVISION OPERATION ORDER NO 30.
===

                                                17/11/17.

1.   The object of the operation is two-fold.

            (a) To prepare a track 20 foot wide from Q.10.a.4.4.
            to RIBECOURT, along which cavalry and light carts
            can pass.

            (b) To repair and improve the road from Q.10.a.4.4.
            to RIBECOURT sufficiently to make it passable
            by lorries.

        For (a), a track of minimum width of 20 feet is required,
        but a metalled surface not being essential deviations can be
        made from the road where a width of 20 feet cannot be got on
        the road alignment.

        For (b), it will be necessary to follow the alignment of
        the existing metalled road, except at the two large craters in
        K.36.c.05.10, and K.36.c.7.7., where timbered diversions will
        be required.

2.   The disposable troops and transport are:-

            121st Field Company, R.E., and attached infantry.
            H.Q. and 2 Sections 150th Field Company, R.E.
              and attached infantry.
            H.Q. and 2 sections 258 (T) Company, R.E.
            16th Royal Irish Rifles (P).
            500 men of labour units.
            Loading parties at METZ, B.W.54, and TRESCAULT,
              (200 in all).
            30 G.S. wagons and 50 teams.

3.   The approximate time available for work is for

            (a) 2 - 3 hours.
            (b) 48 hours.

4. PRELIMINARY ARRANGEMENTS.
        O.C. 121st Field Company, R.E. will arrange to store the
following near B.W.54:-

            (a) Tools detailed in S/50 of 14/11/17.
            (b) Supply of bannerolos 3' high, with streamers
            of tracing tapes.
            (c) Notice boards:-
                NO ROAD   - 20.
                Plain white   - 20.
                  (unlettered)
                Pot of black paint, -   1.
                  and brush
                boards to have 4' poles.

                                                        2/

(2)

O.C. 16th R.I.R. (P) will arrange for each of his Companies to be in possession of 100 banneroles of same type as those made by O.C. 121st Field Company, R.E.

O.C. 121st Field Company, R.E. will arrange for loading all the wagons on "Y" day. These wagons will be parked near METZ.

LOADS.
For Labour units:-
    Brickbats, and 500 sandbags.

For R.E. and Pioneers:-
    Sandbags - 1,000
    Fascines
    6" nails - ¼ cwt.

Each wagon to be marked with a large lettered board "T.R."

5.   The following dumps of material will be available:-

    METZ :-   Tools, pit props, fascines, nails, and road metal.

    B.W.54:-   Tools, pit props, and road metal.

    TRESCAULT:- Pit props, and road metal.

Owing to difficulty of obtaining transport by rail, quantities in dumps cannot be guaranteed.

6. EQUIPMENT.
    R.E. and Pioneers will be equipped as follows:-

    (a) PACK.   Pack will be carried, and in it will be leather jerkin, and a pair of clean socks.

    (b) AMMUNITION.   R.E.   - 100 rounds per man.
                           Pioneers - 200   "

    (c) BOX RESPIRATOR.   (But not P.H. Helmet).

    (d) RATIONS for one day, and one iron ration.

    (e) TOOLS as may be detailed by Officers Commanding units.

Labour units will carry box respirator, and draw such tools as may be required from dump at B.W.54.

7. DISPOSITIONS AT ZERO.

    121st Field Co.R.E. and attached infantry)
        (less 24 sappers)
    H.Q. and 2 Sects. 150th Field Co.R.E.
        and attached infantry   ) Q.15.B. & D.
        (less 1 Officer and 12 sappers)
    H.Q. and 2 Sections 258 (T) Coy.R.E.
    16th Royal Irish Rifles (P)

(3)

Labour Units on rail between present billets, and B.W.54.

Wagons in vicinity of METZ.

Special missions for sappers detached from 121st and 150th Field Companies will be detailed to Officers Commanding those units.

8. Captain H. GOOCH, R.E., 121st Field Company, R.E. will take general charge of work of Labour Units from Zero - ½.

9. On receipt of orders to commence work, units will deal with sectors of road as follows:-

(a) Labour units from Q.10.a.4.4. to Crater in K.36.c.05.10, exclusive of crater, trench crossings, and wire. 400 men will be put on this work, 100 being left to pitch camp and form night party.

(b) 2 Sections 121st Field Company, R.E. and attached infantry - trench crossings and wire of British Support and Front lines.

(c) One Company 18th R.I.R. (P) - diversion round crater in K.36.c.05.10., and road repair or diversion up to, but exclusive of, crater at K.36.c.7.7. and trench crossing near crater at K.36.c.05.10.

(d) One Section 258 (T) Company, R.E., - trench crossing near crater at K.36.c.05.10.

(e) One Company 18th R.I.R. (P) - diversion round crater at K.36.c.7.7., and diversions or road repair up to, but exclusive of, trench crossings at K.36.b.2.3., and intermediate crossings.

(f) One Section 258 (T) Company, R.E. - trench crossing at K.36.c.8.9.

(g) One Section 121st Field Company, R.E. and attached infantry - trench crossing at K.36.b.2.3.

(h) Two Companies 16th R.I.R. (P) - clearance or diversion of road from K.36.b.2.3. to RIBECOURT, exclusive of trench crossings.

(i) One Section 121st Field Company, R.E. and attached infantry - trench crossing at K.36.b.7.8.

(j) Two sections 150th Field Company, R.E. and attached infantry - trench crossings between K.36.b.7.8. and RIBECOURT.

(k) Available transport will move forward, and join units as follows:-

      121st Field Company, R.E. - 6 wagons.
      150th   "   - 8 "
      258 (T) Company, R.E. - 4 "
      16th R.I.R. (P) - 4 "
      Labour Units - 8 "

(4)

10.   Before commencing work, Officers Commanding Companies of Pioneers will post sentries, and place their Lewis Guns so as to protect the working parties from any attack by isolated parties of the enemy.

11.   Sentries will give warning of the approach of the cavalry, when all working parties and transport must be cleared off the track. Captain GOOCH will arrange to detail look-out men to warn Labour Units.

12.   As soon as the track has been cleared for passage of the cavalry, all parties will rest for one hour.

13.   At expiration of one hour's rest, the following action will be taken:-

R.E. and Pioneers will detail one quarter of their total strength to retire to the nearest dug-outs and rest till 4 p.m., when they will form the night party. These men should secure sufficient accommodation for the day party, so that they can rest in their turn. The day party will be split into reliefs, so that work will carry on continuously, every man working four hours and resting two hours, till relieved at 4 p.m.

Labour Units will not detail a night relief, as this has already been arranged, but will work by reliefs in the same way as R.E. and Pioneers.

14.   On resuming work, the efforts of all parties will be concentrated on the clearance and repair of the permanent road alignment.

Officers in charge of sections are at liberty to open or close diversion tracks as may seem desireable in the interests of reconstruction of the metalled road.

15.   Officers sending back wagons for more material must invariably send a guide with a list of the stores needed.

16.   The following runners will be needed:-

121st Field Co.R.E.)   -   Orderly for C.R.E.
)   1 Runner.

150th Field Co.R.E.   -   1 Runner.

258 (T) Company,R.E.   -   1 Runner.

16th R.I.R. (P)   -   1 Runner.

Runners and orderly to report to C.R.E. at ZERO - 1.

(17) ACKNOWLEDGE.

S Campbell

Lt. Colonel, R.E.
C.R.E. 36th Division.

Copies.

No 1. - C.E. IV Corps.
    2. - O.C. 121st Field Coy.R.E.
    3. - O.C. 150th Field Coy.R.E.
    4. - O.C. 258 (T) Coy. R.E.
    5. - O.C. 16th R.I.R. (P)
    6. - O.C. 56th Labour Company.
    7. - O.C. 113th Labour Company.
    8. - Captain Gooch, R.E.
    9. - FILE.
  10. - WAR DIARY.

SECRET.   COPY NO........ 11

C.R.E. 36th DIVISION OPERATION ORDER NO 31.

122nd Field Company, R.E. and 2 Sects. 150th Field Co. R.E.

19/11/17.

1. **EQUIPMENT.**
   Each man will wear steel helmet and carry rifle, 50 rounds ammunition, box respirator, water bottle filled, the unexpired portion of day's ration, iron rations, field dressing, and Iodine ampoule. Attached infantry will carry 100 rounds S.A.A.

2. **MOVING OFF - 122nd FIELD CO.R.E.**
   The Company, plus attached infantry, will move off at ZERO + 2½ to proceed to J.28.d.5.9. where they will halt to await instructions.

   150th FIELD COMPANY, R.E.
   The two sections, plus attached infantry, will be standing by in their billets at ZERO + 2, ready to move off.

3. **TRANSPORT.**
   122nd Field Co.R.E.
   All teams for wagons and the four pack mules will leave horse lines at ZERO + 3 and proceed to J.28.c.3.9. where they will halt.

   150th Field Co.R.E.
   Pack mules to be at J.28.c.3.9. at ZERO + 4.

4. **WORK.**
   122nd Field Co.R.E.
   Two sections, plus 25 infantry, will construct a trestle bridge at approximately K.15.a.4.5.
   Two sections, plus 25 infantry, will construct a WELLDON Trestle bridge at approximately K.20.b.40.65.

   150th Field Co.R.E.
   Two sections, plus 70 infantry, will repair the HERMIES - GRAINCOURT Road, and make bridge approaches in accordance with instructions received from Officers i/c bridging parties. A party will be detailed to put up a screen at the look at K.9.c.70.80, to hide operations on the bridge at K.15.a.4.5.

5. **COMMENCEMENT OF OPERATIONS.**
   On receipt of information from Division that operations may be started, 150th Field Company will immediately move forward. One section 122nd Field Company R.E. and attached infantry will proceed to reconnoitre bridge site at K.15.a.4.5., and set out bridge foundations.
   One section 122nd Field Company R.E. with attached infantry will proceed to reconnoitre bridge site at K.20.b.4.0, and commence work on foundations.
   The Officer i/c Transport will hook in all teams to wagons.
   On receipt of information that the routes on the bridge heads are clear, the two remaining sections of 122nd Field Co.R.E. will immediately move forward with the transport.
   As soon as each wagon has delivered its load of bridging material it will return to R.E. Dump, HERMIES and load up R.E. material to form a dump on the East side of the bridge head
                                                at K.15.a.4.5.

at K.15.a.4.5.

O.C. 122nd Field Co.R.E. will arrange for a loading party of ten men at HERMIES Dump.

6. **COMPLETION OF WORK.**

Officers i/c of parties will immediately report completion of work to Advanced Divisional H.Q. at J.29.b.80.63, HERMIES.

The bridges must not be reported as being complete until the approaches on the East side have been screened from view from the North.

7. **COMMUNICATION**

O. i/c Sections 150th Field Coy. will detail two orderlies to be at Signal Office HERMIES at ZERO. They will be responsible for transmitting all communications from Divisional H.Q. to O.C. 122nd Field Coy. to ZERO + 4.

Immediately on arrival at J.28.d.5.9. O.C. 122nd Field Coy. will send forward an orderly to the Signal Office to relieve one of the orderlies of 150th Field Coy. Each bridging party will have a cyclist orderly. O. i/c Sections 150th Company will also detail one.

Under no circumstances must messages be sent except in writing. Time at which message was sent must also be stated.

8. **ROUTE.**

Men marching, and all transport must comply with instructions given on attached plan, when going through HERMIES.

9. **STRETCHER BEARERS.**

Each party will have two stretcher bearers.

10. **CASUALTIES.**

In the case of casualties, the nearest Aid Post is at K.13.d.6.1.

11. **WATER.**

Drinking water will be brought up by pack mules.

12. **MAPS.**

Each Officer will carry a copy of the following maps
57c N.E. 1/20,000
51b S.E. 1/20,000

13. **DUMPS.**

DEMICOURT
HERMIES.

The Dump at HERMIES should be drawn on first.

14. **PERSONNEL REMAINING BEHIND.**

Nominal roll of men remaining behind and name of Senior N.C.O. i/c to be in C.R.E's Office at 8.30 p.m. to-night.

N. Campbell.

Lt. Colonel, R.E.
C.R.E. 36th Division.

Copies to:-

No 1 to 36th Division "G"
   2 to 36th Division "Q"
   3 to O.C. 122nd Field Co.R.E.
   4 to O.C. Det. 150th "
   5 to 107th Brigade.
   6 to 108th Brigade.

No 7 to 109th Brigade.
   8 to C.R.A. 36th Div.
   9 to A.D.M.S. 36th Div.
  10 to FILE.
  11 to WAR DIARY.

S E C R E T.   COPY NO...... 10

C.R.E. 36th DIVISION OPERATION ORDER NO 58.

28/11/17.

(1) 36th Division (less Artillery, R.E., H.Q., 122nd and 150th Field Companies and 16th R.I.R. (P)) will be transferred from IV Corps to XVII Corps on 29th November, and will move on that date to the FOSSEUX Area.

(2) H.Q., Divisional R.E., 122nd and 150th Field Companies, and 16th R.I.R. (P) will remain as at present located until further orders.

(3) 121st Field Company will move with the Division, and will be administered by Divisional H.Q. from 29th inst., inclusive.

(4) Attached infantry will remain with their respective Field Companies for the present, whether moving or remaining in their present location.

(5) 121st Field Company will move with the 108th Brigade Group, in accordance with attached Administrative Instructions, and will get in touch with 108th Brigade at BEAULENCOURT forthwith as to rations, billets, move of transport etc.

(6) O.C. 121st Field Company will supply 108th Brigade, by wire, with a state showing number of Officers and O.R. vehicles, and horses proceeding by train and by road.

(7) Attention is directed to 36th Division Administrative Instructions dated 28/11/17, copies of which are attached (Field Coys. only).

(8) O.C. 121st Company will hand over to TOWN MAJOR HERMIES, all tents in his possession, and obtain a duplicate receipt for them, one copy of which will be forwarded to this Office. Any trench and area stores will also be handed over to TOWN MAJOR HERMIES.

(9) The units remaining in this area will be rationed from 29th inst., by No 1 Company 36th Div. Train.

(10) The wagons from 14th Reserve Park and 36th D.A.C. will be rationed by 150th Field Company, R.E. from 29th inst   and O.C. 121st Company will arrange this with O.C. 150th Company.

(11) Field Companies ACKNOWLEDGE.

                                                    Captain, R.E.
                                                for C.R.E. 36th Division.

Copies issued :-

No 1 to	121st Field Co.R.E.	No 7 to	36th Divisional Train.
2	122nd Field Co.R.E.	8	No 1 Company, Divl. Train.
3	150th Field Co.R.E.		
4	108th Brigade.	9.	16th R.I.R. (P).
5	36th Division "Q"	10.	WAR DIARY.
6.	C.E. IV Corps.	11.	FILE.

Confidential JK 27

War Diary

C.R.E. 36th Division

for Month of

December 1917

WAR DIARY
or
INTELLIGENCE SUMMARY

(Erase heading not required.)

Army Form C. 2118

Place	Date	Hour	Summary of Events and Information	Remarks and references to Appendices
TRES	1/2/19	12.2 & 1.30	10 R.W.D. enfilading & wiring. Receive the report that fresh squaders indulged into every ??? and no interference by enemy.	
	2/2/19		Enfilment and wiring. But the day only some showed damage at position during wiring. No more cut & Jail not firing ??? ???	
	3/2/19		Enfilment on right of 2/3 in before. Took detail to OC No CoA completed. Asked to CO & Cols. For rest or work not to be done.	
SAILLY LE GRAND	4/2/19		Moved RD. In afternoon. Jaloo & Myers & Breffert 700. Section 1812 C & dug at to METZ - GOIZEN Court road & took 2 Coloned ass RO Var CRS 6 & 27 Dec & Con. in Section Silic over.	
	5/2/19		Staff met L.O. & L.O.I. Saw live to Receive the Guide & Inspected abodes which worked thorough inspection & area which revealed changed conditions. Saw O.C. 122 & 150 2D KDE & RWR (?) & doing average & having banks ??? 121 Pioneers.	

Instructions regarding War Diaries and Intelligence Summaries are contained in F. S. Regs., Part II. and the Staff Manual respectively. Title Pages will be prepared in manuscript.

WAR DIARY
or
INTELLIGENCE SUMMARY
(Erase heading not required.)

Army Form C. 2118

Place	Date	Hour	Summary of Events and Information	Remarks and references to Appendices
SOREL LE GRAND	6/2/17		To line with O.C. 16 R.I.R. (P) arranged details of work for Pioneers & Field Cos 122 & 150 to wire front 121 to wire Reserve Line. Had front. AB	
	7/2/17		To line with O.C. 16 R.I.R. (P) Progress during night of 6/7 fair in Reserve line. poor in front owing to activity of enemy. AB	
	8/2/17		To line with O.C. 121. Saw all Brigadiers. Arranged for demolition of trenches in right brigade area where enemy had made bombing attacks. Progress fair. Thaw. AB	
	9/2/17		To line with Adjt 16 R.I.R. (P). Investigated extension of Reserve Line then along front of 108 I.B. & up [illegible] in L34D & R4A. Back billets of 122 shelled. 1 R.E.O. wounded. AB	
	10/2/17		To Reserve Line with O.C. 150th Fd Co R.E. Work generally progressing favourably. AB	
	11/2/17		Rest. Work of Cos & Pioneers progressing satisfactorily. AB	
	12/2/17		To Reserve Line then round ground between Hindenburg Line and SLUSH TRENCH in search of site for Brigade HQ. AB	
	13/2/17		Progress on night 12/13 fair. Pioneers shelled off their work. 150th Fd Co relieved by Fd Co of 63rd Div & withdrawn to SOREL. AB	

1875 Wt. W593/826 1,000,000 4/15 J.B.C. & A. A.D.S.S./Forms/C. 2118.

WAR DIARY
or
INTELLIGENCE SUMMARY

Army Form C. 2118.

(Erase heading not required.)

Place	Date	Hour	Summary of Events and Information	Remarks and references to Appendices
SARSL.	14/12/17		To METZ H.Q. 16th C.R.P. with O/C M.G.T. CUSINS. R.E. Inn O.C. 121, 122 Pioneers. Inst. working right 13/14 satisfactory. Nil -	
	15/12/17		To METZ with C.R.E. 63rd Div. Re Cotons used for work. Nil right 14/15 satisfactory. Nil.	
	16/12/17		To ALBERT to head M/a. dutus. J. C.R.E. III Army. To O/C CAMPBELL R.E. Coy. Same evng. Work on night 15/16 satisfactory. Rest.	
	17/12/17		To LOUVENCOURT. Blizzard. Snowstorm.	
	18/12/17		To ACHEUX to fort. Snowstorm.	En rode for LUCHEUX Rest.
	19/12/17		To LUCHEUX.	
	20/12/17		To BEAUVRICOURT to 121 Coy in Pioneer. To BOUT DES PRES & 150 Coy. Rest.	
			In afternoon.	
	21/12/17		To PAS to 122 Coy. Then shift Rest.	Generally frost & snow lying.
LUCHEUX	22/12/17		To CANADIAN FORESTRY Coy. Then shift Rest.	
	23/12/17		To 121 Coy. O.S.R.	
	24/12/17		To 150 Coy. O.S.R.	Snowing at intervals.
	25/12/17		To QUERRIEU & Corps. Saw SORE A.D.	Afternoon fine & bright. Light winds.
	26/12/17		Return.	
CORBIE.	27/12/17		C.R.E. moved to CORBIE. Rest.	

Army Form C. 2118.

WAR DIARY
or
INTELLIGENCE SUMMARY.

(Erase heading not required.)

Place	Date	Hour	Summary of Events and Information	Remarks and references to Appendices
CORBIE	28/12/17		C.R.E. and Adj. to QUERRIEU in afternoon to C.E. Conf. Shutting and drifting. Transport of 9/22nd Coy directed to pass night at DAOURS on account of weather. Roads v. bad. 121st & 2nd Coys at WARFUSEE-ABANCOURT.	Appx
"	29/12/17		To 121st Coy, WARFUSEE-ABANCOURT, with intelligence. Company in fair billets, great improvement in BEAUDRICOURT. Horses well stabled. Germany Beginning to Thaw.	Appx
"	30/12/17			Appx
"	31/12/17		C.R.E. returned to TOUTENCOURT for C.O.'s Course.	

Intentional

War Diary

of

CRE 36 Division

for month of January 1941

Army Form C. 2118.

WAR DIARY
or
INTELLIGENCE SUMMARY.
(Erase heading not required.)

Instructions regarding War Diaries and Intelligence Summaries are contained in F. S. Regs., Part II. and the Staff Manual respectively. Title pages will be prepared in manuscript.

Place	Date	Hour	Summary of Events and Information	Remarks and references to Appendices
	3/1/18			
	4/1/18		H.Q. at CORBIE. C.R.E. at O.C.s Course. 5th Army School. TOUTENCOURT.	G/1
	6/1/18		Colonel BRACOVNOT DIRECTEUR DD MATERIAL DE GENIE inspected both adjutant, equipment of 122 Field Coy R.E., the later at TOUTENCOURT with a view . C.R.E. returned from TOUTENCOURT.	G/1
	7/1/18		H.Q. R.E. moved with Division H.Q. to HARBONNIERE. 121 Field Coy moved with 107 Bde Groupe from WARFUSSEE to FRAMERVILLE. 122 Field Coy moved with 108 Bgde Groupe from HAILLES to BAYONVILLERS. 150 Field Coy moved from DOMART to FRESNOY with 109 Bgde Groupe.	
	8/1/18		150th Field Coy RE moved to BILLANCOURT.	
			122 " " " " VOYENNES	
	1/1/18		122 " " " " CARRE PUITS	
			121 " " " " DURY	
			150 " " " " OLLEZY	
	12/1/18		H.Q. R.E. moved with Div. H.Q. to NESLE.	
	13/1/18		122 Field Coy R.E. moved to DURY	
	do		121 " " " from DURY to line (Lft Sector) Billets in le HAMEL	
			150 " " " OLLEZY " " " " " " GRAND SENECOURT	
	14/1/18			

WAR DIARY
or
INTELLIGENCE SUMMARY.
(Erase heading not required.)

Army Form C. 2118.

Place	Date	Hour	Summary of Events and Information	Remarks and references to Appendices
	14/1/18		HQ R.E. moved with Div HQ from NESLE to OLLEZY & took over from C.R.E. 6th French Division.	
	17/1/18		122 Field Coy R.E. from DURY to BRAY-ST-CHRISTOPHE. Detachment of Coy - 121st Coy with Left Brigade but mostly engaged on Divisional Work under C.R.E. 150th Coy with Rt Bgde & similarly employed. 122 Field Coy on general area work — mostly of a "Q" nature.	
	29/1/18		A. FERRIER took up duties as Staff officer & relieved Adjutant of all work in connection of supply of RE stores & materials.	
	31/1/18		Coys working as above described. HQ CRE at OLLEZY. C.R.E. toured (by Secheine) with Corps & Divisional Commanders & C.E.	

Art Potters
Lt. Col. R.E.
C.R.E. 36th Division

Vol 29

Confidential
War Diary
of
C.R.E. 36th Division
for month of February 1918.

Army Form C. 2118.

WAR DIARY
or
INTELLIGENCE SUMMARY.
(Erase heading not required.)

Instructions regarding War Diaries and Intelligence Summaries are contained in F.S. Regs., Part II. and the Staff Manual respectively. Title pages will be prepared in manuscript.

Place	Date	Hour	Summary of Events and Information	Remarks and references to Appendices
OLLEZY	1/2/18	—	C.R.E. to Pioneers (14th K. Rif.) & 121 Field Coy. re work on tracks, causeway & bridge from Tontaine & cross-clues to Castres & a.m. in direction of Urvillers.	[initials]
	2/2/18	—	C.R.E. to 150th Field Coy R.E. re work on Stony Point & Redhill Line, and to R.13A, H.R. & LEJEUNE TRENCH.	[initials]
	3/2/18		Back aero in morning. Visit of C.E. in afternoon.	[initials]
	4/2/18		C.R.E. to Causeway & Stony Point Line. Reconnoitred from St Simon customs prepared bridge crossings.	[initials]
	5/2/18		C.R.E. to Epine de Dallon, reconnoitred I.16c/12d by GIFFECOURT & S.P. GRUGIES.	[initials]
	6/2/18		C.R.E. & Adjt. to ST SIMON to investigate march crossings Franco-Annois.	[initials]
	7/2/18		C.R.E. & R. Eng. Mtr. to Stony Point N° 4 3 and RACECOURSE	[initials]
	8/2/18		C.R.E. to line with Corps Commander.	[initials]
	9/2/18		Reconnaissance canal for desirability of each forward of OLLEZY.	[initials]
	10/2/18		To C.E. Seraucourt to see Pioneers & 121 Coy. To R.E. Dump re anti-tank measures	[initials]
	11/2/18		To whole Stony Point line with C.E.	[initials]
	12/2/18		To GIFFECOURT & RACECOURSE with G.O.C.	[initials]
	13/2/18		To S.P. Line with O.C. 121 & Coy.	[initials]
	14/2/18		Hanneycourt to Major Levan.	[initials]
	15/2/18			[initials]

Army Form C. 2118.

WAR DIARY
or
INTELLIGENCE SUMMARY.
(Erase heading not required.)

Instructions regarding War Diaries and Intelligence Summaries are contained in F. S. Regs., Part II. and the Staff Manual respectively. Title pages will be prepared in manuscript.

Place	Date	Hour	Summary of Events and Information	Remarks and references to Appendices
OLLEZY	16/2/18		To Grand Seracourt to 121 Coy + Pioneers	RPM
	17/2/18		To CUFFECOURT to see Strong Point	28 PM
	18/2/18		To JEANNE D'ARC Strong Point for inspection	10 AM
	19/2/18		Ground to take over Battle zone F + J sectors 20/2/18 instead of 25/2/18	10 PM
	20/2/18		Taking over of F + J sectors with O.C. 201 and O.C. 218.	11 AM
	21/2/18		To see work going on in E.S. sector	11 AM
	22/2/18		To CUFFECOURT to see Strong Point, + the Rancourt Strong Point	10 AM
	23/2/18		To G.I. Seracourt to see 121 + 150 Coys and Pioneers	10 AM
	24/2/18		WE J.O.C. to CUFFECOURT Strong Point - proposed plan considered. Approved plan for Strong Point decided upon. Read of F + J sectors with C.E. Gutters which I started from made more general.	10 AM
	25/2/18			11 AM
	26/2/18			11 AM
	27/2/18		To 121 Coy + North Got transport of 121 Coy	12 AM
	28/2/18		To HAM for C.E.'s conference.	11 AM

JMLewis Major
a/C.R.E. 36 Divn

2353 Wt. W2544/1454 700,000 5/15 D. D. & L. A.D.S.S./Forms/C. 2118.

36th Divisional Engineers

C. R. E.

36th DIVISION

MARCH 1918

Narrative of Operations attached.

War Diary
of
C.R.E. 36th Division
for month of March 1918.

Army Form C. 2118.

WAR DIARY
or
INTELLIGENCE SUMMARY.
(Erase heading not required.)

Instructions regarding War Diaries and Intelligence Summaries are contained in F. S. Regs., Part II. and the Staff Manual respectively. Title pages will be prepared in manuscript.

Place	Date	Hour	Summary of Events and Information	Remarks and references to Appendices
OLLEZY	4.3.18		C.R.E. returned from leave	
	5.3.18		C.R.E. to Battle Zone with Brig. Lewis	
"	6.3.18		C.R.E. to Redoubt Line with O.C. 150th Coy. R.E.	
"	7.3.18		C.R.E. to Redoubt Line	
	8.3.18		C.R.E. to Battle Zone	
	9.3.18		C.R.E. to Redoubt Line with CO. XVIII Corps.	
	10.3.18		C.R.E. to Redoubt Line	
	11.3.18		C.R.E. to Redoubt Line	
	12.3.18		C.R.E. to Gd. Seraucourt re anti-tank arrangements	
	13.3.18		C.R.E. to Gd. Seraucourt (anti-tank) and Mennevis (billets)	
	14.3.18		C.R.E. to Battle Zone with D.C. 121st Inf. Bde.	
	15.3.18		C.R.E. to Pontoise & Grugies with D.C. 122nd Inf. Bde.	
	16.3.18		C.R.E. to Gd. Seraucourt with C.E. re anti tank work	
	18.3.18		C.R.E. to Roupy with Gen. Wilkinson & Bastion and D.C. 150th Wright	
	19.3.18		C.R.E. to Seraucourt for Anti Tank Gun demonstration. To 365 Trustee Coy in Afternoon	

WAR DIARY or INTELLIGENCE SUMMARY

Army Form C. 2118.

Place	Date	Hour	Summary of Events and Information	Remarks and references to Appendices
Ugny	20.3.18		C.R.E. to Canizy. 66 C. G.C. Canal bank to Col Stevenson. 121st Coy & Dumps	
	21.3.18		Enemy offensive opened. One Coy Pioneers set at on to french on L 35a. bn hy height of 21/22 all casernes at SOMMETTE-EAUCOURT less 1 Sec: 121 Coy, 2 Hdqrs to withdraw to L.15. HAMEL – SETRAUCOURT demolition group. 1 Sec. 150th ARTEMPS demolition group. 2 Sec: 150th TUGNY + ST SIMON demolition group. 2 Sec 122 Coy of 150 FSH FARM – L 3rd. Later Hdqrs ordered to PITHON K 28 to view of S. EAUCOURT. Lieut Benson to bridge group to ensure demolition not carried out prematurely. C.A.E. send H.Q. to E.S. TOURLY Report from 12 x lcy group bridge near ST SIMON completed. Norm 21.3.18. ARTEMPS group bridge demolished 7.0 a.m. Lieut RAINIGHT and escort refusing at PITHON. Companies moved to new transport to COL AUVCOURT and demonstration position available. TUGNY group bridge demolished 9.30 AM. Pioneers moved to support 61st Brigade 10.40 AM. ST SIMON RESEAU Bridge demolished shortly after 10.0 AM. Pioneers moving onward with Brigade under OCCC5 Orders 1207 Coy retired under orders to take up Brigade between ARTEMPS and SOMMETTE EAUCOURT and support from there. C.R.E. and H.Q. to FRENCHES. Bridges moved later to CHARMES for return.	
FRENCHES	23.3.18		C.R.E. to GERONCOURT. Arct BENSON RE to CHARMES for return. Bridle companies ordered to take up defensive position & cover GERONCOURT. Transport to west of FRETOY under command of Major Haly. Preparation of demolition and of FRETOY command. C.R.E. and H.Q. to BEAUREVE. 2nd Lieut BREEDEN R.E. wounded.	

WAR DIARY or INTELLIGENCE SUMMARY

Army Form C. 2118.

(Erase heading not required.)

Place	Date	Hour	Summary of Events and Information	Remarks and references to Appendices
BEAULIEU	24.3.18	10 AM	CRE to FRETOY to organise demolition of bridge. Adjutant attended meeting of CE to found Divisions to consolidate.	
		12 noon	Report from Capt FAIRMAN R.E. that field operated and other works under construction P 36 & 50. Pioneers were composed of 2 B.N.R.E.'s.	
			on our 660, P 346 out to P 36 & 50. Pioneers were composed of 2 B.N.R.E.'s.	
			Returned and on return wagons to TACHAM to meet of FRENCH troops.	
			Transport & trans...res ordered to MARGNY en ceisse.	
			100 authn. cavalry B.Qr. JM CRAIG R.E. of 2nd BN CANADIAN Rly TROOPS taken over & command of by C.R.E.	
ROYE	25.3.18	2.0 PM	CRE and HQ to ROYE.	
		4.0 PM	CRE to MQ to MARICOURT to reconnoitre & re-organise men of CANADIAN Rly TROOPS withdrawn to this area south...	
NOYON?			Brit & Aust men ANDECHY. Companies on futures. 121 Oz INFANTRY, 122 Oz TRENCHES.	
GUERBIGNY	26/3/18	5.0 PM	CRE went H.Q. to GUERBIGNY	
		10.0 AM	Supplies transport of companies ordered to proceed to MARICOURT (6) by O and at supt area.	
		10.30	CRE to FRONTIER at train and last pigeon to sort sort sort	
		2.30 PM	CRE to PONTIERE is positions in direction of HARICOURT & HARICOURT. Preparation for demolition of bridge at BECQUIGNY movement.	
		3.30 PM	Continued to BERNY with FRENCH troops.	Maj MJ.D. KERR wounded
		5.0 PM	4 Section Royal Eng? Ordered to report to BERNY R... under BAN FRASER	Capt PATRICIAN wounded
		6.00 PM	CRE to ANDSY HQ at CAIVESNES	Lieut KENNOX "
		6.00 PM	CRE HQ to CAIVESNES	Lieut NORMAN wounded and missing
		7.0 PM	Transport of R.E. companies at CAIVESNES	Capt? R.E. WALL missing
			Brigade Indicated Bond SAVART to ABBEVILLE	
ERICOURT?	27.3.18	3.0 PM	CRE to MARICOURT. Surplus Transport moved back Lieut BENSON to ABBEVILLE	
		9.30 PM	CRE to HARICOURT 150 by one Ordinated returned to R... P...	
		5.30 PM	...gdt... ... SERAUCOURT ... Bgd... NICKINSON and ambulance stop at 122 W.C? at HARICOURT for demolition	
SOURDON	28.3.18		... and hidden train lorry. 121st and 122nd to IMBENY. 122 to BRIVIVILLERS	
			Companies to Mr...'s from all sides and d line coyt in worst N.W. of DAVESNY, 121 & KIRK	
ESBERTOY?	29.3.18		CRE & 2 MALLIS? Bde DIV d'... here wood Imp hours. Companies moving to area to VERONNES, also GOR KIRK to MENZILLY	
WAVILLY	30/3/18	noon	Order for entrainment of Companies nominal Transport & material of CRE one Bde next to FLIXECOURT	
VILLERY	31.3.18		CRE's HQ to GNAMCHES 121 and 122 6, 6, to DARGNIES 150 & 6 to EBERVILLERS	

2353 Wt. W.2541/4454 700,000 5/15 D. D. & L. A.D.S.S./Forms/C. 2118.

36th Division "G"

Herewith a narrative of the operations carried out between 21st and 28th March, 1918, together with a report on the demolition of bridges and a copy of the instructions issued to Field Companies and Pioneers in case of enemy attack.

It is regretted that these instructions are not quite complete, as some of the amendments have been lost.

Captain, R.E.
for C.R.E. 36th Divn.

29/4/18.

SECRET

NARRATIVE OF OPERATIONS

Between 21st and 28th MARCH, 1918.

At the opening of the German offensive on March 21st 1918, the disposition of the Field Companies R.E. was as follows :-

121st Field Coy.R.E. — H.Q., Transport and 4 Sections at G.1.b. and 2.d.(Sheet 66c).

122nd " " " — H.Q., Transport and 2 Sections at G.9.c.1.5. (Sheet 66c).
2 Sections ESSIGNY STATION G.6.a.(Sheet 66c).

150th " " " — H.Q., Transport and 1½ Sections HAMEL G.1.b. (Sheet 66c).
2½ Sections MARSH FARM L.34.d.1.0.(Sheet 66d).

16th R.I.R.(P). — H.Q., at GRAND SERAUCOURT. 2 Companies at SOMME Dugouts A.26.(Sheet 66c). 1 Company JEANNE D'ARC B.25.b.(Sheet 66c).

On the order "MAN BATTLE STATIONS". Demolition parties went out as follows :-

2/Lt.Norman R.E. and 1 Section 121st Field Coy.R.E. to HAMEL-SERAUCOURT Group.
Lt.Brunyate R.E. and 1 Section 150th Field Coy.R.E. to ARTEMPS GROUP.
2/Lt.C.L.Knox R.E. and 1½ Sections 150th Field Coy.R.E. from MARSH FARM to TUGNY GROUP.
Lt.Stapylton-Smith R.E. and 1 Section 150th Field Coy.R.E. from MARSH FARM to ST.SIMON GROUP.

H.Q. and 3 Sections of the 121st Field Coy.R.E. stood by at LE HAMEL. H.Q. and 2 Sections of the 122nd Field Coy.R.E. stood by at G.9.c.1.5. the two sections in railway cutting at ESSIGNY STATION were very heavily gas shelled, and surprised by the enemy who entered the cutting from the east. The two officers and about twenty men succeeded in rejoining their unit. One Section 150th Field Coy.R.E. and H.Q. 150th Field Coy.R.E. moved to a site west of TUGNY (L.15.c.and d (Sheet 66d) where the transport of the 121st and 150th Field Companies R.E. was collected. Transport of 122nd Field Coy.R.E. went to L.27.c.9.7. (66d).

16th R.I.R.(P) concentrated 2 Companies N.W. of GRAND SERAUCOURT at SOMME Dugouts.

No.1 Company 16th R.I.R.(P) consisting of 9 Officers and 150 men, was entirely cut off in JEANNE D'ARC redoubt by the enemy and did not rejoin the battalion.

The pontoon wagons of the three Field Companies R.E. were collected and parked at OLLEZY in case it should be necessary to build new pontoon bridges over the SOMME and ST.QUENTIN CANALS. Bridging Equipment was obtained from C.E.XVIII Corps for this purpose and was also parked at OLLEZY.

At 8.0 a.m. 21/3/18 two sections 122nd Field Coy.R.E. under Lt. T.K.Knox R.E. and 2/Lt.Ewens R.E. were ordered to construct a new foot bridge at L.35.c.3.7. This work was completed by 9.0 p.m. and the two sections billeted for the night in MARSH FARM.

At 10.0 a.m. Capt.Withington R.E.122nd Field Coy.R.E. and details from his transport repaired the pontoon bridge at L.33.a.34.(66d). This transport then rejoined the transport of the other two Companies at L.15.d.

Shortly after noon 2/Lt.Norman R.E. completely destroyed a pontoon bridge and a foot bridge at FONTAINE LES CLERCS. At 2 P.M the remaining sections of 122nd Field Coy.R.E. left GRAND SERAUCOURT and joined their transport. At 3 p.m. H.Q. and 3 Sections of 121st Field Coy.R.E. were withdrawn from LE HAMEL to L.15.d. and No.2 & 3 Companies of Pioneers were ordered to construct a track for artillery East of

2/

ST. SIMON, transport being provided by a reserve park detachment located in that village.

22/3/18. During the night of 21st/22nd the three Companies less demolition parties were concentrated with their transport at PITHON and the 16th R.I.R.(P) bivouaced at OLLEZY.

C.R.E. and H.Q. moved to ESTOUILLY.

2/Lt.I.T.V.Norman R.E. and 1 Section 121st Field Coy.R.E. successfully demolished the HAMEL-SERAUCOURT Group of bridges between 10.15 p.m. 21st and 4.0 a.m. 22nd.

The ARTEMPS Group was demolished at 6.0 a.m. 22/3/18 by Lt. Brunyate R.E. and half a Section 150th Field Coy.R.E.

Both Officers and men then rejoined their units at PITHON.

The TUGNY bridges were demolished at 9.30 a.m. 22/3/18 by 2/Lt C.L.Knox R.E. and 1½ Sections 150th Field Coy.R.E.

Great gallantry was displayed by this Officer who, when a fuze junction had failed, personally lit the instantaneous fuze to fire a charge. The bridge was successfully destroyed and 2/Lt.C.L.Knox escaped unhurt. During the same period Lt.Stapylton-Smith R.E. and 1 Section 150th Field Coy.R.E. successfully destroyed the ST.SIMON Group. These two detachments rejoined their unit later in the day.

All these bridges were destroyed in the presence of the enemy in one case the hostile infantry being actually on the bridge.

About 9.0 a.m. 22/3/18 the Pioneers were ordered to SOMMETTE EAUCOURT to start work on a line of strong points between that village and OLLEZY. Tools were drawn from HAM by pontoon wagons and dumped along this line.

The Field Companies marched with transport and concentrated at GOLANCOURT, C.R.E. and H.Q. moving to FRENICHES. During the afternoon Lt.R.E.Walsh R.E. and No.3 Section 121st Field Coy.R.E. took over from 18th Corps Troops the destruction of bridges in HAM and along the line of the SOMME to OLLEZY. It was found that the broad gauge railway bridge near PITHON had not been prepared for demolition, but an N.C.O. and two men were detached to do all possible damage to it. Doubtful reports have since been received that French railway troops destroyed this bridge. The destruction of the other bridges was carried out during the night 22nd/23rd and the morning of the 23rd. After completion Lt.Walsh rejoined his Company at GOLANCOURT.

23/3/18. During the 23rd the Pioneers were attached by order of 36th Div. to 9th R.Ir.Fus. and were in action all day on the line of the SOMME.

At 10.0 a.m. the transport of the Field Companies and Pioneers was ordered to move to FLAVY LE MELDEUX and later to a site West of FRETOY in U.23.a.(66d), where they parked for the night. The dismounted sections were ordered to take up a line covering GOLANCOURT under command of Major H.M.Fordham R.E. They accordingly took up a position from BONNEUIL FARM westwards in conjunction with details of Machine Gunners and other troops, the whole being under command of Major Lowe of the M.G.Corps.

In the evening C.R.E. and H.Q. moved to BEAULIEU and orders were issued to Major J.H.Otway R.E. then in command of H.Q. and mounted sections of the three Field Companies to prepare for demolition bridges West of FRETOY and CAMPAGNE.

During the night 23rd/24th the Pioneers fought a retiring action falling back to a line West of VILLESELVE. The Field Companies were forced to fall back with the rest of the troops under Major Lowe to a position near BONNEUIL CHATEAU Wood, P.29.b.(66d).

24/3/18. At dawn on the 24th Lt.Blagden R.E.121st Field Coy.R.E. was wounded and evacuated. After 7.0 a.m. the Companies dropped back to a line held by the 20th French Division P.34.d.23., P.35.c.52.(66d).

Major R.A.H.Lewin R.E. returned from leave during the day and took over command of the 121st Field Coy.R.E.(his unit) sending Capt. H.Scoch to transport lines.

- 3 -

Tools were brought up to the line by lorry for 62nd French Division.

The C.R.E. went out at 9.30 a.m. to see bridges West of FRETOY.

The two bridges in U.23.b. were prepared for demolition and handed over to a detachment of Trench Mortars. One bridge West of CAMPAGNE was also prepared and left in charge of the C.S.M. and 2 sappers of 122nd Field Coy.R.E. who destroyed it at 6.0 p.m. 25/3/18.

On the night of the 24th Field Companies and Pioneers were drawn out of the line and marched to BEAULIEU. Transport went to MARGNY aux CERISES.

25/3/18. On the 25th C.R.E. and H.Q. moved to AVRICOURT. Field Companies and Pioneers with transport joined Brigade groups round this village.

At 6.0 p.m. C.R.E. and H.Q. commenced march to GUERBIGNY, 121st Field Coy.R.E. to same place, 122nd Field Coy.R.E. to ERCHES, 150th Field Coy.R.E. and Pioneers to WARSY sheet 66a.

26/3/18. At 10.0 a.m. on 26th The dismounted portion of the 121st Field Coy.R.E. joined the 107th Brigade and took up positions in old trenches Q.23.c. near the ANDECHY-GUERBIGNY Road, tool carts and water cart being kept at GUERBIGNY. The dismounted portion of the 122nd Field Coy.R.E. went into action with the 108th Brigade at ERCHES. 150th Field Coy.R.E. stood by in WARSY. Pioneers were put in Divisional Reserve. Major W.J.Allen took over command of this unit vice Lt.Col. C.F.Meares D.S.O. who was admitted to hospital.

All transport less tool carts of 121st and 150th Companies moved to GRIVESNES and LE PLESSIER.

At 2.0 p.m. C.R.E. moved to FRIGHIERES.

150th Company moved under verbal orders from 36th Div."G" to BECQUIGNY where one section under 2/Lt.C.L.Knox R.E. prepared the AVRE Crossing for demolition. At 5.0 p.m. 1 Section under Lt.Stapylton-Smith R.E. marched with tool carts to MARE ST MONTIERS to prepare for destruction the crossings of the river at this village and at BOUILLANCOURT.

Orders were sent to Capt.Withington R.E. 122nd Field Coy.R.E. to prepare the bridge at HARGICOURT for demolition. At about 7.0 p.m. C.R.E. and H.Q. moved off to GRIVESNES.

In the afternoon 16th R.I.R.(P) were sent into action under 108th Brigade to close a gap between ERCHES and BOUCHOIR.

27/3/18. During the night 26th/27th Major M.J.D.Kerr R.E. 122nd Field Coy.R.E. was wounded, command of dismounted portion passing to Lt.T.K.Knox R.E.

This Company was holding a line through ERCHES.

121st Field Coy.R.E. was holding a line with the 107th Brigade West of ERCHES. Lt.Walsh R.E. of this unit did some valuable patrol work at this time and identified enemy transport on the ROYE-AMIENS Road.

150th Field Coy.R.E. less one Section were at BECQUIGNY.

During the 27th Lt.T.K.Knox R.E. 122nd Field Coy.R.E. was wounded by shrapnel and evacuated the command passing to 2/Lt.Fagan R.E. the Company now being in the line between P.6.central and P.12.a. 2/Lt.Fagan got in touch with 36th Div. at K.32.b. and came under orders of the 107th Brigade. At about 12 noon the 107th Brigade were forced to fall back and the Field Companies and Pioneers had to conform to their movements. During the withdrawal Major R.A.H.Lewin R.E. and 2/Lt.I.T.V.Norman R.E. were both severely wounded but were carried to an A.D.S. and evacuated. Lt.R.E.Walsh R.E. was also wounded but was not evacuated and has been missing since that date.

H.Q. and 3 Sections 150th Field Coy.R.E. marched during the morning to MAREST MONTIERS leaving a small detachment with the French at BECQUIGNY.

C.R.E. and H.Q. went to HARGICOURT.

4/

- 4 -

Surplus transport of Companies and Pioneers was sent to ABBEVILLE under Lt.T.K.Benson R.E. and the remainder of the transport moved under Major J.H.Otway R.E. to AUBVILLERS.

At 4.0 p.m. C.R.E. ordered 150th Company to advance towards BOUSSICOURT where they joined up with the French and held a line South of that village.

The detachment left at BECQUIGNY destroyed the bridge there at 9.30 p.m. after the French had withdrawn.

At 6.30 p.m. C.R.E. and H.Q. moved to SOURDON.

28/3/18.   During the night 27th/28th and morning of the 28th the Division was relieved. The Field Companies concentrated at EPAGNY and HAINNEVILLE and the 16th R.I.R.(P) at CHAUSSOY. In the evening C.R.E. and H.Q. moved to ESSERTAUX.

Before leaving Lt.Stapylton-Smith R.E. 150th Field Coy.R.E. destroyed the bridge at MAREST MONTIERS under orders from the French.

The bridge at HARGICOURT was handed over ready for demolition by Capt.Withington R.E. to 9th Cie.du Genie under orders of General LAVIGNY of 5th French Cavalry Division. This bridge was afterwards destroyed by the French.

During the whole operations communication was kept up by means of mounted and cyclist orderlies, the latter in particular being found very successful.

The Casualties in the Field Companies were nearly 50 per cent and those of the 16th R.I.R.(P) nearly 60 per cent.

On the 29th March the Division moved out to rest.

REPORT ON THE DEMOLITION OF BRIDGES DURING OPERATIONS

FROM 21st to 28th MARCH, 1918.

PART I. THE ST.QUENTIN CANAL.

Grouping, Location and description of Bridges.

1. In the 56th Divisional Area the bridges over the ST.QUENTIN CANAL and the River SOMME were divided into groups as follows :-

(a) HAMEL-SERAUCOURT GROUP comprising

Pontoon Bridge) at FONTAINE LES CLERCS A.15.d.3.7.(Sheet 66c
Foot bridge   )   N.W.)

Bridge 40 heavy trestle bridge) A.26.c.1.2.   "
Foot Bridge   )

Bridge 35 A) to take M.T. G.2.c.4.4.   "
   "   35 B)

   "   34 A   trestle to take M.T. G.1.b.9.2.   "
   "   C   trestle at G.7.b.2.8.   "
   "   35 C) HAMEL LOCK.
Foot Bridge)

(b) ARTEMPS GROUP.

33 A   Trestle Bridge.
33 B   Steel girder 80' span L.17.a.   (Sheet 66d)

32 A   Trestle Bridge.
32 B   Plate girder bridge. L.17.c.   "

(c) TUGNY GROUP.

No.31 "RAILWAY BRIDGE" heavy wooden pile bridge
                              L.22.a.1.5.   "

30 a 66d (N.E.) L.21.d.2.3.
30 b 66d (N.E.) L.21.d.2.4.

Foot bridges a   L.21.c.99.40.
             b   L.27.a.99.40.

                                    Bridges 29 a)
Bridges 27 a) L.21.d.4.8.   b) L.21.b.
         b   )
                                             c)
         28 a) L.21.d.2.9.   d) L.20.d.
         b   )

(d) ST.SIMON GROUP.

Pontoon Bridges "Y" L.35.a.30.30. (Sheet 66d).
                 "R" R.6.a.80.00.   "

Foot bridges 13, 14, 22, 17B, 18A, 19B and a new one constructed by 122nd Field Coy.R.E. at L.35.c.20.80 on 21/3/18.

Bridge 16A Heavy wood trestle for M.T.) Across ST.QUENTIN Canal
       17A   "   "   "   "   "   ) on OLLEZY- ST.SIMON
       16B Steel lattice girder   ) Road. in L.34.c.
                                         (Sheet 66d).

These four groups made up what was known as the "Southern Sector", and the responsibility for the demolition of all bridges in the Southern Sector rested with the C.R.E. 56th Division in accordance with orders received from C.E. 18th Corps.

2. Distribution of R.E. responsible for demolitions.

Group.	Officer i/c.	Party.	Unit.	Location.
HAMEL-SERAUCOURT	2/Lt.I.T.V.Norman	1 Sect.	121st Fd.Co.R.E.	HAMEL.
ARTEMPS	Lt.W.M.V.Brunyate	½ "	150th "	HAMEL.
TUGNY	2/Lt.C.L.Knox	1½ "	150th "	Marsh Farm, near ST. SIMON.
ST.SIMON	Lt.Stapylton-Smith.	1 "	150th "	Marsh Farm.

3. General Method of Demolition.

There were four types of bridges viz :-

(1) Steel lattice and plate girder bridges

(2) Wooden trestle and pile bridges

(3) Pontoon bridges

(4) Pile foot bridges for infantry in file.

CHARGES. The explosives used were guncotton for the three first types and ammonal tubes for the last.

The Charges as calculated were made up and stored near sites in special boxes. These boxes were fitted into boxes or shelves permanently fastened to the members to be destroyed. Owing to the newness of the wood employed it was found necessary to use a loose fit and to provide a number of small wooden wedges for the purpose of tightening up. Every charge was numbered and lettered to correspond to its bridge and member.

Firing was carried out by the electric exploder. As an alternative the time and safety fuze system was also prepared and put in place.

On the steel girder bridges the charges were applied in the usual way to cut the flanges, and the lattices at an intersection. No charge was laid to destroy the abutments.

On the wooden pile bridges the charges were applied in two ways on each bridge,

(a) A long charge on a horizontal shelf just under the road bearers designed to destroy both piles and superstructures.

(b) A long charge on a sloping shelf attached to piles designed to cut the piles at different heights.

The pontoon bridges were rendered useless by scuttling the boats.

The foot bridges were demolished by means of Zinc Tubes 2½" diam. and 2 metres long filled with ammonal fired by time and instantaneous fuze.

4. COMMUNICATION. By cyclist orderly direct to C.R.E's office. During the whole of the operations it was found that cyclist orderlies were eminently successful.

5. AUTHORITY. The bridges were demolished under orders from C.R.E. or Brigade Commander.

6. NARRATIVE. "MAN BATTLE STATIONS" was ordered shortly after 4 a.m. 21/3/18. The demolition parties immediately went to their stations and prepared for demolition. Shortly after noon the pontoon bridge and foot bridge at FONTAINE LES CLERCS were completely destroyed although they had been previously rendered unserviceable by hostile fire. Shortly after 10.15 p.m. Bridge No.40 and a foot bridge North of the SUCRERIE at LE HAMEL were destroyed under orders from the Infantry.

There was heavy hostile fire on the approaches to these bridges and the electric firing leads were cut three times. During this period the Division was pivoting on its left and swinging back on its right flank so as to conform to the movement of the troops on the right, the intention being to take up a line behind the SOMME from ARTEMPS southwards and facing East. At 11.45 p.m. the 107th Infantry Brigade having crossed the river and canal, they ordered the destruction of bridges 35 A and 35 B. This order had only just been carried out when 109th Infantry Brigade sent a message to delay destruction as they wished to cross, however, 2/Lt.Norman R.E. guided their troops over another way. At 3.0 a.m. 22/3/18 Bridge 34 A over Canal Between GRAND SERAUCOURT and HAMEL was demolished by order of 109th Infantry Brigade. Next, Bridge C was blown at 3.15 a.m. At 3.45 a.m. Bridge 33 C and foot bridge at HAMEL LOCK were blown by orders of the same Brigade.

Demolition of HAMEL-SERAUCOURT Group was reported complete at 7.0 a.m. by 2/Lt.Norman R.E.
No casualties occurred in the parties.

ARTEMPS GROUP. Demolition was commenced at 4.0 a.m.
No.36 A a wooden trestle bridge and No.33 B a large 90' span steel girder bridge being destroyed. Bridges 32 A trestle bridge and 32 B plate girder were fired at 4.30 a.m.

TUGNY GROUP. This group comprising 13 bridges in all was successfully demolished shortly after 9.30 a.m. 22/3/18.
In one case the time fuze having failed the officer in charge 2/Lt.C.L.Knox R.E. lit the instantaneous fuze with a match. He escaped unhurt.

ST.SIMON GROUP. Destruction of this group commenced at about 8.0 a.m. 22/3/18. Pontoon bridges "Y" and "R" were dismantled and the boats scuttled. Six foot bridges were demolished about 9.45 a.m. the destruction of the seventh was delayed owing to the failing of the fuze. Trestle bridges 16 A and 17 A and the large lattice girder bridge 16 B were successfully destroyed at about 9.50 a.m.

All the above bridges were destroyed in the presence of enemy. Hostile artillery kept a continual barrage on the approaches in order to prevent demolition being carried out. This barrage being increased to a great intensity each time a charge was fired.

PART II.   SOMME AND SOMME CANAL.

At 12 noon 22/3/18 under orders from XVIII Corps, Lt.Walsh R.E. and No.3 Section 121st Field Coy.R.E. took over from Corps Troops the demolition of bridges over the SOMME, SOMMETTE and SOMME CANAL between HAM and OLLEZY, comprising 3 bridges between DURY and OLLEZY, 4 bridges at SOMMETTE EAUCOURT, 3 wooden trestle bridges for light railway, a broad gauge railway bridge, steel span; a wooden road bridge on the HAM-JUSSY Road and a pair of steel girder bridges on the HAM-NOYON Road, making a total of 14 bridges.

It was found that a small bridge over the SOMMETTE between DURY and OLLEZY had been prematurely destroyed before taking over. The remainder of this group were blown about 1.30 p.m. 22/3/18. The SOMMETTE EAUCOURT bridges were blown about midnight 22/3/18, and of the group of light railway bridges one was to be destroyed by explosives and the other two by fire. The fire effectually destroyed the bridges for purposes of traffic, but left them still passable for infantry. No preparations had been made for the demolition of the broad gauge railway bridge owing to the fact that both Lt.Walsh R.E. and the N.C.O. he put on the bridge have since become missing, reports as to the action taken are confusing. Lt.Walsh left an N.C.O. and two men to do as much damage as they could by destroying the wooden piles of the abutments. Sergeant Grice R.E. of 121st Field Coy.R.E. states that the N.C.O. 2nd/Cpl.Wheeler reported that French troops laid a charge and destroyed the bridge.

- 4 -

The bridge on the HAM-JUSSY Road was blown at 6.0.a.m. 23/3/18 and the pair of bridges on the HAM-NOYON Road at 7.30 a.m.

PART III.   OPERATIONS FROM 23rd ------27th MARCH, 1918.

On the withdrawal of the line westward, orders were issued on evening 23/3/18 by C.R.E. to Major J.H.Otway R.E. then in command of H.Q. and mounted sections of the three Field Companies located East of FRETOY U.23.a. (Sheet 66d), to prepare for demolition the bridges over the Canal West of FRETOY and CAMPAGNE, 2 trestle bridges in U.23.b. were prepared and handed over to a detachment of Trench Mortars personnel specially detailed by Division to hold this crossing. One large trestle bridge for M.T. (CAMPAGNE) was also prepared and was blown under orders of the French, by a detachment of the 122nd Field Coy.R.E. on the 24/3/18. A small foot bridge was left standing as it was not considered of any importance.

On the 26/3/18 a reconnaissance was made of the crossings of the AVRE and GUERBIGNY, WARSY and BECQUIGNY, it was considered advisable to destroy the bridge at BECQUIGNY and one section of the 150th Field Coy.R.E. was detailed to carry this out under 2/Lt.C.L.Knox R.E. French troops were at this time holding the line of the AVRE. An N.C.O. and small detachment was left with the French for the purpose of firing the charge. This was done successfully on the 27/3/18 after the French had completely withdrawn and the enemy were on the opposite bank of the river.

No.3 Section 150th Field Coy.R.E. under Lt.Stapylton-Smith R.E. was ordered on the 26/3/18 to prepare the bridges Riviere des 3 Doms at HAREST MONTIERS and BOUILLANCOURT. These were both brick arch bridges and the charge was placed by digging a trench along the crown of the arch. The bridge at HAREST MONTIERS was demolished about 11.30 p.m. on 27/3/18, but the one at BOUILLANCOURT was not destroyed owing to the presence of French troops. Trees were felled across the road at this place.

On the 26/3/18 Capt.Withington R.E. 122nd Field Coy.R.E. and details from H.Q.section prepared bridge at HARGICOURT for demolition and was instructed to destroy 5th Army Reserve ration supply in case of necessity. The Division however was relieved by the French on the night of the 27th/28th and Capt.Withington R.E. handed over his work to them and withdrew.

A personal letter to this officer from the French N.C.O. reports successful destruction.

S E C R E T.

E/14/69/1.

AMENDMENT TO "INSTRUCTIONS TO R.E. AND PIONEERS IN CASE OF ENEMY ATTACK" - 28/2/18.

After "Demolish" ------Groups, Detailed Instructions
    Para 1 (c) add "Completion to be reported to this office by phone, telegram or orderly".

1/3/18.

(Sd) G.McIldowie, Capt.R.E.
for C.R.E. 36th Division.

To all recipients of my E/14/69 dated 28/2/18.

SECRET. E/14/69/5.

AMENDMENT TO "INSTRUCTIONS TO R.E. AND PIONEERS IN CASE OF ENEMY ATTACK" - E/14/69, dated 28/2/18.

14/3/18.

In accordance with Fifth Army S.G. 907/82 dated 5/3/18, the 60 c.m. Railway Bridge at L.22.a.1.5., included in the TUGNY Group (my E/14/69 dated 28/2/18 - Schedule of Bridges, page 2) will be known as No.131.

(Sd) J.McIldowie,Capt.R.E.
for C.R.E. 36th Division.

To all recipients of my E/14/69 dated 28/2/18.

S E C R E T.

AMENDMENT TO "INSTRUCTIONS TO R.E. AND PIONEERS IN CASE OF ENEMY ATTACK" No.E/14/69 dated 28/2/18.

❉❉

As the Bridge demolition detachment of 150th Field Coy. R.E. is now at L.34.d.1.0. the following amendments are necessary, in the Detailed Instructions :-

<u>Para.1.b.4th line from foot of page.</u> for "The BRAY ST.CHRISTOPHE detachment" read "TUGNY Group detachment of the 150th Field Coy.R.E. from L.34.d.1.0".

<u>Para.1.b.</u> Delete the two paras at top of page 2 and substitute :-
Demolition parties for TUGNY Group and ST.SIMON Group will be despatched immediately from L.34.d.1.0.
    The TUGNY party will be reinforced on arrival at TUGNY by the half section of 150th Field Coy.R.E. as detailed in 1 (b)(last 6 lines at foot of page 1).
    These parties will make final preparations for the destruction of the bridges in their group.

<u>Para.1.d.</u> (Sixth line). For "Detachment 150th Field Coy.R.E. at BRAY ST CHRISTOPHE" read "Detachment 150th Field Coy.R.E. at L.34.d.1. and for "BRAY ST CHRISTOPHE in last line but 2 of para.1 (d)" read "L.34.d.1.0.

    Amendment to Schedule of Bridges - Page 3 :-

    Delete bridges "X" and "Y".

                                            (Sd) G.McIldowie, Capt.R.E.
6/3/18.   for C.R.E. 36th Division.

    To all recipients of my E/14/69 dated 28/2/18.

SECRET.   E/14/69.

INSTRUCTIONS FOR R.E. AND PIONEERS IN CASE OF ENEMY ATTACK.

Map reference - France Sheets 66d & c - 1/40,000.

GENERAL INSTRUCTIONS.

1. In the event of an attack becoming imminent, the order "MAN BATTLE STATIONS" will be issued from Corps H.Q., and will be communicated to Field Companies by the C.R.E., and to 16th R.I.R.(P) by 36th Division "G".

2. On receipt of this order the following action will be taken :-

    (a) The Companies of the 16th R.I.R.(P) will move back to GRAND SERAUCOURT, the Battalion will be under the orders of the C.R.E.

    (b) The Field Companies will remain at their present positions, all Sections out at work or on detachment (except as given below in the DETAILED INSTRUCTIONS), including Sections with Div.Artillery, rejoining their Company H.Q.
    The Companies will be under the orders of the C.R.E.

    (c) Bridge Demolition detachments will be sent out as shewn in the following DETAILED INSTRUCTIONS.

DETAILED INSTRUCTIONS.

1. On receipt of the order "MAN BATTLE STATIONS":-

    (a) Personnel and transport will be held in readiness to move immediately on receipt of instructions.
    One cyclist and one mounted orderly will be detailed immediately by each Company, to report to this office.
    Men and horses should be carefully selected, and should have two days rations and forage with them.
    16th R.I.R.(P) will similarly detail one mounted and one cyclist orderly.

    (b) BRIDGES.
    O.C.121st Field Coy.R.E. will send out the parties already detailed for the demolition of the bridges in the HAMEL-SERAUCOURT Group, and make final preparations for their demolition.
    On completion of demolitions, or if withdrawn for any reason, the parties will rejoin their unit.

    O.C.150th Field Coy.R.E. will arrange as follows :-
    A demolition party from Company H.Q. consisting of one Officer and half a section R.E. will immediately be despatched to make final preparations for the demolition of all bridges in the ARTEMPS Group.
    This party will be accompanied by transport and material as laid down in para.1.(d) below.
    The remaining half section will be sent to TUGNY, to a rendezvous previously arranged, to await the arrival of the BRAY ST.CHRISTOPHE detachment of 150th Field Coy.R.E.
    This half section will be at the disposal of O.C. Detachment 150th Field Coy.R.E. for work on either TUGNY or ST.SIMON Group.

                                                            Detachment.

Detachment 150th Field Coy.R.E. will vacate BRAY ST.CHRISTOPHE, and O.C.Detachment and all details will take up their H.Q. at FARM HOUSE in the MARSH at L.34.d.1.0. They will be accompanied by transport etc,, as laid down in para.1 (d) below.

Demolition parties at TUGNY Group and ST.SIMON Group, composed of the half section joining them at TUGNY and remainder of the detachment, will be posted en route. These parties will make final preparations for destruction of bridges in their group.

If withdrawn for any reason, demolition detachment will rendezvous at Farm L.34.d.1.0. On completion of demolitions, parties will make their own way to the rear, and endeavour to get in touch with this office.

Orderlies will be detailed as follows :-

One at Telephone, Area Commandants Office, ARTEMPS
One   "   173 Bde. R.F.A. Wagon Lines, TUGNY.
One   "   36th D.A.C., H.Q. ST.SIMON.
Three cyclist orderlies to C.R.E's office OLLEZY.

All orderlies should know their way to any of the bridges in any of the three above mentioned groups.

(c) Demolition parties will act on the order from this office "Demolish Bridge ----" or "Demolish ----- Group".

The list of bridges in the various groups is given in the attached Schedule.

(d) O.C.concerned will arrange that sufficient transport is available for each demolition detachment to move stores required for their work to the various sites in one trip.

To ensure this, sufficient transport will be kept in readiness at 150th Field Coy.R.E. H.Q., 121st Field Coy.R.E. H.Q., and detachment 150th Field Coy. at BRAY ST.CHRISTOPHE, to take materials required for the ARTEMPS Group, SERAUCOURT Group, and TUGNY and ST.SIMON Groups respectively.

Till final arrangements are made for storage of materials on site they will be located as follows :-

SERAUCOURT GROUP   -   121st Field Coy.R.E.
ARTEMPS   "   -   150th   "
TUGNY   "   -   BRAY ST.CHRISTOPHE.
ST.SIMON   "   -   In dug-out at L.34.c.5.8, near Bridge No.16 B.

2. It is possible that it may be necessary to withdraw Field Coys and Pioneer transport (except any wanted for immediate use or for operations) now in GRAND SERAUCOURT and LE HAMEL to lines in a less advanced position.

Sites for picket lines should be reconnoitred by O.C. as follows :-

122nd Field Coy.R.E. - In the vicinity of ARTEMPS.
16th R.I.R.(P)   -   "   "
121st Field Coy.R.E. - } L.15.c.8.5. (between HAPPENCOURT-TUGNY
150th   "   "   "   - }   Road and the SOMME Marshes).

Sites finally selected should be reported to this office by 6.0 p.m. 2nd prox.

The decision to withdraw transport, as outlined above, is left to Os.C. Units.

Men.

3. Men employed at their trades at the R.E. Dump, GRAND SERAUCOURT will rejoin their unit on the order "MAN BATTLE STATIONS". The staff employed on the receipt and issue of R.E. stores will remain there.

4. ACKNOWLEDGE.

28/2/18.

(Sd) G.McIldowie, Capt, R.E.
for C.R.E. 36th Division.

Distribution.

3 Copies	to	121st Field Coy.R.E.
2	"	122nd " " "
5	"	150th " " "
3	"	16th R.I.R.(P).
1	"	36th Division "G".
1	"	36th Division "Q".
1	"	C.E. XVIII Corps.
3	"	36th Divl.Artillery.
1	"	A.P.M. 36th Division.
1	"	A.D.M.S. 36th Division.
1	"	Area Commandant, ARTEMPS.
1	"	Town Major, GRAND SERAUCOURT.
1	"	Town Major, ST.SIMON.
1	"	Area Commandant, BRAY ST.CHRISTOPHE.
1	"	36th Divl.Signal Coy.R.E.

INSTRUCTIONS FOR R.E. AND PIONEERS IN CASE OF ENEMY ATTACK.

Schedule of bridges referred to in para 1 (d) of DETAILED INSTRUCTIONS.

28/2/18.

Reference Maps
Sheets 66c and d.
1/40.000

Group.	Locality.	No.	Map reference.	Load.	Remarks.
G.SERAUCOURT	HAMEL	A	G.1.b.9.2.	7 Tons.	34a.
-do-	G.SERAUCOURT)	B	G.2.c.4.5.	9 Tons.	35a) Grouped as bridge
	G.SERAUCOURT)		G.2.c.5.5.	3 Tons.	35b) B.
-do-	HAMEL)	D	A.26.c.2.7.	2½ Tons	40
	HAMEL)		A.26.c.2.8.	Footbridge.	Infantry in single file.
-do-	G.SERAUCOURT	C	G.7.b.3.8.	Horse transport.	
-do-	HAMEL LOCK	E	L.12.a.9.7.	Horse transport.	Not mentioned in Corps list.
-do-	FONTAINE-les-CLERCS.	F	A.15.d.35.75.	-do-	Pontoon Bridge.

INSTRUCTIONS FOR R.E. AND PIONEERS IN CASE OF ENEMY ATTACK.

Schedule of Bridges - Page 2.

28/2/18.

Group.	Locality.	No.	Map-reference.	Load.	Remarks.
ARTEMPS	ARTEMPS	32 a.	L.17.a.6.8.	Lorries.	
-do-	-do-	32 b.	L.17.a.6.7.	17 Tons one axle.	
-do-	-do-	33 a.	L.17.a.6.1.	Horse transport.	
-do-	-do-	33 b.	L.17.a.6.0.	17 Tons one axle.	
TUGNY	TUGNY	27 a.	L.20.d.9.9.	10 Tons.	
-do-	-do-	27 b.	L.20.b.9.0.	9 Tons.	
-do-	-do-	28 a.	L.21.a.7.2.	14 Tons.	
-do-	-do-	28 b.	L.21.a.7.3.	Horse transport.	
-do-	-do-	29 a.	L.21.d.2.9.	17 Tons one axle.	
-do-	-do-	29 b.	L.21.a.10.05.	7 Tons.	
-do-	-do-	29 c.	L.21.a.1.1.	Horse transport.	
-do-	-do-	29 d.	L.21.c.95.75.	Infantry in file.	
-do-	-do-	30 a.	L.21.d.2.3.)	8 Tons.	
-do-	-do-	30 b.	L.21.d.2.4.)		
-do-	-do-	—	L.22.a.1.3.	60 c.m. engines and tractors.	To be known as "Railway Bridge". Not mentioned in Corps List.

INSTRUCTIONS FOR R.E. AND PIONEERS IN CASE OF ENEMY ATTACK.

Schedule of Bridges - Page 3.   28/2/18.

Group.	Locality.	No.	Map reference.	Load.	Remarks.
St.SIMON.	ST.SIMON	13	L.33.a.7.2.	Infantry in file.	
--do--	--do--	14	L.33.d.2.9.	--do--	
--do--	--do--	16 a.	L.34.c.1.8.	9 Tons.	Bridges 21 b.(6 tons) at R.8.a.9.8. and 21 c (Infy. in file) at R.8.a.5.6. are not included in Schedule. These should be demolished if time permits. They are both E. of Canal, and bridge a small stream.
--do--	--do--	16 b.	L.34.c.2.9.	17 Tons one axle.	
--do--	--do--	17 a.	L.34.c.25.95.	6 Tons.	
--do--	--do--	17 b.	L.34.a.5.3.	Infantry in file.	
--do--	--do--	18 a.	L.34.a.9.7.	--do--	
--do--	--do--	18 b.	L.34.b.2.7.	--do--	
--do--	--do--	21 a.	R.6.a.3.7.	--do--	
--do--	--do--	X	L.34.b.9.1.	--do--	Not mentioned in Corps list.
--do--	--do--	Y	L.35.c.9.4.	--do--	
--do--	--do--	22	M.1.d.3.7.	--do--	

```
TOTALS :-   GRAND SERAUCOURT GROUP  - 8
            ARTEMPS GROUP           - 4
            TUGNY GROUP             -11
            ST.SIMON GROUP          -12
                                    ----
                        Total    35 Bridges.
```

36th Divisional Engineers

C. R. E.

36th DIVISION.

APRIL 1918.

WA 31

War Diary

of

6. R.E. 36th Division

for month of April 1918

Army Form C. 2118.

WAR DIARY
or
INTELLIGENCE SUMMARY.
(Erase heading not required.)

Instructions regarding War Diaries and Intelligence Summaries are contained in F. S. Regs., Part II. and the Staff Manual respectively. Title pages will be prepared in manuscript.

Place	Date	Hour	Summary of Events and Information	Remarks and references to Appendices

WAR DIARY
INTELLIGENCE SUMMARY
(Erase heading not required.)

Army Form C. 2118.

Place	Date	Hour	Summary of Events and Information	Remarks and references to Appendices
	11/4/18	—	CRE in office. Visited CRE 30th Div in morning.	AM
	12/4/18	—	Lt T.R. BENSON RE took over duties as Staff Officer from Lt A. FERRIER RE	AM
	15/4/18	—	(to 150th Field Coy RE as 2nd in command).	
		—	knew of proposed withdrawal. CRE with GOC reconnoitred proposed new line.	AM
	16/4/18	—	CRE & GSO1. made a further reconnaissance of proposed new line, both front & support lines, & proposed withdrawal connection between 36th Div. line & line of Div on right. In afternoon CRE &	April
			GSO1. reconnoitred line on Canal Bank.	
	17/4/18	—	2/Lt CL KNOX 150th Field Coy RE was personally congratulated by Div. commander for his coolness & bravery whilst destroying 13 bridges	AM
			at TUGNY on the Somme following the enemy's attack 21/3/18.	
	18/4/18	—	CRE & GSO1. reconnoitred 2nd line of Defence on wire & gaps in same — arranged for bounding into 41st Div. on right & Belgian Division on left.	AM
	19/4/18	—	CRE with GOC inspected Westrype defences & belodryrePwJupe	AM
	20/4/18	—	CRE with GOC & Byles Major here & Mr Byle reconnoitred Vlamertinghe - Brielen lines	AM

WAR DIARY

INTELLIGENCE SUMMARY.

(Erase heading not required.)

Army Form C. 2118.

Place	Date	Hour	Summary of Events and Information	Remarks and references to Appendices
	21/4/18	—	Advanced Div. H.Q. moved from Canal Bank to Border Camp. (A 30 B.)	
	22/4/18	—	CRE & GSO1 visited M Bde re head defence whole sector. CRE & GSO1 & Bussex Divisional 150 Rd Coy RE. re working the system.	
	25/4/18	—	CRE visited Westrep & arranged demolition of Deep Dugouts there with OC 122nd Field Coy RE.	
	26/4/18	—	CRE visited Bielew defences with GSO1 in morning. In afternoon to Canal Bank defences with OC 150th Field Coy RE. United Bde fashion 107 & 109 in. Bde re front line.	
	27/4/18	—	CRE to advanced Div H.Q. moved from Border Camp to Dragon Camp (A15 B 57) B4.	
	28/4/18	—	CRE in office. Transport 121 Field Coy, A 150 Field Coy, Transport 92 Septem 4.122 Field Coy moved with their Syf Coys. to X Camp (A 16 c 36), A 10. a O 2 & A 3 c 14 respectively.	
	29/4/18	—	CRE in office.	
	30/4/18	—	CRE in office.	

Robert A. McKenzie
Lieut. Colonel, R.E.
C.R.E. 36th (Ulster) Division.

SECRET & URGENT.   Copy No.....11

C.R.E. 36th Division order No.2.
==============================

28/4/18.

1. MOVES.

The instructions re moves of Field Companies, R.E. and 16th
R.I.R.(P), issued by wire on 27/4/18 are cancelled and the following
substituted :-

The 16th R.I.R.(P) complete with transport, and the dismounted
portion of the 121st Field Company R.E. will remain in their
present camps for the time being.

The transport of the 121st Field Company and the 122nd and 150th
Field Companies complete will move to their Brigade Group Areas as
ordered yesterday i.e.

121st Field Coy.R.E.	to 107th Brigade Group.	A. 16.c.2.5.
122nd " " "	to 108th " "	A. 3.c.3.5.
150th " " "	to 109th " "	A. 10.a.0.2

Completion of moves and location of H.Q. and transport lines
will be reported to this office by wire.

2. WORK.

121st Field Coy.R.E. will carry on with BRIELEN Defences, the
scheme now being a continuous line.

122nd Field Coy.R.E. will get in touch with 108th Brigade
A.22.b.7.7. and assist them in completion of GREEN LINE.

16th R.I.R.(P) will place two companies at disposal of 121st
Field Coy.R.E. for work on BRIELEN Line, commencing 29th instant.

Tramway service for working parties of 121st Field Company and
16th R.I.R.(P) will be arranged. Details will follow.

3. ACKNOWLEDGE.

Robert M. MacKenzie.
Lt.Colonel, R.E.
C.R.E. 36th Division.

Issued at 11.15 a.m.
────────────────

Distribution of copies:-

No.1 to 121st Field Coy.R.E.   No.7 to 36th Divisional Train.
  2 to 122nd   "   "   "   8 to 107th Brigade.
  3 to 150th   "   "   "   9 to 108th Brigade.
  4 to 16th R.I.R.(P)   10 to 109th Brigade.
  5 to 36th Division "G".   11 to WAR DIARY.
  6 to 36th Division "Q".   12 to File.

WO 32

War Diary

of

C.R.E. 36th Division

for month of May 1916.

Confidential.

WAR DIARY or INTELLIGENCE SUMMARY

Army Form C. 2118.

Place	Date	Hour	Summary of Events and Information	Remarks and references to Appendices
	1/5/18	-	C.R.E. in office in morning. To 2nd Army with A.A.& Q.M.G. letter in the day.	
	2/5/18	-	C.R.E. in office to meet B.G.G.S. 2nd Corps. (B.G.G.S. did not arrive) C.R.E. to Blue line in morning.	
	3/5/18	-	C.R.E. & G.S.O.1 to Graham Line & Belgian corresponding line.	
	4/5/18	-	122 Field Coy RE moved from Ripley Camp to Border Camp. (near H.Q. only)	
	5/5/18	-	C.R.E. in office	
	6/5/18	-	do	
	7/5/18	-	do	
	8/5/18	-	122 Field Coy RE	
			Rear H.Q. & sections moved from Border Camp to HOSPITAL FARM Camp. 150 Field Coy RE took over demolitions on Canal from S. army boundary to Salvation Corner & demolition of wells Cross Roads from 233 Field Coy RE 41st Div.	
	15/5/18	-	150th Field Coy RE handed over to 122 Zuchley RE demolition of Antique 30 36 a 4 & causeways 34 a 45 b.	
	17/5/18	-	1 section /122 Field Coy attached to 36 Div. Arty. for work on emplacements & O.Ps.	
	19/5/18	-		
	20/5/18	-	C.R.E. Belgian Division on left visited C.R.E.	
	21/5/18	-	C.R.E. in office.	
	22/5/18	-		
	23/5/18	-	C.R.E. visited Graham Line & Border Line with G.O.C.	
	24/5/18	-	C.R.E. visited Green Line.	

Army Form C. 2118.

WAR DIARY
or
INTELLIGENCE SUMMARY.
(Erase heading not required.)

Instructions regarding War Diaries and Intelligence Summaries are contained in F. S. Regs., Part II. and the Staff Manual respectively. Title pages will be prepared in manuscript.

Place	Date	Hour	Summary of Events and Information	Remarks and references to Appendices
25/5/18	→		C.R.E. – office	
	26/5/18		C.R.E. to firing line with G.S.O.1.	
	27/5/18		121 Infantry Bde returned. R.E. talking life in forward work	
			C.R.E. visited Brigade HQrs with G.O.C.	
	28/5/18		C.R.E. 49 Div. visited C.R.E.	
	30/5/18		C.R.E. – office.	

[signature]
Captain R.E.
for Lieut. Colonel, R.E.
C.R.E. 36th (Ulster) Division

SECRET.   Copy No..........

C.R.E. 36th DIVISION OPERATION ORDER NO 3.
****
                                                  27/5/18.

1.   The following reliefs will take place on the 29th instant, and will be completed by 10 p.m. on that date. Details of reliefs to be arranged between Os.C. Units concerned.

   121st Field Company, R.E. will relieve 122nd Field Company, R.E. and will take over all work at present in hand, including the demolitions allocated to 122nd Field Company in my S.E. 22 of the 17th instant.
   They will also provide, as far as possible, any R.E. supervision required by 107th Brigade for works East of the CANAL.

   122nd Field Company, R.E. will take over accommodation at present occupied by 121st Field Company, R.E. at BROMWELL CAMP.
   O.C. 122nd Field Company will arrange to relieve the section of 121st Field Company at present attached to the C.R.A. The relieving section of 122nd Field Company must be of the same strength as the section of 121st Field Company at present attached to the R.A. (1Officer and 30 O.R.)
   O.C. 122nd Field Company will take over all work at present in charge of 121st Field Company on the GREEN and BRIELEN LINES. For this purpose two companies of Pioneers will be provided for work on the BRIELEN LINE and one company of Pioneers and 100 R.A.M.C. for work in connection with the GREEN LINE.

   150th Field Company, R.E. will remain as at present on the CANAL BANK, and their work is not changed.

   HORSE LINES will remain as at present, and 121st and 150th Field Companies will leave a nucleus of at least one section in them to enable the front line sections to have a few days rest in rotation.

2.   Completion of reliefs to be reported to this Office by wire.

3.   Field Companies ACKNOWLEDGE.

                                          Robert H. Mackenzie

                                          Lt. Colonel, R.E.
Issued at 1 p.m.   C.R.E. 36th Division.

              Distribution of copies:-
   No 1-2 to 121st Field Co. R.E.   No 10 to 16th R.I.R. (P).
      3-4 to 122nd   - : -   11 to 107th Brigade.
      5   to 150th   - : -   12 to 108th   "
      6-7 to C.R.A. 36th Division.   13 to 109th   "
      8   to 36th Division "G"   14 to C.E. II Corps.
      9   to   - : -   "Q"   15-16 WAR DIARY.
              17-18   -   FILE.

****

Confidential

WO 33

War Diary

of

C.R.E. 36th Division

for month of June 1916.

Army Form C. 2118.

WAR DIARY
or
INTELLIGENCE SUMMARY.

C.R.E. 36th Divn.

(Erase heading not required.)

Place	Date	Hour	Summary of Events and Information	Remarks and references to Appendices
	1/6/18		CRE handing over to CRE 12th Belgian Inf. Division. CRE took Belgian and given list of Button lines.	
	2/6/18		Handing over to Belgians.	
	3/6/18		122nd Coy RE relieved by Belgians & moved to camps near St Jan ter BIEZEN. Vacated by 49th West Divs.	
	4/6/18		12th Field Coy RE & 150th Field Coy RE relieved by Belgians & moved to camps near ST JAN TER BIEZEN. Vacated by 49th West Division. CRE's office moved from DRAGON CAMP to COUTHOVE CHATEAU.	
	5/6/18		2 Coys working on farm lines & East Poperinghe line S. of POPERINGHE - VLAMERTINGHE Road. Hd CRE Corps Troops (IInd Corps) one day training.	
	6/6/18		CRE in office.	
	7/6/18		CRE visited CRE 33rd Division.	
	8/6/18		CRE in office.	
	9/6/18		CRE attended joint church parade of 3 Field Coys & afterwards inspected mess horses wagons & camps.	
	10/6/18		CRE in office. 150th Field Coy working on GREEN LINE from Railway at H 8 b to H 14 a 2 8 & 122 on E. Poperinghe line from POPERINGHE - VLAMERTINGHE Road to G 11 d 47.	
	11/6/18		122nd & 150th Field Coys moved from ST JAN TER BIEZEN to PROVEN.	
	12/6/18		12th Field Coy moved from ST JAN TER BIEZEN to PROVEN.	
	13/6/18		CRE in office.	

Army Form C. 2118.

WAR DIARY
or
INTELLIGENCE SUMMARY.
(Erase heading not required.)

Instructions regarding War Diaries and Intelligence Summaries are contained in F. S. Regs. Part II. and the Staff Manual respectively. Title pages will be prepared in manuscript.

Place	Date	Hour	Summary of Events and Information	Remarks and references to Appendices
	14/6/18		121st Field Coy relieved 150th Field Coy on section of front line H 8 b to 14 14 a 2 8. Coys now employed on Intours. — 121st Field Coy RE in Army Line as above. 150th Field Coy in E. Poperinghe Line from POPERINGHE-VLAMERTINGHE Road to POPERINGHE — BUSSEBOOM Road. 150th Field Coy training.	
	15/6/18		CRE in office.	
	16/6/18		Sunday. CRE in office.	
	17/6/18		121st Field Coy withdrawn from GREEN LINE & employed on E. POPERINGHE Line from POPERINGHE — VLAMERTINGHE Road to Corps Boundary at Railway at A22 central. Work consisting in clearing crops, widening hedges & firm to give field of fire for E. Poperinghe Line.	
	18/6/18		C.R.E. to E. Poperinghe line with G.O.C.	
	19/6/18		C.R.E. in office.} Capt R.E. & O.C. 122 Field Coy R.E. made reconnaissance of Tracks 1, 2 & 3 C.R.E. in office.} across Aa marshes between WATTEN and ST. OMER.	
	20/6/18		C.R.E. in office.	
	21/6/18		C.R.E. to E. Poperinghe Line with G.O.C. & G.S.O.1.	
	22/6/18		CRE in office.	
	23/6/18		150th Coy RE took over work of 122 Field Coy RE in E. Poperinghe Line. 122nd Field Coy Training. C.R.E. to see CRE Hqd Div. T/Major H. OTWAY 122. took over command of 150th Field Coy vice Major H.M. FORDHAM M.C.	
FORDHAM M.C.	24/6/18		CRE to 466th Field Coy 46 Div in 24th T/Major H. GOOCH M.C. RE took over command 121st Field Coy RE vice Major OTWAY. T/Lieut. T.K. KNOX M.C. RE from 122 Field Coy RE to 121st Field Coy vice Major GOOCH.	

Army Form C. 2118.

WAR DIARY
or
INTELLIGENCE SUMMARY.
(Erase heading not required.)

Place	Date	Hour	Summary of Events and Information	Remarks and references to Appendices
	26/6/18		C.R.E. in office.	
	27/6/18		C.R.E. to G.H.Q. demonstration of Anti-Tank land mines.	
	28/6/18		121 Field Coy. to RUBROUCK area for musketry.	
	29/6/18		C.R.E. in office.	
	30/6/18		C.R.E. & Adjt. to RUBROUCK to 121 Field Coy. R.E.	

Robert Mackay
Lieut. Colonel, R.E.
C.R.E. 36th (Ulster) Division

SECRET.   Copy No........

C.R.E. 36th DIVISION OPERATION ORDER NO 8.

Ref. BELGIUM & FRANCE
Sheet 27   28/8/18.

1. The 36th Division is being relieved in the line by the 35th Division between the 29th and 31st August, 1918.

2. Movements and reliefs of Field Companies, R.E. on the 30th/31st instant will be as follows:-

   150th Field Company will relieve 122nd Field Company in the forward area by midnight 30th.instant.

   On relief, the 122nd Field Company will move complete to camp at P.8.d.2.8.

   150th Field Company will retain their present horse lines at EECKE (Q.26.a.8.5).

   121st Field Company will hand over accommodation at MONT DES CATS (R.19.b.3.7) to 203rd Field Company, R.E. They will also hand over billets for H.Q. and 2 sections at R.26.c.15.20, for one section at R.33.b.5.0, for one section at R.21.c.00.25 to 204th Field Company, R.E.

   On completion of relief, 121st Field Company will move complete to camp in P.33.b., to accommodation arranged with the Area Commandant ST. MARIE CAPPEL.

   Except in the case of the relief of 122nd Field Company by 150th Field Company, all reliefs will be completed by 4 a.m. on 31st instant.

3. Advance parties from 35th Division are reporting as under, at 10 a.m. on 29th inst., to take over work, billets, etc.

   2 Officers and 2 N.C.Os. from 205th Field Company, R.E. to 122nd Field Company, R.E. at Left Brigade H.Q. (R.24.c.4.2.)

   1 Officer and 2 N.C.Os. from 203rd Field Company, R.E. and 2 Officers and 2 N.C.Os. from 204th Field Company, R.E. to 121st Field Company, R.E. at R.19.b.3.7.

4. 204th Field Company, R.E. is taking over all work connected with KNOX'S CAUSEWAY.

   205th Field Company, R.E. is taking over all outstanding work from 122nd Field Company, R.E., with the exception of the Brigade H.Q. dug-outs which are being taken over by 150th Field Company, R.E.

5. Details of reliefs, and handing over of works, plans, etc., will be arranged between Os.C. concerned.

6. 150th Field Company, R.E. will come under the orders of C.R.E. 35th Division for all matters connected with work and tactics at midnight 30th/31st instant.

7. **DIVISIONAL R.E. DUMPS.**
Control of R.E. Dump, GODE., will pass to C.R.E. 35th Division at 9 a.m. on 30th instant.

Taking over party from 35th Division is arriving on 29th inst., and will be accommodated at the Dump from that date.

Handing over stock-sheets will be made out in duplicate and forwarded to this Office.

The two sections of 150th Field Company, R.E. at present working at the Dump will rejoin their Company on the morning of 30th instant.

The 35th Divisional R.E. Dump at CASSEL will be taken over by C.R.E. 36th Division at the same time, and a representative will report to C.R.E. 35th Division at CASSEL on 29th inst. to take over.

8. Attention is directed to extracts from 36th (Ulster) Division Administrative Instructions No 29, which will follow.

9. Completion of reliefs will be wired to this Office by code word "CHEERS", and the exact locations of New H.Q. and sections will be forwarded to this Office when moves are complete.

10. C.R.E's Office will close at TERDEGHEM at 10 a.m. 31st inst. and will open at P.28.a.9.3. at the same hour.

11. ACKNOWLEDGE.

Issued at ....

Lt. Colonel, R.E.
C.R.E. 36th Division.

Distribution of copies :-

No 1 to 121st Field Co.R.E. (Forwd).	No 18 to 36th Signal Co.R.E.
2 to " " (Rear).	19 to C.E. X Corps.
3 to 122nd " (Forwd).	20 to D.A.P.M. 36th Divn.
4 to " " (Rear).	21 to A.D.M.S. "
5 to 150th "	22 to D.A.D.V.S. "
6- 9 to C.R.E. 35th Division.	23 to S.C. C-of-E.
10 to 36th Division "Q"	24 to S.C. Non-C-of-E.
11 to " "G"	25 to 16th R.I.R. (P).
12 to C.R.A. 36th Division.	26 to Area Comdt. No 2.
13 to 107th Infy. Bde.	27 to " " No 3.
14 to 108th "	28 to WAR DIARY.
15 to 109th "	29 to "
17 to 36th Divisional Train.	30 to FILE.

SECRET.   C.R.E. No C.E. 4/6.

O.C. 121st Field Company, R.E.
O.C. 122nd Field Company, R.E.
O.C. 150th Field Company, R.E.
O. i/c R.E. Dump, GODE.

   (1)   The 36th Division will remain in the line for the present. My operation order No 8 is therefore cancelled.

   (2)   121st Field Company, R.E. will remain in its present billets and horse lines, and will continue the work at present in hand.

   (3)   150th Field Company, R.E. will relieve 122nd Field Company, R.E. by midnight to-night, 30th/31st August, in the forward area, and will take over all work from 122nd Field Company, R.E.

   (4)   122nd Field Company, R.E. will take over any work being done by 150th Field Company, and will also supply the necessary sections for work at R.E. Dump, GODE.

   (5)   All details as to relief will be arranged between O.C. concerned.

   (6)   122nd and 150th Field Companies will retain their present horse lines, and should the accommodation for the relieved men of 122nd Field Company at BECKE be insufficient, O.C. 122nd Field Company will arrange with O.C. 150th Field Company to take over part of the billets vacated by 150th Field Company on their move forward.

   (7)   The Field Companies, R.E. of the 35th Division are returning to the billets occupied by them previous to to-day.

   (8)   Any fresh instructions as to work will be issued later.

   (9)   Completion of relief of 122nd Field Company by 150th Field Company will be wired to this Office by code word "CHEERS".

   (10) Field Companies, R.E. ACKNOWLEDGE.

                                            Capt. Adjt. R.E.
                                            for C.R.E. 36th Division.
30/8/18.

            Copies to 36th Div. "G" and "Q"
                      C.E. X Corps.
                      C.R.E. 35th Division.
                      X Corps Rear

WR 34

War Diary

of

C.R.E. 36th Division

for month of July, 1918.

WAR DIARY
or
INTELLIGENCE SUMMARY.

Army Form C. 2118.

Place	Date	Hour	Summary of Events and Information	Remarks and references to Appendices
	1/7/18		C.R.E. in office.	Map Sheet 27 (France)
	2/7/18		C.R.E. saw C.R.E. 34 Div. to see C.R.E. 121 Coy R.E. moved from PROVEN to near ST. JAN TER BIEZEN, 150th Coy R.E. hutts. 122nd Fd Coy moved from RUBROUCK and to near ST JAN TER BIEZEN	
	3/7/18		121st Field Coy R.E. moved from ST JAN TER BIEZEN to 0.30 c 04, 122nd Coy to Q 26 B 72 150th Field Coy to D 26 c 42. H.Q. R.E. moved from COUTHOVE CHATEAU to CASSEL. C.R.E. to MONT DES CATS to C.R.E. 41st (French) Division & commenced taking over.	
	4/7/18		C.R.E. to MONT DES CATS to C.R.E. 41st (French) Division & then to Esquelbecq to C.E. Xth Corps.	
	5/7/18		C.R.E. to MONT DES CATS to 41st French Div. to take over. Conference at CRE's office CASSEL with 3 Field Coy Commanders & O.C. 16th R. W. Ry. (P) at which all details of relief (Times, Labour, Billets, work etc.) were settled.	
	6/7/18		C.R.E. in office. Adjt. R.E. to Mont Des Cats to settle details of Coy over of R.E. Stores, dumps, plant etc.	
	7/7/18		C.R.E. moved to Advanced Div HQR at Mont des Cats. Adjt R.E. & office etc remaining at CASSEL for the present.	
	8/7/18		C.R.E. visited 121 & 122 Coys R.E. with French C.R.E. C.R.E. visited all 3 Infantry Bgde. H.Q., the 16th R. W. Ry (P), 121 Field Coy R.E. & H.Q. 35 Div. Visited 122 Coy in afternoon. Conference of Field Coy Commanders in afternoon.	
	9/7/18		Rear H.Q. moved from CASSEL to Terdeghem. C.R.E. to conference with C.E. Xth Corps.	

WAR DIARY
or
INTELLIGENCE SUMMARY.

Army Form C. 2118.

(Erase heading not required.)

Place	Date	Hour	Summary of Events and Information	Remarks and references to Appendices
	10/7/18		GSO 1. CRE at Conference with G.O.C., 3 Brigade Commanders & 3 Bgde Majors	
	11/7/18		CRA & A.A. & Q.M.G. re defence of Divisional Sector. CRE to H.Q. 9th Division	
	12/7/18		CRE with G.S.O.1. in reconnaissance of Mont NOIR, also in new line intent support line in Divisional Sector.	
	13/7/18		CRE & GSO 1 visited O.P.s in Left Bgde Sector.	
	14/7/18		CRE round with advanced H.Q. truck from MONT DES CATS to TERDEGHEM. Out with GSO 1. in morning.	
	15/7/18		CRE in office. Visited by CRE 9th Division.	
	16/7/18		CRE in office.	
	17/7/18		CRE in office. Visited by C.E. xth Corps.	
	18/7/18		CRE with GSO 2 to defences of MONT NOIR and Blue line in Divisional area.	
	19/7/18		CRE to Blue Line, Right Sector, with G.O.C. at night. Met O.C. 121 Coy on ground and went round work.	
	20/7/18		CRE — office.	
	21/7/18		CRE — office. Interview with O C 150 Coy re relief of 122nd Coy by 150th Coy in line.	
	22/7/18		CRE inspecting —	

Army Form C. 2118.

WAR DIARY
or
INTELLIGENCE SUMMARY.
(Erase heading not required.)

Instructions regarding War Diaries and Intelligence Summaries are contained in F. S. Regs., Part II. and the Staff Manual respectively. Title pages will be prepared in manuscript.

Place	Date	Hour	Summary of Events and Information	Remarks and references to Appendices
	22/7/18		(continued) 150th Field Coy relieved 122 Field Coy in line in left Sector on night of 22/23	
	23/7/18		CRE to ARQUES to see MOIR Pill Box.	
	24/7/18		CB X th Corps visited CRE. — in afternoon CRE 29 th Div visited CRE.	
	25/7/18		CRE. with CRE 29 th Div. to proposed Div H.Q. & other works in Mont des Cats & Kokereele.	
	26/7/18		CRE in office. visited by C.E. X th Corps. G.S.O.1. G.H.Q. M.G. demonstration at Camiers	
	27/7/18		with G.O.C. & G.S.O.1.	
	28/7/18		CRE in Office. Conference with O.s.C. 121 & 150 in afternoon.	
	29/7/18		CRE with A.A. & Q.M.G. to Back areas in office in afternoon	
	30/7/18		CRE in office. Conference with seconds in command of Field Coys.	
	31/7/18		CRE to Blue line with G.S.O.3 — also to 107 & 108 Bgdes.	

Robert H. Mackenzie
Lieut. Colonel, R.E.
C.R.E. 36th (Ulster) Division

SECRET.   Copy No.... 10.

C.R.E. 36th DIVISION OPERATION ORDER NO 6.
==

21/7/18.

Reference 36th (Ulster) Division Operation Order No 209 dated 20th instant.

1. 150th Field Company, R.E. will relieve 122nd Field Company, R.E. in the Left Subsector on the night 22nd/23rd July, 1918.

2. Details of relief will be arranged direct between Os.C. Companies.

3. All maps, photographs, plans, Works Orders, etc., will be exchanged by Os.C. Units concerned.

4. The command of MONT NOIR Post will pass from O.C. 122nd Field Company to O.C. 150th Field Company at 6 a.m. 23rd instant. The garrison provided by 16th R.I.R. (P) will not be relieved.

5. On the night of 22nd/23rd, all work on the BLUE LINE etc. will be supervised by the 122nd Field Company, to enable 150th Field Company to study details of same on the spot, as there will be no working parties provided by 108th or 109th Brigades on the night of 23rd/24th, work being continued on the night of 24th/25th. by 108th Bde.

6. Relief will be completed by 6 a.m. 23rd instant.

7. Completion of relief will be reported to this Office by code word "REJOICE".

8. 122nd and 150th Field Companies, and 16th R.I.R. (P) ACKNOWLEDGE.

Robert H. MacKenzie
Lt. Colonel, R.E.
C.R.E. 36th Division.

Distribution of copies :-

No 1 to 122nd Field Co. R.E.   No 7 to 108th Infy. Bde.
   2 to 150th   "   8 to 109th   "
   3 to 16th R.I.R. (P).   9 to 36th Signal Co.R.E.
   4 to 36th Divn. "G"   10 to WAR DIARY.
   5 to   "   "Q"   11 to FILE.
   6 to C.E. X Corps.

War Diary VII 35

of

O.C. E 316ᵗʰ Division

for month of August 1916

Confidential

Army Form C. 2118.

WAR DIARY
or
INTELLIGENCE SUMMARY.
(Erase heading not required.)

Instructions regarding War Diaries and Intelligence Summaries are contained in F. S. Regs., Part II. and the Staff Manual respectively. Title pages will be prepared in manuscript.

Place	Date	Hour	Summary of Events and Information	Remarks and references to Appendices
	1/8/18	—	CRE in office	
	2/8/18	—	CRE with GSO2 to 107 & 108 Inf Bgdes. Also made reconnaissance in direction of MURAL FARM (X 17 b) before in afternoon	
	3/8/18	—	CRE in office	
	4/8/18	—	CRE to Commemoration Service (4th Anniversary of War) at TERDEGHEM. Visited by CE 10th Corps. Office in afternoon.	
	5/8/18	—	CRE in office.	
	6/8/18	—	CRE with A.A.Q.M.G. to Army H.Q. to presentation of V.C. to 2/Lt C.L. KNOX RE 150th Field Coy. by H.M. THE KING	
	7/8/18	—	CRE with C.R.A. to battery positions left group. 122 Field Coy relieved 150th Field Coy with Schroeder in front of 7/8th. Details Order No 7 dated 6/8/18 attached	
	8/8/18	—	CRE with GSO2 to Blue Line.	
	9/8/18	—	CRE with CRA turned all artillery positions in Div Area	
	10/8/18	—	CRE at Conference held by G.O.C. & staff, Bgde Commanders & staffs.	
	11/8/18	—	CRE at Memorial Service at TERDEGHEM (march past) attended by H.M. the KING.	
	12/8/18	—	CRE in office.	
	13/8/18	—	CRE with GSO1 to works in forward Div. Area. Conference with Field Coy Commanders.	
	14/8/18	—	CRE in office. Visited by O.C. 122 in evening.	
	15/8/18	—	CRE with GSO2 & OC 122 Field Coy to inspect proposed HQ — aft instructor forward area.	
	16/8/18	—	C.R.E. visited by CE Xth Corps in morning, to Conference in afternoon to 30 Div HQ CREs 30th & 35th present	
	17/8/18	—	CRE Divl Area Interview with OC 121 & 122 at H of MUS Cats reported	

WAR DIARY
or
INTELLIGENCE SUMMARY.

Army Form C. 2118.

Place	Date	Hour	Summary of Events and Information	Remarks and references to Appendices
	17/8/18 (contd)		of RE by Major Gen 35th Div also present. Subject of conference - work tendered by Corps Tps units mentioned. Visited by CRE 30th Div in evening.	
	18/8/18		CRE Flew with GSO I in morning. Office in afternoon.	
	19/8/18		C.R.E. in office.	
	20/8/18		CRE to line. Inspected R.E. dump GOEWAERSVELDE.	
	21/8/18		CRE in office.	
	22/8/18		CRE to line. Visited 121 & 122 Coys.	
	23/8/18		CRE visited O.C. 205 Fielding R.E. re work being carried out by 205.	
	24/8/18		CRE in office	
	25/8/18		CRE turns Visited 109 Bgde & saw O.C. 122 re new Bgde H.Q. visited Headquarters of all Units Corps.	
	26/8/18		CRE visited by C.B. 10th Corps. CRE 35 Div. re details of relief of 36 by 35 Div.	
	27/8/18		CRE in office.	
	28/8/18		CRE to line with CRE 35 free work on hand. In office with CRE 35 in afternoon handing over.	O.O. No 2
	29/8/18		CRE to Conference (handing over) with CREs 31st Div & 35th Div.	
	30/8/18		CRE in office. Relief of 36th by 35th Div Cancelled in view of enemy retirement O.O. No 3 therefore Cancelled. 150th Coy relieved 122 Coy in forward area in evening.	
	31/8/18		Entered H.Q. (Divisional) opened at MONT DES CATS at 10 a.m. CRE to new H.Q. Brig Gen H.Q. New H.Q.	

Rhodes H. Mackenzie
Lieut. Colonel, R.E.
CRE 36th (Ulster) Div

SECRET.   Copy No.........

C.R.E. 36th DIVISION OPERATION ORDER NO 7.

4/8/18.

Reference 36th (Ulster) Division Order No 215 dated 4/8/18.

1. 122nd Field Company, R.E. will relieve 150th Field Company, R.E. in the Left Subsector on the night 7th/8th August, 1918.

2. Details of relief will be arranged direct between Os.C. Units concerned.

3. All maps, photographs, plans, Works Orders, etc., will be exchanged by Os.C. Companies.

4. The command of MONT NOIR Post will pass from O.C. 150th Field Company to O.C. 122nd Field Company at midnight 7th/8th instant. The garrison provided by 16th R.I.R. (P) will not be relieved.

5. Owing to relief, no working parties will be provided by 108th or 109th Brigades on the night of 8th/9th inst.

6. Relief will be completed by 6 a.m. 8th instant.

7. Completion of relief will be reported to this Office by code word "WALES"

8. 122nd and 150th Field Companies, and 16th R.I.R. (P) AKNOWLEDGE.

Robert M. Mackenzie
Lt. Colonel, R.E.
C.R.E. 36th Division.

Issued at Midnight.

Distribution of copies :-

No 1 to 122nd Field Co. R.E.   No 6 to C.E. X Corps.
   2 to 150th   "   7 to 108th Infy. Bde.
   3 to 16th R.I.R. (P).   8 to 109th   "
   4 to 36th Divn. "G"   9 to 36th Signal Co.R.E.
   5 to   "   "Q"   10 to WAR DIARY.
           No 11 to FILE.

Confidential

War Diary

— of —

C.R.E. 36th Division.

September 1918.

Army Form C. 2118.

WAR DIARY
or
INTELLIGENCE SUMMARY.
(Erase heading not required.)

Instructions regarding War Diaries and Intelligence Summaries are contained in F. S. Regs., Part II. and the Staff Manual respectively. Title pages will be prepared in manuscript.

Place	Date	Hour	Summary of Events and Information	Remarks and references to Appendices
	1/9/18	—	Rear H.Q. moved from TERDEGHEM to ST. SILVESTRE CAPPEL. Location of H.Q. Field Corps HQ in Interim. 121st at MONT DES CATS. 122nd at ECKE. 150th at BAILLEUL ASYLUM.	AP
	2/9/18	—	Advanced Div HQ moved from MONT DES CATS to ST JANS CAPEL. Rear HQ from ST SILVESTRE CAPPEL to ECKE. 121st Field Coy UE from Mont des Cats to SCHAEXKEN. 122nd Recing from ECKE to R.21.a.9.2. (sheet 27)	AP
	3/9/18	—	CRE to NEUVE EGLISE with A.A.&Q.M.G. in morning. In afternoon to same place with G.S.O.1. Rear Div. HQ moved from ECKE to MONT DES CATS.	AP
	4/9/18	—	Visited Pioneers, visited by CE Xth Corps. To 29th Div "g" & 108th & 107th Replies in lieu & 30th Div "g" advanced. 150 a Tuesday Rear HQ to Horshaven moved from BERTHEN to BAILLEUL ASYLUM.	AP
	5/9/18	—	CRE in office. Visited 107 & 108 Byls & Bdes HQ forward in afternoon. Rear Div HQ moved from MONT DES CATS to ST. JANS CAPEL	AP
	6/9/18	—	CRE visited by CE XII Corps re forward roads & water supply	AP
	7/9/18	—	CRE in office.	AP
	8/9/18	—	CRE in office.	AP
	9/9/18	—	CRE in office.	AP
	10/9/18	—	CRE with G.S.O.1. & O.C 121 Field Coy to 107 Bgde HQ reference new Bgde HQ.	AP
	11/9/18	—	CRE in office.	AP

Army Form C. 2118.

WAR DIARY
or
INTELLIGENCE SUMMARY.
(Erase heading not required.)

Instructions regarding War Diaries and Intelligence Summaries are contained in F. S. Regs., Part II. and the Staff Manual respectively. Title pages will be prepared in manuscript.

Place	Date	Hour	Summary of Events and Information	Remarks and references to Appendices
	12.9.18		CRE to II Army HQ.	
	13.9.18		CRE in office	
	14.9.16		CRE took over temporary command of 107 Inf. Bde vice Br. Gen. Shorts (wounded) returning office of I/CRE. To I Corps HQ re Dump in more forward area. To Ballieul Asylum with a view in afternoon to choose site.	
	15.9.18		150 (Coy) returned 121st by in forward work in evening. To Russell, 107 Bde. HQ & Meuri Eglise. Visited 121 Fld Coy forward.	
	16.9.18		To $\mathbb{I}^R$ Corps RE dump & 107 Bde. HQ. Visited by CEX Corps re work & reviewing of man light tramways.	
	7.9.18		Div HQ moved ST JANS CAPPEL TO CHATEAU at M32.a.6.1. (Ref. 26)	
	8.9.18		Office. To CRG 30 Div in evening. Received orders for moves of field Coys in ready for 30th Div.	
	9.9.18		To 150 Coy + RE dump Bailleul re moves. 121 by moves from SCHERPENBERG to ST SYLVESTRE CAPPEL area with 107 Bde. 2 sections 133 by moved from NEUVE EGLISE to BAILLEUL telephone in relief by 30th DIV.	
	20.9.18		HQ RE moved from ST JANS CAPPEL CHATEAU to ESQUINE CAMP 27 K H I Field Coys moved small head quarters. Bde groups.	

WAR DIARY
~~INTELLIGENCE SUMMARY~~

Army Form C. 2118.

(Erase heading not required.)

Instructions regarding War Diaries and Intelligence Summaries are contained in F. S. Regs., Part II. and the Staff Manual respectively. Title pages will be prepared in manuscript.

Place	Date	Hour	Summary of Events and Information	Remarks and references to Appendices
	21.9/18		121 Field Co R.E. at ESQUELBEC. 122 + 150 Field Coys at EECKE. 16th Batt R.I.R. (P) Bde 27/E 20 a.1.8.	AP
	22/9/18		122 Co. moved to 26/A 21.6.2.9.	AP
	23/9		150 Field Co. moved to 28/A 20.d.35. CRE returned from 107 Inf Bde on return of B.G. Brock R.F.A.	AP
	24/9		C.R.E. proceeded on leave to U.K. Major W. Smyth A/CRE.	AP
	25/9		Visited 121 Field Co. G.O.C. Div. inspected 121 Field Co at 2 pm.	AP
	26/9		A/CRE visited 150 + 122 Field Coys during morning. 121 Field Coy moved to 27/P 28 c.7.4.	AP
	27/9		R.E. HQ moved to 27/F 22 c.9.9. A/CRE visited 121 Field Co R.E.	AP
	28/9		A/CRE moved to join Adv. Div. HQ at I.8.c.6.0. (YPRES) at 6.30 hrs. 150 Field Coy transferred to REIGERSBERG CHATEAU area, 4 sections to 28/H.12.a.7.1. 122 Field Co to 28/H.6.d.10.0.	AP
	29/9		4 sections 150 Coy moved to 28/J.8 central. 4 sections 150 Coy moved to 28/V.8.6.6.2. 121 & 122 Coys moving complete to 28/H.6.6.5.	AP
	30/9/18		R.E. near HQ moved to 28/I.8. central. C.R.E. to forward area with Div. 'G'. 2 road repairs in forward areas.	AP

Sgd Potts D/HRE for
C.R.E. 36th Division.

Vol 37

WAR DIARY

of

C.R.E. 36th Division

for month of October 1918.

Confidential

Army Form C. 2118.

WAR DIARY
or
INTELLIGENCE SUMMARY.
(Erase heading not required.)

Instructions regarding War Diaries and Intelligence Summaries are contained in F. S. Regs., Part II. and the Staff Manual respectively. Title pages will be prepared in manuscript.

Place	Date	Hour	Summary of Events and Information	Remarks and references to Appendices
YPRES	1/10/18		LOCATIONS of Units as follows:- Ref Sheet 28. 121 Field Coy. at J.12.c.5.7. 122 Field Coy. H.Q. and transport H.B.B.25. 150th Coy H.Q. and transport H.B.B.25. 4 sections J.8.b.5.5. 16th Batt. R.I.R.(P) at J.12.d.23. R.E. H.Q. at I.8.central. A/CRE reconnoitring roads for repair BROODSEINDE - BERCELAERE area, was with G.S.O.2. and A.A. & Q.M.G in evening.	
JUNCTION CAMP	2/10/18		Div. H.Q. with R.E. H.Q moved to JUNCTION CAMP 28/C.27.c.9.8. A/CRE out all day on roads in forward area. 150 Field Coy moved complete to BERCELAERE J.12.d.5.3.	
"	3/10/18		A/CRE in office during morning. Reconnoitring accommodation and roads in BERCELAERE - GHELUVELT area in afternoon. Interviewed G.S.O.1, inspected	
"	4/10/18		A/CRE moved to forward Div. Hqrs. at K.7.d. (Sheet 28). O.C. 122 Field to called to report progress. forward areas. O.C. 122 Field Coy to moved to 28/J.18.d.5.8. A/CRE at conference with Div. Comm. & G. Staff. 122 Field Coy. moved to 28/J.18.d.5.8. A/CRE at conference later.	
"	5.10.18		at 2p.m. and Field Coy. commanders confirmed later. A/CRE with Divion G in forward area.	
"	6.10.18		A/CRE with Divion G in forward area.	
"	7.10.18		A/CRE with Divion G in forward area.	
"	8.10.18		Divisional Hqrs G moved from 28/K.7.a to junction cross. A/CRE remaining at the forward location, 28/K.7.d.	

Army Form C. 2118.

WAR DIARY
or
INTELLIGENCE SUMMARY.
(Erase heading not required.)

Instructions regarding War Diaries and Intelligence Summaries are contained in F.S. Regs., Part II. and the Staff Manual respectively. Title pages will be prepared in manuscript.

Place	Date	Hour	Summary of Events and Information	Remarks and references to Appendices
JUNCTION CAMP.	9/10/18		Visited near Div. Hdqrs. Made reconnaissance and arranged dispositions for defence of BECELAERE according to Div. defence scheme. Conference of field Cory. commanders at 2/pm, called by O/C RE.	
	10/10/18		A/C.R.E. at forward Div. Hdqrs. with 9503. C.R.E. returned from leave to U.K.	
	11/10/18		C.R.E. in office at JUNCTION CAMP 28/C.27.c.9.8. Visited field Cops. or forward area. Saw Major Smyth (late acting C.R.E.) with regard to work in hand + impend operations. Conference with Div commander in morning.	
	12/10/18		C.R.E. moved with Advanced Div. to 28/K.7.d. Conference of Coy. commanders and O.C. Pioneer Batt. (16 R.I.R.) at noon. Called on C.R.E. 35th Div. & arranged about Pioneer work on roads. In office remainder of day. Engineer-in-Chief called to see C.R.E.	
	13/10/18		Working in office remainder of day. Interview with O.C.'s Field Companies + Pioneers in morning.	
	14/10/18		Directing operations from forward office.	
	15/10/18		Rear Div. H.Q. moved to 28/K.14.d.3.1. Advanced H.Q. with C.R.E. moved to SHILLING FARM L.22.6.2.6. Return to Divisional Form L.15.c.9.0	

WAR DIARY
or
INTELLIGENCE SUMMARY.

Army Form C. 2118.

Place	Date	Hour	Summary of Events and Information	Remarks and references to Appendices
	16.10.18		Directing operations from the office re Field Coy work. Had an interview with CRE 41st Div. and arranged handing over to Division in the afternoon. Adv Div HQ moved to COMEDIAN CROSSING in evening 22/F26a44. Formation of Field Coys 121st at 29/4.6 t.2.9. 122 at 29/9 2 c 20. 150 at 28 t 87. (28) Pioneer Batt. at L.12 a.10.40. after relief by 41st Division. REAR Divl HQ moved up to join Advanced at COMEDIAN CROSSING CRE and Div Commander to see CE II Army re supply of additional pontoons for bridging the LYS.	APPENDIX 'A' is a report of these operations
	17/10/18			
	18.10.18		'G' and CRE moved to new area and established Div HQ at LENDELEDE A 18 d 3 2. Start 29 Inv taken over from 2nd Bdy. Pioneer 109 Bde to line north 150d Field & RE. Location as follows 121st Field Co 29 B.9 c 42 with Horse lines at A 23 c.19. 122 Field Co in reserve at 9 2 c. 20. 150th Co B 15 a 19 transport at B H d 25 75. Pioneers at A 15 A 3. 2. Rear Div HQ still at COMEDIAN CROSSING	

WAR DIARY or INTELLIGENCE SUMMARY.

Army Form C. 2118.

Place	Date	Hour	Summary of Events and Information	Remarks and references to Appendices
	19/10/18		C.R.E. with Div Commander to inspect Lys between Oyghem and BAVICHOVE with a view to crossing same by pontoons. C.E. II Corps called to see C.R.E. re same. Interview with Field Coy commanders. Arranged details of bridging operations. Two additional Pontoons allotted by C.E. II Army for use on the LYS. Enemy directly observing all crossing the LYS by 150 & 121 Field Coys. O.C. Pioneer Batt. called regarding repairs to roads in the Divisional area. One company employed.	
	20/10/18		C.R.E. in office in morning. 122 Field Coy moved with 105 Bde. Group to LENDELEDE 29/A.17.d.11. C.R.E. to RIVER LYS in afternoon to inspect medium pontoon bridge at light footbridges just up by 121 Field Coy & 150 Field Coy. Interviews with Army Officer, Pioneer Batt, B.G.R.A. G.O.C. G.S.O.1 and O.C. 122 Field Coy R.E.	

DETAILS OF OPERATIONS of Div Field [illegible] APPENDIX "B"

Army Form C. 2118.

WAR DIARY
or
INTELLIGENCE SUMMARY.
(Erase heading not required.)

Instructions regarding War Diaries and Intelligence Summaries are contained in F. S. Regs., Part II. and the Staff Manual respectively. Title pages will be prepared in manuscript.

Place	Date	Hour	Summary of Events and Information	Remarks and references to Appendices
LENDELEDE	21/10/18		C.R.E. in Office. Remainder of 121 & 150 Field Coy transferred moved forward to 29/A.23.c.6.9. In compliance of hereis assembly field engs in ferry bridge approaches across the Lys at 29/B.14.c.6.4. Open for field artillery.	APPENDIX C.- operations of 150 Field Coy R.E. 13-21st Oct.
	22/10/18		C.R.E. to the Lys. Inspected bridges and improvements to approaches including plank road laid by 121 Field Coy. Crossed the Lys and visited forward positions. C.R.E. to Office in the afternoon.	
	23/10/18		C.R.E. in Office.	
	24/10/18		CRE and HQrs 'G' staff moved to 29/I.3.b.36. C.E. II Corps called and left message that Pontoons borrowed from 7th Pontoon Park should be returned by the CRE for use in crossing L'ESCAUT (SCHELDE)	
	25/10/18		150th Field Co R.E. moved across the Lys to 29/C.21.a.5.3. 122 Field Co RE moved to 29/C.13.c.5.3. C.R.E. in Office. Major Abbott, O.C. 150 Field Co + Capt Spendley O/c Bridge Hop party called to see CRE	APPENDIX D received.

WAR DIARY
or
INTELLIGENCE SUMMARY.

(Erase heading not required.)

Army Form C. 2118.

Place	Date	Hour	Summary of Events and Information	Remarks and references to Appendices
	26/10/18.		C.R.E. worked in office all day. Morning issued instructions to the Field Coys. regarding relief by 34th Division. 121 and 122 Coys to dismantle the two pontoon bridges. 150 Field Cy. moved to B.21.a.5.5. 122 Field Co. sent one section to 28/R.14.c.5.0 to meet guides from X Corps and took over maintenance of bridges at HALLUIN. Handing over to 34th Division. C.R.E. in office. 150 and 122 Coys. moved to Linselles area.	
	27/10/18		121 Field Co. moved to Aalbeke 29/N.29.a.0.6. Divisional Headquarters moved from II Corps Area to X Corps area at BELLEGHEM M.27.a.0.3. C.R.E. to HALLUIN and MENIN re bridge maintenance.	
	28/10/18		122 Field Co.R.E. move complete to 28/R.24.a.4.7. 150th Field Co.R.E. moved to St. ANNE N.19.a.0.0. C.R.E. to X th Corps and General Army in morning. CRE Corps tools called. Sent instructions to Companies regarding training and reconstruction. O.C. 121 Field Co. called to see the CRE.	
	29/10/18			

Army Form C. 2118.

WAR DIARY
or
INTELLIGENCE SUMMARY.
(Erase heading not required.)

Place	Date	Hour	Summary of Events and Information	Remarks and references to Appendices
	30/10/18		C.E. II Army called to see C.R.E. Conference and Reviewed Commanders and O.+C. branches. To see all Field Coys. and inspect general state of same. In office during the afternoon.	
	31/10/18		C.R.E. to 122 and 121 Field Coys with Lt. Green in the morning and in the office in the afternoon.	

Robert M. Mackenzie
Lieut. Colonel, R.E.
C.R.E. 36th (Ulster) Division

APPENDIX A

C.R.E., 36th Division.

On the morning of the 16th October, 1918, it was arranged to bridge the River LYS at COURTRAI (sheet 29, H.25.d.1.7.)

The 122nd Field Company, R.E., was detailed to throw the bridge across the river, while the Commanding Officer of the 9th ~~Inniskilling~~ Irish Fusiliers made all arrangements for landing and covering parties also for a smoke screen and Trench Mortar fire on selected targets.

The artillery were also to cooperate by putting down a barrage on a high bank about 200 yards on the right front, but failed to do so. The smoke screen on the right was poor, but might have been sufficient if the artillery barrage had been provided as promised.

By 12-30 hours the pontoons were brought forward to within 30 yards of the river bank, behind houses. The pontoons were unloaded and all stores laid out in readiness under the shelter of a wood pile by 13-00 hours.

At 14-00 hours the smoke screen was put down, and the T.M. Batteries and Lewis Guns opened fire on selected targets.

By 14-05 hours it was considered that the smoke screen was thick enough and bridging could commence.

2/Lt. J.J.A.FAGAN, R.E., took the first party down to the river with half a pontoon and launched it successfully. A Lewis Gun team and three riflemen were ferried across in this, and a Sapper party landed who put in a rope anchorage. 2/Lt. FAGAN superintended the further ferrying of infantry until he was wounded.

Meanwhile, 2/Lt. A.J.TOWLSON, R.E., had launched the next boat and started bridging. All available infantry having been ferried across, the boat thus employed was brought into position to complete the bridge. It was now about 14-15 hours. The shore baulks and last bay were got across from this boat, but the chessing was never completed, as No. 3 boat was by this time in a sinking condition owing to M.G. fire.

The Infantry who were on the far side had dealt successfully with the M.G's in the buildings on the left, but the smoke screen was insufficient to mask the bridge from the M.G's on a high bank 200 yards away on the right front.

About one rifle section got across the bridge, but the far shore bay which was not completed, opened up, and owing to the sinking condition of one of the pontoons the bridge broke up.

At 14-10 hours 2/Lt. A.J.TOWLSON, R.E., had been killed and 2/Lt. J.J.A.FAGAN, R.E. wounded. Capt. E.A.WHEATLEY, R.E. then took charge of the whole situation, and carried on all parties, until he was wounded about 14-40 hours.

At 14-45 hours the M.G. fire was very intense, and 3 Officers and 24 O.R's, including most of the senior N.C.O's were casualties, so the bridging party was ordered to withdraw.

(Sd) W. SMYTH,
Major, R.E.,
O.C. 122nd Field Coy., R.E.

18/10/18.

War Diary

APPENDIX 'B'

NARRATIVE of OPERATIONS on 19th and 20th Oct., 1918.
BRIDGING OF RIVER LYS by 121st Field Coy RE Ref. Sheet 29

Three bridging wagons with complete bridging equipment, were taken up to B.24.d.9.9. at 03-00 hours and equipment unloaded and placed amongst farm buildings.

At 19-00 hours Capt. KNOX and II Lieut. DELAHEY with Nos. 2 and 4 Sections launched the two pontoons and tied ropes on for towing. At 19-25 hours the infantry arrived and 3 N.C.O's and 3 Sappers rowed the first two boat loads across the river and then stayed on the east bank to tow the boats across during subsequent trips. After two trips had been made, the enemy sent up flares and turned machine guns on the site of the operations. The remainder of the two Coys. of Infantry and the Machine Gun Sections were safely ferried across, in spite of heavy M.G. fire, and no casualties were sustained, all the men being ferried across by 20-00 hours.

The building of the bridge was then commenced, Nos. 1 and 3 Sections being held in reserve. About 21-00 hours the enemy put down a heavy barrage of H.E. and gas shells right along the river. A light bridge was constructed, using half pontoons, but it was found that the width of the river was 83 feet, which was 3 feet more than was estimated beforehand. I decided to try and launch a trestle, and had the parts carried down and assembled on the river bank. The shells were falling very close and making work difficult. Before the assembling of the trestle was completed, a gas shell fell amongst the party and killed 4 men and wounded several others. No.1 Section was called on to get the wounded away, and No.3 to take the place of the wounded men, as the 4 Sections altogether only mustered 73 men to commence with. Several men on the bridge head were also hit, and it was only the magnificent example set by Capt. KNOX II Lieut. DELAHEY and some others that the work went on whilst the wounded were still lying there. The shelling caused further delay, and as the infantry were nearly due, it was decided to draw on the reserve pontoons of 150 Coy., instead of launching the trestle and so save time. Word was sent to Lieut. STAPYLTON-SMITH of 150 Coy., and he brought the pontoons down at the gallop, and the bridge was then completed. Three minutes after, the first platoon of the 1st Inniskillings arrived. The 109th Brigade crossed without casualties. At 04-30, 20/10/18, the shelling again increased, and the bridge got a direct hit, which destroyed the superstructure of part of the bridge, and damaged one pontoon. Magnificent work was again done, and the bridge repaired before the next Battalion was due to cross, viz., at 06-00 hours.

At daybreak material was collected for the construction of a permanent foot bridge, which was completed during the day, and has been very much used.

Robert H. MacKenzie
Lt. Colonel, R.E.,
C.R.E., 36th Division.

22/10/18.

War Diary

APPENDIX 'C'.

Narrative of Operations by 150th Field Coy., R.E., 13th Oct.-21st Oct.1918.

In the operations carried out by the II Corps commencing on the 14th October, 1918, the 150th Field Coy., R.E. was attached to the 109th Infantry Brigade and the following special tasks were allotted to the unit:-

(1). To assist the assault waves to cross the HEULEBEEKE, between 28/L.15.b.3.6. and L.16.c.6.1., by placing light infantry bridges across.

(2). To carry out any necessary repairs on the roads in the area to be captured by the Brigade, with especial reference to the bridges over the HEULEBEEKE at MOORSEELE, GULLEGHEM and HEULE.

Preparations were completed by the afternoon of the 13th October, the Company being organised on the following basis:-

No.1 Section, under II Lieut. C.L.KNOX, V.C., R.E., and one wagon attached to 1st Batt. R. Innis. Fusiliers, for the purpose of carrying forward infantry bridges.

No.2 Section, under II Lieut. R. CHARLESWORTH, R.E.

No.4 Section, under Lieut. W.M.W. BRUNYATE, each with a specially loaded bridging wagon attached in readiness to repair any craters or other gaps in the MOORSEELE-HEULE road.

Fighting transport, consisting of above mentioned wagons, a trestle wagon loaded with 15 feet of superstructure and spare timber, and a double tool-cart were all under the general control of Lieut. J.B. STAPYLTON-SMITH, M.C., R.E.

At 19-00 hours on the 13th, II Lieut. C.L.KNOX, V.C., and No.1 Section moved off into battle position with the 1st R. Innis. Fusiliers at JAGO FARM, 28/L.13.c. At 03-30 on the 14th, Nos. 2 and 4 Sections and fighting transport moved into a reserve position at ARKMOELEN, 28/K.16.b., arriving about 05-00. Capt. A. FERRIER, R.E., and II Lieut. R. CHARLESWORTH, R.E. then went forward to 109 Brigade Headquarters at BASS FARM, 28/K.18.c.

II Lieut. C.L. KNOX, V.C., and No.1 Section successfully bridged the HEULEBEEKE with the first wave, but the infantry bridges proving somewhat short, other crossings were constructed with local materials. Casualties were, 1 killed, 1 died of wounds, 4 wounded.

As the enemy carried out no demolitions to roads in the area captured by the 109th Brigade, the remainder of the unit was not called on to go into action. The whole Company, less horse lines, was concentrated on the night of the 14th, at COHEN HOUSE, 28/L.16.a. and fighting transport at ORAM FARM at 28/L.15.d.

On the ~~Company~~ 15th, the Company stood by for orders. Two pontoons, with wagons and teams complete, were attached to the 122nd Field Company, R.E., taking subsequent part in the bridging operations carried out by that unit on the 16th October, at COURTRAI.

On the 16th October, the Company moved to LEDEGHEM, and remained there until 13-30 on the 18th, when it moved to ABSUL, 29/B.15.a., with horse lines at WINKEL St. ELOI. During the afternoon of the 18th, Capt. FERRIER and II Lieut CHARLESWORTH visited the H.Q. of the 11th Belgian Infantry Regiment, from whence II Lieut. CHARLESWORTH went forward with a guide to gain information about the approaches to the LYS near OYGHEM. Capt. FERRIER returned to VLUGERY FARM and remained there all night in close touch with 109th Brigade.

At 22-20 on the 18th October, Lieut. J.B. STAPYLTON-SMITH, M.C. and II Lieut. CHARLESWORTH with No.2 Section went forward with two pontoons and placed them in concealment in OYGHEM, in case an attack should be ordered at dawn of the 19th.

At 07-30 on the 19th, Lieut. W.M.W. BRUNYATE, R.E., went up to OYGHEM and made a most valuable daylight reconnaissance of the LYS and its approaches in 29/C.14.a. and c. The information he gained, decided, without a doubt, the site at which a bridge was subsequently placed.

Just before dusk on the 19th, Lieut. J.B. STAPYLTON-SMITH and II Lieut. CHARLESWORTH, with two teams of horses and No. 2 Section went to OYGHEM and collected the pontoons, and took them to a reserve position in the farm at C.19.a.9.7.

In the meanwhile, Nos. 1 and 4 Sections, II Lieut. KNOX, V.C., and Lieut. BRUNYATE, with 2 trestle wagons, followed later by 2 pontoons belonging to No.7 Pontoon Park, under Capt. FERRIER, moved into position at the farm at C.13.a. central. Having arrived at this position, Capt. FERRIER and II Lieut. KNOX went forward to gain touch with No.2 Section and the pontoons, and also the 121st Field Coy., R.E. on the river bank in C.19.a. Touch having been gained, II Lieut. KNOX returned to his Section. Capt. FERRIER remained in a house at C.19.a.5.3.

During the night, O.C. 121st Field Company, R.E. asked for another pontoon, and Lieut. J.B. STAPYLTON-SMITH, M.C., and II Lieut. CHARLESWORTH with No.2 Section brought the wagon down to the bridge at C.19.a.45.10. under heavy shell fire and unloaded the boat. At this stage, one driver and 5 horses were killed in the farm C.19.a.9.7.

Word was received from O.C. 121st Field Coy., R.E. at 02-50 on the morning of the 20th, that the 107th Infantry Brigade had completely passed over the LYS. Instructions were accordingly sent to Lieut. BRUNYATE and II Lieut. KNOX, with Nos. 1 and 4 Sections, to investigate the river bank and start bridging if possible. The material was all brought down to the site, when these two Sections came under shell fire and were forced to scatter, one man being killed. At this time, owing to the situation on the left flank not being clear, orders were issued to stop bridging until later.

Shortly after 08-00 on the 20th, the situation on the left was reported clear, and bridging operations were again ordered to start. Capt. FERRIER and Lieut. J.B. STAPYLTON-SMITH, having previously made a rough reconnaissance of approaches to the bank, a medium bridge was constructed at C.14.c.7.5., the first transport passing over at 14-15. A certain delay was caused in the construction of the bridge owing to the shortage of pontoons.

During the 21st October, the Company was employed on maintenance of the pontoon bridge, construction of roadways, and a light footbridge.

36th Division "G"
Chief Engineer, 2nd Corps.
War Diary.

Robert H. MacKenzie.

Lt. Colonel, R.E.,
C.R.E., 36th Division.

23/10/18.

APPENDIX 'D'.

The Army Commander wishes to express his appreciation of the very valuable services rendered by all officers, N.C.O.s, and men of the Royal Engineers in the construction of bridges for the passage of troops across the R. LYS and other streams.

The manner in which this work has been carried out reflects the highest credit on them and has contributed in no small degree to the success of the operations.

                            (sd) J. PERCY,
                                 M.G.G.S.
22.10.18.   Second Army

                              Second Army G.241
                              II Corps 188 G.
                              36th Division G.T. 336

II Corps.

The attached expression of the Army Commander's appreciation of the work of the Royal Engineers is forwarded. Will you kindly have it communicated to all R.E. in Corps and Divisions, including Tunnelling Companies.

                            (sd) J. PERCY,
                               M.G.G.S.
22nd October 1918.   Second Army.

- 2 -

G. R. E.

    Forwarded.

                                      A.M. Thomas Lt Col
25th October 1918.   36th (ULSTER) Division.

WD 38

War Diary

of

C.R.E. 36th Division

for the month of November 1916.

WAR DIARY or INTELLIGENCE SUMMARY

Army Form C. 2118.

Date	Hour	Summary of Events and Information	Remarks and references to Appendices
1/11/18	—	Locations of Units R.E. as follows. Headquarters R.E.- S29/N.27.c.9.1 121 Field Co.R.E. 29/M.29.d.2.9.), 122 Field Co.R.E. S.28/R.24.a.3.6.), 150 Field Co R.E. 29/N.19.a.0.0. Pioneer Batt. (16.R.I.R.) at S29/S.16.d.13. Division Front of action. Field Companies employed making fontails Infantry bridges over failures of operations. C.R.E. together with Field Company Commanders and C.O. 16th R.I.R. inspected the River LYS at MENIN. Samples of light Infantry floating bridges and a discussion on suitable designs and field trial and proposals inspected for construction of these were made.	
2/11/18	—	C.R.E. in office in morning. In afternoon with G.O.C. & Field Coys to see samples of temporary light bridges.	
3/11/18	—	C.R.E. with A.A. & Q.M.G. in morning. In afternoon with G.S.O.1. to MOUSCRON to new Div H.Q. 121st & 122nd Field Coys moved to MOUSCRON. Div H.Q. moved from BELLEGHEM to MOUSCRON.	
4/11/18	—	C.R.E. in office all day	
5/11/18	—	C.R.E. and office 150 Hh Field Coy R.E. moved to MOUSCRON.	
6/11/18	—	C.R.E. in office	
7/11/18	—	C.R.E. in office	
8/11/18	—	Orders received for move of 3 Field Coys R.E. (+Pioneer Batt) to AUTRYVE (Sheet 29 V & d) for Bridging M.9473/M657 750000 E.1.0 D.Fuite.Std. Finance 2 Bridges over the Schildt & one over the COURTRAI - BOSSUYT	
9/11/18	—	Canal at BOSSUYT (V.13c) in contemplation	

WAR DIARY / INTELLIGENCE SUMMARY

Army Form C. 2118.

Place	Date	Hour	Summary of Events and Information	Remarks and references to Appendices
	10/11/18	—	121, 122 & 150 Field Coys RE. moved from MOUSCRON to AUTRYVE. CRE visited them there in the afternoon. Fresh instructions received from CE XIth Corps as follows:— One Field Coy to repair heavy Bridge at BOSSUYT. (over Canal) Two Field Coys on heavy Pontoon Bridge over SCHELDT near AVELGHEM – ESCANAFFLES.	
	11/11/18	—	CRE greeted todays "Parliamentary" news. Major N Smyth M.C. R.E. a/CRE but remain at AUTRYVE. CRE's office remain at MOUSCRON with a/Adjt R.E. Work arranged by CE Xth Corps this evening as follows:— 121 Coy at BOSSUYT (no Pontoon) 122 & 150 on Bridges for "A" Lorries at V 28 b 1.3. over the river HAIE.	
	12/11/18 & 13/11/18	—	150th Field Coy moved to Sheet 29/V23 c 55. on 12th inst	
	14/11/18	—	Adjt R.E. with GSO3 to Field Coys at AUTRYVE	
	15/11/18	—	Adjt RE with AAQMG to Field Corps of Pioneer Battalion at AUTRYVE.	
	16/11/18	—	Orders received from 9 for move of Field Corps RE to their Bgde groups in 17th inst N.J.	
	17/11/18	—		
	18/11/18	—	121st & 122nd Field Coys from AUTRYVE to MOUSRON. 150th Field Coy from V 23 c 55 to RUDDERVOORDE (sheet 29/T 11 B)	
	19/11/18	—	150th Field Coy moved from RUDDERVOORDE to RONCQ (sheet 28/X 13 B & 9) CRE returned from leave.	
	20/11/18	—	CRE visited all three Field Coys	
	21/11/18	—	CRE to conference with CE XVth Corps	
	22/11/18	—	CRE to 121 & 122 Field Coys	

WAR DIARY
or
INTELLIGENCE SUMMARY.

(Erase heading not required.)

Army Form C. 2118.

Place	Date	Hour	Summary of Events and Information	Remarks and references to Appendices
	24/10/18		CRE in office. Visited by CE 2nd Army Commander.	
	28/10/18		Conference of Army Commanders at CinC's office.	
	29/10/18		CRE to educational conference at 15th Corps HQ.	
			The following documents are attached:-	
			(1) Letter from the E. in C. to CRE congratulating the Divisional RE on their work in forcing the Hotlys etc. at Courtrai.	
			(2) Letter from C.E. 2nd Army with Army Commander's appreciation of work done by the RE.	
			(3) Short description of a medium trestle bridge built across the Lys at Sheet 29/I E.19.B.2.2 by the 121st Field Coy R.E.	

Capt. & Adjt., R.E.
1st C.R.E., 36th Division.

C.R.E.,
36th DIVISION.

No................
Date...............

G.H.Q.,
7/11/18.

Dear Mackenzie,

I have just been reading the account of the bridging of the LYS by your very gallant Field Companies. I had heard about it before. I am thankful to say that all our Engineers have done good and gallant work all along the line, and we are all - back here at G.H.Q. - very proud of them.

Please express our admiration of their deeds to the Officers and men concerned, in the specially difficult task that fell to the 36th Division.

The Commander-in-Chief is very interested to hear of all these doings; he cannot of course particularise, but I shall, if I get the opportunity, read him a few extracts from your report. I fear you had heavy casualties.

Yours sincerely,
(Sd) G.M. HEATH.

- (2) -

O.C. 121st Field Company, R.E.
O.C. 122nd Field Company, R.E.
O.C. 150th Field Company, R.E.

The above copy of a letter received from the Engineer-in-Chief, G.H.Q., is forwarded for your information. *I need hardly say with what pride & pleasure I received the above letter.*

War Diary

Robert H. Mackenzie
Lt. Colonel, R.E.,
C.R.E., 36th Division.

8/11/18.

Second Army,
E. 1099.

C.R.E., 36th Division.

    Reference your reports on operations of 121st, 122nd, and 150th Field Companies, R.E.

    The following remarks by the Army Commander are forwarded for information:-

> " Please say that I have read these reports.
> " Express to the C.O's, Officers and men my
> " appreciation of the very gallant and
> " skillful manner in which the operations
> " were carried out."

    Please give the Companies my warm congratulations on this splendid work.

(Sd) F. M. GLUBB,
Major-General,
Chief Engineer, Second Army.

2/11/18.

Short Description of Medium Bridge built across the RIVER LYS at
S/29.C.19.b.2.2. on the 23rd Octr., 1918, by the 121st Field Coy., R.E.

The River at this point was approximately 100 feet wide, with a very uneven soft bottom and with 13 feet of water at the deepest point.

A trestle bridge with 10'0" roadway was put across, the trestles being 10'0" centres, except in two cases, where they were erected 8'6" and 11'6" respectively, in order to miss deep holes in the river bottom. Each trestle consisted of 3 legs made from trees cut locally 9" to 7" diameter with two 10"x 3" timbers on edge for transoms and two 7"x 2" diagonals and ledgers, the whole being spiked together with 10" nails and timber dogs where necessary. Each trestle was diagonally braced to the next one with 3" timber as it was launched.

The smaller trestles were launched into position on skids from the bridge head, the larger ones had their *ledgers* made in box shape and were floated into position and held there by means of ropes. This box was then filled with stones and the trestle sunk into position.

The trestles were forced into position into the mud from 12" to 18" by putting down a temporary deck, and getting the Section of Sappers to jump simultaneously on the structure. The longest trestle was about 17' 6" high. The roadway consisting of 10"x 3" planks was carried on seven 3"x 10" road bearers, and was 10'0" overall in width; 8'6" ribbands were used, giving a clear roadway of 8'9", and a heavy handrail was run on each side.

Twenty Sappers were employed on the Bridge, and one Platoon of Pioneers on the immediate approaches. The time taken to complete the job was 2½ days.

The approaches were made of granite blocks with a covering of broken brick.

All materials were collected locally, with the exception of timber dogs and nails.

On the afternoon of the 25th October, 1918, a large convoy of French 3 ton lorries passed over the bridge, two at a time, without affecting it in any way.

(Sd) Robert H. MacKenzie

Lt. Colonel, R.E.,
C.R.E., 36th Division.

5/11/18.

War Diary

VII 39

War Diary
of
CRE 36? Division

for month of December 1917

WAR DIARY
or
INTELLIGENCE SUMMARY.

Army Form C. 2118.

Place	Date	Hour	Summary of Events and Information	Remarks and references to Appendices
	1/12/18	—	Location of RE units - HQ RE as follows, 121st Field RE in MOUSCRON, 122nd Field Coy RE in MOUSCRON, 150th Field RE in RONCQ. HQ. Div. R.E. in MOUSCRON with Div. HQ.	Ynd
	6/12/18	—	Divisional Parade on Flying Ground HALLUIN. 48 sections from each Field Coy + Signal Coy. March past & inspected by G.O.C. Division.	Ynd
	8/12/18	—	One officer + 33 men from each Coy, the whole being under the command of Capt Allen RE (attached 121 Field Coy) were sent to HALLUIN to work under CRE 39 Div on Bridges over the River LYS (Belarus). Work commenced on 9th.	Ynd
	16/12/18	—	Divisional Parade on HALLUIN Aerodrome as on 6th but O division was inspected by Lt. General Sir Beauvoir de Lisle commanding the 15th Corps.	Ynd
	18/12/18	—	Bridging detachment under CRE 39 Div completed their work on the 3rd Bridge over the River LYS on the MENIN - HALLUIN Road, & rejoined their units.	Ynd
			On other dates of this month work was of a routine nature & no incident occurred worthy of inclusion in the diary	Ynd

[signature]
Capt. & Adjt., R.E.,
1st C.R.E., 36th Division.

Vol 40

WAR DIARY

of

C.R.E. 36th Division

for month of January 1919

WAR DIARY
or
INTELLIGENCE SUMMARY.

(Erase heading not required.)

Army Form C. 2118.

Place	Date	Hour	Summary of Events and Information	Remarks and references to Appendices
	1/1/19	—	Location of Units :— 121st Field Coy R.E. — MOUSCRON	
			122 " " " MOUSCRON	
			150 " " " RONCQ	
			H.Q. R.E. MOUSCRON (with Divn H.Q.)	
	9/1/19	—	Capt. F.M. Newton R.E. (T.F.) arrived & took up duties as Adjutant.	
	16/1/19	—	Capt. F.M. Newton being posted as 2nd in command 201st Field Coy R.E. proceeded to take up his duties.	
	17/1/19	—	C.R.E. attended CE XV Corps' conference on R.E. Memorial & Educational Schemes.	
	21/1/19	—	Lieut W.A. Delahey M.C. R.E. 121st Field Coy R.E. took over duties as Assistant Adjutant.	
	26-1-19		Capt. G. McFarquhar R.E. proceeded to U.K. for demobilization.	
	27-1-19		Lieut W.A. Delahey, 121st Field Co R.E. appointed Adjt. from this date.	
	30-1-19		C.R.E. attended C.E. II Corps conference on R.E. Memorial Scheme.	

W A Delahey
Capt. & Adjt. R.E.
for C.R.E., 36th Division.

WAR DIARY

of

C.R.E. 36th Division

for month of February 1919.

WAR DIARY
or
INTELLIGENCE SUMMARY.

(Erase heading not required.)

Army Form C. 2118.

Place	Date	Hour	Summary of Events and Information	Remarks and references to Appendices
	1/2/19		Location of Units — 121st Field Coy RE — MOUSCRON 122 " " " — MOUSCRON 150 " " " — RONCQ H.Q. RE — MOUSCRON (~~2nd Div H.Q.~~) C.R.E. attended Conference at C.E. 10 - 5th Army — for discussion on R.E. Demand Scheme.	
	4/2/19		C.R.E. proceeded to MICHELHAM Home for 2 weeks convalescence.	

SADOS. 36th Div.
Vol 4

www.ingramcontent.com/pod-product-compliance
Lightning Source LLC
Chambersburg PA
CBHW081434300426
44108CB00016BA/2363